Transmission and Generation in Medieval and Renaissance Literature

Transmission and Generation in Medieval and Renaissance Literature

ESSAYS IN HONOUR OF
JOHN SCATTERGOOD

Karen Hodder and Brendan O'Connell

EDITORS

FOUR COURTS PRESS

Set in 10.5 pt on 12.5 pt Ehrhardt for
FOUR COURTS PRESS LTD
7 Malpas Street, Dublin 8, Ireland
www.fourcourtspress.ie
and in North America by
FOUR COURTS PRESS
c/o ISBS, 920 N.E. 58th Avenue, Suite 300, Portland, OR 97213.

A catalogue record for this title
is available from the British Library.

ISBN 978–1–84682–338–1

Printed in England
by CPI Group (UK) Ltd, Croydon, CR0 4YY

Contents

Acknowledgments

This collection of essays has been in development for an unusually long period, and the editors would like to thank all the contributors for their patience and dedication as the project came slowly to fruition, but above this for the excellence of their contributions to the volume. Because of the long delay in bringing the book to print, the blame for any omission of relevant recent scholarship must lie with the editors, rather than the individual contributors.

We would also like to thank Amanda Piesse for her role in organizing the original study day on Age and Youth in Medieval and Early Modern Literature in honour of John Scattergood, and for her continued support and encouragement.

This project would not have been possible without financial support, and we would like to thank the Provost of Trinity College Dublin, Prof. Patrick Prendergast, and Prof. Darryl Jones, Head of the School of English, Trinity College Dublin, for the generous contributions which enabled us to complete the volume.

Finally, we would like to thank Four Courts Press (and in particular Martin Fanning) for publishing the volume and for their advice and assistance in the final stages of preparation of the manuscript.

Contributors

CLÍODHNA CARNEY, a former student of John Scattergood's, is a lecturer in the English Department at the National University of Ireland, Galway. She has published a number of articles, and is currently working on a book-length study of Chaucer.

DARRAGH GREENE, a former student of John Scattergood's, did his doctoral research on divine speech and personal relationship to God in medieval literature. He has research interests in medieval English drama, medieval mysticism, Chaucer and Dante, has published on *The Kingis Quair*, and teaches medieval literature in Trinity College Dublin and University College Dublin.

KAREN HODDER, now retired, lectured in the Department of English and Related Literature, York. Her research interests include both medieval literature and the medievalism of the eighteenth and nineteenth centuries.

ERIK KOOPER, now retired, lectured in the Department of English Language and Culture at Utrecht University. His research interests lie in the intersection between history, culture and literature, and he has published widely on medieval romance, courtly literature and chronicles.

FRANCIS LENEGHAN, a former student of John Scattergood's, is a lecturer at St Peter's College, Oxford. His research focuses on Old English literature, particularly ideas of kingship and nation in heroic poetry and Alfredian writing, and he has published a number of works on Anglo-Saxon literature.

FRANCES MCCORMACK, a former student of John Scattergood's, is a lecturer in the English Department at the National University of Ireland, Galway. Her research interests focus on Chaucer, mystical writings, and Wycliffism and Lollardy, and she has published a monograph on *Chaucer and the Culture of Dissent* and is working on a book-length study of compunction and shame in Old English literature.

EILÉAN NÍ CHUILLEANÁIN, now retired, lectured in the School of English, Trinity College Dublin. She has published widely on the literature of the English Reformation and European Renaissance. Well known as a poet and translator, she has published several volumes of poetry.

BRENDAN O'CONNELL, a former student of John Scattergood's, lectures in the School of English, Trinity College Dublin. His research focuses on Chaucer and the *Gawain*-poet.

9

NIAMH PATTWELL, a former student of John Scattergood's, lectures in the School of English, Drama and Film, University College Dublin. Her research and publications focus on Chaucer and on religious vernacular writings of the late middle ages.

JOHN J. THOMPSON is chair of English Textual Cultures at Queen's University, Belfast. He is the author of a number of books and articles on topics relating to the pre-modern history of the English book and other aspects of late medieval literature and culture.

List of publications by John Scattergood

BOOKS

Politics and Poetry in the Fifteenth Century (London, 1971)

The Works of Sir John Clanvowe: The Boke of Cupide and The Two Ways, ed. V.J. Scattergood (Cambridge and Totowa NJ, 1975)

English Court Culture in the Later Middle Ages, ed. V.J. Scattergood and J.W. Sherborne (London, 1983)

John Skelton: The Complete English Poems, ed. John Scattergood (London, 1983)

Literature and Learning in Medieval and Renaissance England: Essays Presented to Fitzroy Pyle, ed. John Scattergood (Dublin, 1984)

Oxford Guides to Chaucer: The Shorter Poems [A.J. Minnis, with V.J. Scattergood and J.J. Smith], (Oxford, 1995)

Reading the Past: Essays on Medieval and Renaissance Literature (Dublin, 1996)

Texts and Their Contexts: Papers from the Early Book Society, ed. John Scattergood and Julia Boffey (Dublin, 1997)

Text and Gloss: Studies in Insular Learning and Literature Presented to Joseph Donovan Pheifer, ed. Helen Conrad O'Briain, Anne Marie D'Arcy and John Scattergood (Dublin, 1999)

The Lost Tradition: Essays on Middle English Alliterative Poetry (Dublin, 2000)

Italian Culture: Interactions, Transpositions, Translations, ed. Cormac Ó Cuilleanáin, Corinna Salvadori and John Scattergood (Dublin, 2006)

Manuscripts and Ghosts: Essays on the Transmission of Late Medieval and Early Renaissance Literature (Dublin, 2006)

The Kemble Lectures on Anglo-Saxon Studies, 2005–2008, ed. Alice Jorgensen, Helen Conrad-O'Briain and John Scattergood (Dublin, 2009)

Occasions for Writing: Essays on Medieval and Renaissance Literature, Politics and Society (Dublin, 2010)

POETRY

In Leonardo's Garden (Dublin, 2007)

For Another Year (Dublin, 2009)

ARTICLES AND CONTRIBUTIONS TO BOOKS

'The Authorship of *The Boke of Cupide*', *Anglia* 82 (1964), 137–49.

'*The Boke of Cupide*: An Edition', *English Philological Studies* 9 (1965), 47–83.

'An Unpublished Middle English Poem', *Archiv für das Studium der neuren Sprachen und Literaturen* 203 (1966), 277–82.

'*The Two Ways*: An Unpublished Religious Treatise by Sir John Clanvowe', *English Philological Studies* 10 (1967), 33–56.

'An Inedited Manuscript of *The Stacions of Rome*', *English Philological Studies* 11 (1968), 51–4.

'Two Medieval Book-Lists', *The Library* 23 (1968), 236–9.

'Political Context, Date and Composition of *The Sayings of the Four Philosophers*', *Medium Aevum* 38 (1968), 157–65.

'Adam Davy's *Dreams* and Edward II', *Archiv für das Studium der neuren Sprachen und Literaturen* 206 (1969), 253–60.

'"The Debate between Nurture and Kynd": An Unpublished Middle English Poem', *Notes and Queries* 215 (1970), 244–6.

'Unpublished Middle English Poems from British Museum MS Harley 1706', *English Philological Studies* 12 (1970), 35–41.

'On British Museum MS Harley 1753', *Review of English Studies* 21 (1970), 337–8.

'Skelton's "Ryotte": "A Rustye Gallande"', *Notes and Queries* 219 (1974), 83–5.

(with Dennis Casling) 'One Aspect of Stanza-Linking', *Neophilologische Mitteilungen* 75 (1974), 79–91.

'The Manciple's Manner of Speaking', *Essays in Criticism* 24 (1974), 124–46.

The New Cambridge Bibliography of English Literature, ed. George Watson, Ian Roy Willison and John Drayton Pickles, 5 vols (Cambridge, 1969–77), I (1974), cols. 455–60 (Tales), 459–68 (Chronicles), 473–8 (Prophecies).

'Revision in Some Middle English Political Verses', *Archiv für das Studium der neuren Sprachen und Literaturen* 211 (1974), 287–99.

'*Winter wakeneth al my care* … lines 11–15', *English Philological Studies* 14 (1975), 59–64.

(with Ruth Pitman) 'Some Illustrations of the Unicorn Apologue from *Barlaam and Ioasaph*', *Scriptorium* 21 (1977), 85–90.

'The Originality of *The Shipman's Tale*', *The Chaucer Review* 11 (1977), 210–31

'A Caxton Prologue and Chaucer', *The Chaucer Newsletter* 2 (1980), 14–15.

'A Note on the Moral Framework of Donne's *The Sunne Rising*' *Neuphilologische Mitteilungen*, 92 (1981), 307–14.

'Chaucer and the French War: *Sir Thopas* and *Melibee*' in *Court and Poet: Selected Proceedings of the Third Congress of the International Courtly Literature Society*, ed. Glyn S. Burgess (Liverpool 1981), pp 347–71.

'*Sir Gawain and the Green Knight* and the Sins of the Flesh', *Traditio* 37 (1981), 347–71.

(with T.P. Dolan) 'Middle English Prose' in *The New Pelican Guide to English Literature*, Vol. 1 *Medieval Literature*, ed. Boris Ford (London, 1982), pp 103–20.

'Chaucer's Curial Satire: *The Balade de Bon Conseyl*', *Hermathena* 133 (1982), 29–46.

'Literary Culture at the Court of Richard II' in *English Court Culture in the Later Middle Ages*, ed. V.J. Scattergood and J.W. Sherbourne (London, 1983), pp 29–43.

'Proverbial Verses in Trinity College Dublin MS 212', *Notes and Queries* 227 (1983), 29–43.

'*The Battle of Maldon* and History' in *Literature and Learning in Medieval and Renaissance England: Essays Presented to Fitzroy Pyle*, ed. V.J. Scattergood (Dublin, 1984), pp 11–24.

'*The Parlement of the Thre Ages*', *Leeds Studies in English*, n.s. 14 (1983), 167–81.

'Sir John Clanvowe' in *Dictionary of the Middle Ages*, ed. Joseph L. Strayer (New York, 1982–9), III (1983), 408.

(with Myra Stokes) 'Travelling in November: Sir Gawain, Thomas Usk, Charles of
Orleans and the *De Re Militari*', *Medium Aevum* 53 (1984), 78–83.

'An Unrecorded Fragment of the *Prose Lancelot* in Trinity College MS 212', *Medium
Aevum* 53 (1984), 301–6.

'Skelton and the Elegy', *Proceedings of the Royal Irish Academy* 84 (1984), 333–47.

'Perkyn Revelour and *The Cook's Tale*', *The Chaucer Review* 19 (1984), 14–23.

'Sir Gawain and the Green Knight' in *The Arthurian Encyclopedia*, ed. Norris J Lacy
(New York and London, 1986), pp 506–11.

Contributions on *The General Prologue, The Shipman's Tale* and *The Manciple's Tale*
in *The Riverside Chaucer*, ed. Larry D. Benson (Boston, 1986).

'Skelton and Traditional Satire: *Ware the Hauke*', *Medium Aevum* 55 (1986), 203–16.

'Political and Social Issues in Chaucer: *Lak of Stedfastnesse*', *The Chaucer Review* 21
(1987), 469–75.

'*Winner and Waster* and the Mid-Fourteenth-Century Economy' in *The Writer as
Witness: Literature as Historical Evidence*, ed. Tom Dunne (Cork, 1987), pp 39–57.

'Chaucer in the Suburbs', in *Medieval Literature and Antiquities*, ed. Tom Burton and
Myra Stokes (Cambridge, 1987), pp 145–62.

'*Lenvoy a Bukton* and Proverbs', *Nottingham Medieval Studies* 31 (1987), 98–107.

'Skelton's Lyrics: Tradition and Innovation', *The Fifteenth Century*, ed. David A.
Lampe, ACTA 12 (Binghamton NY, 1988 [for 1985]), pp 19–39.

'The "Busyness" of Love': A Theme in Chaucer's Dawn Songs', *Essays in Criticism*
37 (1987), 110–20.

'Fashion and Morality in the Late Middle Ages' in *England in the Fifteenth Century:
Proceedings of the 1986 Harlaxton Symposium*, ed. Daniel Williams (Woodbridge,
1987), pp 255–72.

'*The Contention between Liberality and Prodigality*: A Late Morality', in *Early English
Drama*, ed. Al Tricomi, ACTA 13 (Binghamton NY, 1987), pp 153–67.

'Two Unpublished Poems from Trinity College Dublin MS 490', *Review of English
Studies*, 38 (1987), 46–9.

'A Graveyard Formula in *Hamlet* V. i. 115–131', *Notes and Queries* 35 (1988), 470–1.

'Insecurity in Skelton's *Bowge of Courte*' in *Genres, Themes, and Images in English
Literature from the Fourteenth to the Fifteenth Century*, ed. Piero Boitani and Anna
Torti (Tübingen, 1988), pp 191–214.

'Skelton and Heresy', in *Early Tudor England: Proceedings of the 1987 Harlaxton
Symposium*, ed. Daniel Williams (Woodbridge, 1989), pp 157–70.

'The Jongleur, the Copyist, and the Printer: The Tradition of Chaucer's *Wordes unto
Adam, his Own Scriveyn*', in *Courtly Literature: Culture and Context. Proceedings of
the Fifth Triennial Congress of the International Courtly Literature Society, Dalfsen,
The Netherlands, 9–16 August 1986*, ed. Keith Busby and Erik Kooper, Utrecht
Publications in General and Comparative Literature 25 (Amsterdam, 1990), pp
499–508.

'John Skelton's *Garlande of Laurell* and the Chaucerian Tradition' in *Chaucer
Traditions: Studies in Honour of Derek Brewer*, ed. Barry Windeatt and Ruth Morse,
(Cambridge, 1990), pp 122–38.

'The Date and Composition of George Ashby's Poems', *Leeds Studies in English* 21
(1990), 167–76.

'The London Manuscripts of John Skelton's Poems' in *Regionalism in Late Medieval Manuscripts and Texts: Essays Celebrating the Publication of a Linguistic Atlas of Late Mediaeval English*, ed. Felicity Riddy (Cambridge, 1991), pp 171–82.

'Old Age, Love, and Friendship in Chaucer's *Envoy to Scogan*', *Nottingham Medieval Studies* 35 (1991), 92–101.

'The Early Annotations to John Skelton's Poems', *Poetica* 35 (1992), 53–63.

'George Ashby's *Prisoner's Reflections* and the Virtue of Patience', *Nottingham Medieval Studies* 37 (1993), 102–9.

'*The Tale of Gamelyn*: The Noble Robber as Provincial Hero', in *Readings in Medieval English Romance*, ed. Carol M. Meale (Cambridge, 1994), pp 159–94.

'Chaucer's *Complaint of Venus* and the "Curiosite" of Graunson', *Essays in Criticism* 44 (1994), 171–89.

'Simon Fish, *A Supplication for the Beggars* en de Protestantse Polemiek', in *Antwerpen, Dissident Drukkerscentrum: De Rol van de Antwerpse Drukkers in de Godsdienststrijd in Engeland (16de Eeuw)*, ed. D. Imhof, Gilbert Tournoy, Francine de Nave, and Ingrid van de Wijer (Antwerp, 1994), pp 71–8; and entries on pp 95, 96–7, 99, 100, 103–4, 104–5, 106, 108–9, 121–2.

'Skelton's *Magnyfycence* and the Tudor Royal Household', *Medieval English Theatre* 15 (1993), 21–48 (appeared 1995).

'Misrepresenting the City: Genre, Intertextuality and William FitzStephen's *Description of London (c.1173)*', in *London and Europe in the Later Middle Ages*, ed. Julia Boffey and Pamela King, Westfield Publications in Medieval and Renaissance Studies (London, 1995), pp 1–34.

'The Short Poems' in A.J. Minnis, J.J. Smith and V.J. Scattergood, *Oxford Guides to Chaucer: The Shorter Poems* (Oxford, 1995), pp 455–512 .

'*An Old Man's Prayer* and Bastard Feudalism' in *Expedition nach der Wahrheit: Poems, Essays, and Papers in Honour of Theo Stemmler*, ed. Stefan Horlacher and Marion Islinger (Heidelberg, 1966), pp 119–30.

'Courtliness in Some Fourteenth-Century English Pastourelles', in *The Court and Cultural Diversity: Selected Papers from the Eighth Triennial Congress of the International Courtly Literature Society 1995*, ed. Evelyn Mullally and John Thompson (Cambridge, 1997), pp 161–78.

'*Pierce the Ploughman's Crede*: Lollardy and Texts' in *Lollardy and Gentry in the Later Middle Ages*, ed. Margaret Aston and Colin Richmond (Stroud, 1997), pp 77–94.

'Patience and Authority', in *Essays on Ricardian Literature, in Honour of J.A. Burrow*, ed. A.J. Minnis, Charlotte C. Morse and Thorlac Turville-Petre (Oxford, 1997), pp 295–315.

(with Guido Latre) 'Trinity College Dublin MS 75: A Lollard Bible and Some Protestant Owners' in *Texts and Their Contexts: Papers from the Early Book Society*, ed. John Scattergood and Julia Boffey (Dublin, 1997), pp 223–40.

'Charles of Orleans', 'John Clanvowe', 'Adam Davy', 'Henry Scogan', 'John Skelton' in *Medieval England: An Encyclopedia*, ed. Paul E. Szarmach, M. Teresa Tavormina, and Joel T. Rosenthal (New York and London, 1998), pp 170–1, 192–3, 232, 675, 701.

'Eating the Book: *Riddle 47* and Memory', in *Text and Gloss: Studies in Insular Learning and Literature Presented to Joseph Donovan Pheifer*, ed. Helen Conrad

O'Briain, Anne Marie D'Arcy and John Scattergood (Dublin, 1999), pp 119–27.
'Dressing the Part in *Magnyfycence*: Allegory and Costume' in *Tudor Theatre: Allegory* ✏
  in the Theatre, THETA: Essays on Semiotics of Theatre 5 (Bern, 2000), pp 55–
  75.
'John Leland's *Itinerary* and the Identity of England' in *Sixteenth Century Identities*,
  ed. Amanda J. Piesse (Manchester, 2000), pp 58–74.
'National and Local Identity: Maps and the English "Country-House" Poem' in *(Re)*
  Mapping the Centres: Membership and State, ed. Trevor Harris, Actes du Colloque
  G.R.A.A.T. 22 (Tours, 2000), pp 13–27.
'Authority and Resistance: The Political Verse' in *Studies in the Harley Manuscript:*
  The Scribes, Contents, and Social Contexts of British Library MS Harley 2253, ed.
  Susanna Greer Fein (Kalamazoo, 2000), pp 163–201.
'A Defining Moment: The Battle of Flodden and English Poetry' in *Vernacular*
  Literature and Current Affairs in the Early Sixteenth Century: France, England and
  Scotland, ed. Jennifer Britnell and Richard Britnell, Studies in European Cultural
  Transition 6 (Aldershot, 2000), pp 62–77.
'*The Libelle of Englyshe Polycye*: The Nation and its Place' in *Nation, Court and*
  Culture: New Essays on Fifteenth-Century English Poetry, ed. Helen Cooney
  (Dublin, 2001), pp 28–49.
'"Iste Liber Constat Johanni Mascy": Dublin, Trinity College, MS 155', in *Middle*
  English Poetry: Texts and Traditions. Essays in Honour of Derek Pearsall, ed. A.J.
  Minnis, York Manuscripts Conferences: Proceedings Series 5 (York and
  Woodbridge, 2001), pp 91–101.
'The Cook's Tale' in *Sources and Analogues of the Canterbury Tales*, ed. Robert M.
  Correale and Mary Hamel, 2 vols (Cambridge, 2002–5), I (2005), pp 75–86.
'Making Arrows: *The Parliament of Fowls*, 211–217', *Notes and Queries* 247 (2002),
  444–7.
'Writing the Clock: The Reconstruction of Time in the Late Middle Ages', *European*
  Review: Interdisciplinary Journal of the Academia Europaea, 11 (2003), 453–74.
'Chaucer's Joke against the Egle: *The House of Fame*, 1011–1017', *Notes and Queries*
  249 (2004), 233–4.
'Validating the High Life in *Of Arthour and of Merlin* and *Kyng Alisaunder*', *Essays in*
  Criticism 54 (2004), 323–50.
'George Ashby' in *Oxford Dictionary of National Biography*, ed. H.C.G. Matthew and
  Brian Harrison, 60 vols (Oxford, 2004), II, 619–20.
'John Skelton' in *Oxford Dictionary of National Biography*, ed. H.C.G. Matthew and
  Brian Harrison, 60 vols (Oxford, 2004), L, 834–40.
'The Shipman's Tale' in *Sources and Analogues of the Canterbury Tales*, ed. Robert M.
  Correale and Mary Hamel, 2 vols (Cambridge, 2002–5), Vol. II (2005), pp 565–
  81.
'The Love-Lyric before Chaucer' in *A Companion to the Middle English Lyric*, ed.
  Thomas G. Duncan (Cambridge, 2005), pp 39–67.
'Humanism in Ireland in the Sixteenth Century: The Evidence of Trinity College
  Dublin MS 160' in *Italian Culture: Interactions, Transpositions, Translations*, ed.
  Cormac Ó Cuilleanáin, Corinna Salvadori and John Scattergood (Dublin, 2006),
  pp 69–89.

'"The Eyes of Memory": The Function of the Illustrations in Dublin, Trinity College Library MS 505', in *Readers and Writers of the Prose Brut*, ed. William Marx and Raluca Radulescu, Trivium 36 (Lampeter, 2006), pp 203–26.

'Thomas Wyatt's Epistolary Satires and the Consolations of Intertextuality' in *Building the Past/Konstruktion der eigenen Vergangheit*, ed. Rudolf Suntrup and Jan Veenstra, Medieval and Early Modern Culture 7 (Frankfurt, 2006), pp 67–83.

'"The Unequal Scales of Love": Andreas Capellanus' *De Amore* and Some Later Texts' in *Writings on Love in the English Middle Ages*, ed. Helen Cooney (New York, 2006), pp 63–79.

'London and Money: *Chaucer's Complaint to his Purse*' in *Chaucer and the City* edited by Ardis Butterfield, Chaucer Studies 37 (Cambridge, 2006), pp 162–73.

(with Karen Hodder) '*Wynnere and Wastoure 407–414* and *Le Roman de la Rose 8813–8854*' in *People and Texts: Relationships in Medieval Literature. Studies Presented to Erik Kooper*, ed. Thea Summerfield and Keith Busby, Costerus New Series 166 (Amsterdam and New York, 2007), pp 99–109.

'A Pocketful of Death: Horology and Literature in Renaissance England' in *On Literature and Science: Essays, Reflections, Provocations*, ed. Philip Coleman (Dublin, 2007), pp 43–61.

'"Portraying a Life": Skelton's Flytings and Some Related Poems', in *John Skelton and Early Modern Culture: Papers Honoring Robert S. Kinsman*, ed. David R. Carlson, Medieval and Renaissance Texts and Studies 300 (Tempe, AZ, 2008), pp 189–214.

'Introduction', Helen Waddell, *Mediaeval Latin Lyrics, with an introduction by John Scattergood* (Dublin, 2008), pp v–xviii.

'Two Medieval Service Books', in *Treasures of the Royal Irish Academy Library*, ed. Bernadette Cunningham, Siobhan Fitzpatrick and Petra Schnabel (Royal Irish Academy: Dublin, 2009), pp 50–5.

'John Mitchell Kemble (1807–1857)' in *The Kemble Lectures on Anglo-Saxon Studies 2005–2008*, ed. Alice Jorgensen, Helen Conrad-O'Briain and John Scattergood (Dublin, 2009), pp 1–11.

'On the Road: Langland and Some Medieval Outlaw Stories' in *Medieval Alliterative Poetry: Essays in Honour of Thorlac Turville-Petre*, ed. John A. Burrow and Hoyt N. Duggan (Dublin, 2010), pp 195–211.

'The Date of Sir John Clanvowe's *The Two Ways* and the "Reinvention of Lollardy"', *Medium Aevum* 79 (2010), 116–20.

'Erasing Oldcastle: Some Literary Reactions to the Lollard Rising of 1414' in *Heresy and Orthodoxy in Early English Literature, 1350–1680*, ed. Eiléan Ní Chuilleanáin and John Flood (Dublin, 2010), pp 49–74.

'Reading Between the Lines in Philip Larkin's *Naturally the Foundation Will Bear your Expenses*' in *Post: A Review of Poetry Studies* II (2010), 32–40, http://post.mater-dei.ie/pages/post-ii-poetry

'Alliterative Poetry: Religion and Morality' in *A Companion to Medieval Poetry*, ed. Corinne Saunders (Oxford, 2010), pp 329–48.

'Alliterative Poetry and Politics' in *A Companion to Medieval Poetry*, ed. Corinne Saunders (Oxford, 2010), pp 349–66.

Introduction

It is a tribute to the extraordinary legacy of John Scattergood that this is the second festschrift dedicated to a scholar who has left such an indelible impression on the study of medieval and renaissance literature. The first festschrift dedicated to John (the volume edited by Anne Marie D'Arcy and Alan J. Fletcher and published by Four Courts Press in 2005) constitutes an exceptionally generous and stimulating tribute to the robust and wide-ranging historicism championed by John throughout his remarkable career. While many of the essays in the present volume also acknowledge and extend the historicist spirit of John's work, the editors and contributors have chosen to pay particular tribute to John's legacy as a teacher and personal supervisor of research in medieval and renaissance literature, which has profoundly shaped the character of medieval and renaissance literary studies in Ireland and further afield.

The essays in the present volume emerged from a study day on the theme of Age and Youth in Medieval and Early Modern Literature, which was organized by Amanda Piesse to mark John's retirement as Professor of Medieval and Renaissance Literature at the School of English, Trinity College Dublin. The theme of Age and Youth provided a conceptual focus to this study day and provides the thematic coherence of the papers presented in this volume, each of which addresses relationships between generations in the medieval and early modern periods, either literally or in terms of literary transmission. The collection reflects on the dynamic relationship between the generations and the ways in which this relationship not only ensures the preservation and transmission of knowledge, but also serves to generate provocative new ideas, approaches and questions. Indeed, the volume might be said to embody just such a dynamic relationship since, in addition to a number of John's friends and colleagues, several essays in the volume by former students provide an affectionate and appropriate acknowledgement of the tensions inherent in the master/student relationship, recognizing at once both the debt to past masters and the challenges produced by new models of thought.

The essays in this volume coalesce around a number of different themes. Some focus on genealogy, considering the importance of royal genealogy in literary and historical texts, or as a metaphor for the process of intellectual transmission. Others deal with methods of education and instruction, and the process of personal, moral and cultural development throughout an individual life. Many, following the example of John Scattergood, consider the intersection of literature and history, while all address the energetic tensions between past and present, the preservation and transmission of the old learning and the generation of the new.

In the opening essay, Francis Leneghan addresses precisely this relationship between the old ways and the new in his consideration of the originality of the Scyld Scefing episode in *Beowulf*, which carefully traces how the *Beowulf* poet reshapes traditions from Danish royal history and other sources to create the story of this royal founder figure. Indeed, he posits that the poet was so successful in presenting Scyld Scefing as an authentic part of the Danish royal tradition that some elements of the story were used as sources for the remote stage of the West Saxon royal genealogy.

Moving into the period of Middle English vernacular writing, Erik Kooper also attests to the importance of genealogy with his focus on the Middle English chronicles, considering the works of writers including Robert of Gloucester, Thomas Castleford and Robert Mannyng, and the traditions of Higden/Trevisa and the Prose Brut. In a thoughtful extension of one of John Scattergood's insights into the relationship of politics and poetry, he highlights how personal attitudes colour the choices of the chronicle writer no less than the poet. His study juxtaposes the chronicle accounts of three twelfth-century kings (Henry I, Stephen and Henry II) and the difficulties they had with their heirs, as each faced exceptional challenges to their attempts to secure the transmission of power to the next generation.

In a very direct way, the essay by Brendan O'Connell picks up where Kooper's study leaves off, by considering one of the most important works produced in the eventful reign of Henry II, Richard FitzNigel's *Dialogue of the Exchequer*. O'Connell demonstrates that the dialogue form of the text is heavily influenced by the turbulent historical circumstances of the day, as FitzNigel connects disruption in the line of legitimate monarchic succession with the disruption of intellectual transmission, highlighting both Stephen's usurpation of Henry I and the rebellion of Henry II's sons. He argues, however, that the model of intellectual transmission developed by FitzNigel recognizes that debate between the generations is essential to the generation of new questions and approaches, and suggests that the *Dialogue* provides an important context for the open-ended debate poems of the Middle Ages, including the *Owl and the Nightingale*.

Darragh Greene's essay focuses on the *Parliament of the Thre Ages*, a debate poem in which allegorical representatives of the three ages of man consider what it means to live well. Challenging traditional readings of the poem as a closed text in which the figure of Elde puts an end to the dispute between Youthe and Medill Elde, Greene argues that the text is radically more open-ended than is commonly believed, and that the apparently magisterial figure of Elde is in fact guilty of committing the informal fallacy known as *ignoratio elenchi*, by introducing an irrelevant thesis and missing the point under discussion. As allegorical personifications, each character remains unable to continue in a meaningful dialogue, leaving it up to the reader to move beyond the *aporia* of the poem's conclusion to engage with the ethical problem at the heart of the debate.

In a very different way, the relationship between the different stages of a human life is also to the fore in Niamh Pattwell's reinterpretation of the later life of Isabelle of France (*c.*1295–1358). Building on an approach pioneered by John Scattergood, she highlights the importance of a neglected manuscript, British Library Cotton Galba E XIV, which details the financial transactions of Isabelle's household from October 1357–8. Pattwell's approach provides fresh and compelling evidence about the later years of Isabelle's life, demonstrating that, contrary to popular opinion, and despite the confiscation of her lands in 1330 following the accession of her son, Edward III, Isabelle managed to forge a significant place at the heart of a strong coterie of cultural exchange. As well as highlighting some tantalizing connections to the works of Chaucer and Mandeville, Pattwell argues persuasively that despite the political turmoil of the middle years of her life, Isabelle's youthful engagement with the best of European art, music and literature continued undiminished into her final years.

Clíodhna Carney's essay on Chaucer's 'Franklin's Tale' also considers the relationship between the different stages of human life, with a focus on ethical development. It takes as its starting point the relationship between the generous father and the spendthrift son articulated by the Franklin in his words to the Squire. From here, Carney's analysis expands to consider the tale's fundamental ethical question about the relationship between virtue and social status, and the principle of *generositas virtus, non sanguis*. Carney's subtle interpretation addresses several key interpretive cruxes of the Tale, and, importantly, highlights the process of personal development whereby the rebellious son becomes the conservative father.

Taking as her theme the relationship between the old ways and the new, Frances McCormack considers the heterodoxy of Sir John Clanvowe's *The Two Ways*, a work brought to prominence by John Scattergood's 1967 edition. McCormack's careful reading responds sensitively to the strategies by which Clanvowe (one of the so-called Lollard Knights) articulates his doctrinal positions, highlighting the ways in which the Lollard movement distinguished itself from the contemporary, earthly Church by harking back to the example provided by the old ways of the apostolic Church.

Tensions between Church and State are to the fore in Eiléan Ní Chuilleanáin's analysis of the accounts of the Princes in the Tower in Shakespeare's *Richard III* and Thomas More's *History of Richard III*. She traces a nuanced account of the ways in which More complicates a tradition of immunity attached to consecrated places and persons, and explores how this is altered in Shakespeare's dramatic presentation of the episode. Drawing on both contemporary historical debates about the role of sanctuary and the then recently published works of Tacitus, she builds a compelling picture of the intersection between the representation of childhood innocence and the changing role of sanctuary in the sixteenth-century, giving a vivid account of the ways in which writers such as More and Shakespeare breathe new life into old texts and traditions.

The uses to which early modern readers turn ancient texts and traditions is also exemplified, in a markedly different sense, by John J. Thompson's essay, which considers the reception among seventeenth-century readers of a fifteenth-century manuscript celebrating English history (Dublin, Trinity College Library MS 505). In his study, Thompson builds on John Scattergood's argument that the genealogical and historical material found in this manuscript, along with the townscapes included in the decorative roundels accompanying the text, act as 'eyes of memory' for its readers. Thompson's meticulous account of the surprising history of this manuscript adds a remarkable Irish dimension to the evidence of English and Welsh interest in the material contained in this fascinating document.

Closing the volume, Karen Hodder's essay also deals with the later reception of medieval works, here focussing on Wordsworth's engagement with Chaucer's 'Manciple's Tale'. It highlights Wordsworth's lifelong commitment to Chaucer as the 'morning star of English poetry' within the context of eighteenth- and nineteenth-century medievalism. She demonstrates, in particular, Wordsworth's sensitive reading of the language of the 'Manciple's Tale', noting the significance of his engagement with Chaucer for his own poetic development. Her essay marks a fitting conclusion to the volume both in its emphasis on a work which was the subject of one of John Scattergood's most influential studies, and by stressing a commitment to the politics of art which has characterized John Scattergood's exceptional contribution as a scholar and teacher.

Reshaping tradition: the originality of the Scyld Scefing episode in *Beowulf*

FRANCIS LENEGHAN

Just as the writers of medieval romances might develop old characters and episodes from the various 'matters' of Britain, France, Rome and England in new, original ways, Anglo-Saxon heroic poets appear to have freely adapted Germanic legends to suit their own immediate poetic ends. New characters could be skillfully inserted into a well-known setting, or a new tale could be told about an established figure. In a culture which valued tradition above originality, new tales had to be passed off as old. *Beowulf* is a self-consciously traditional poem, composed in what J.A. Burrow has recently termed the 'auxetic' or superlative mode, the main function of which is to praise the deeds of great men.[1] In the opening lines the poet also casts himself in the role of the 'traditional narrator',[2] engaging a listening audience in a collective act of remembrance of past glories (ll. 1–3):

> Hwæt, we Gardena   in geardagum
> Þeodcyninga   þrym gefrunon
> hu þa æþelingas   ellen fremedon!   (*Beowulf*, ll. 1–3).[3]

The inherited nature of the story is emphasized throughout by the use of phrases such as *ic gefrægn* and *ic hyrde*.[4] The highly allusive manner in which the poet deploys Germanic legendary material certainly implies that his audience was already familiar with much of this material.[5] For example, the comparison between the necklace given to Beowulf and the *Brosinga mene* (l. 1199) evokes the stories of Hama and Eormanric, alluded to in *Deor* (ll. 21–6) and

---

1 J.A. Burrow, *The Poetry of Praise* (Cambridge, 2008), pp 2, 13 and 29–60. 2 See W. Parks, 'The Traditional Narrator and the "I Heard" formulas in Old English Poetry', *Anglo-Saxon England*, 16 (1987), 45–66; U. Schaefer, 'Rhetoric and Style', in R.E. Bjork and J.D. Niles (eds), *A 'Beowulf' Handbook* (Exeter, 1997), pp 105–24 at 120. 3 'Listen! We have heard of the might of the people-kings of the Spear-Danes in days of yore, how those athelings achieved glory!' All citations are taken from R.D Fulk, R.E. Bjork and J.D. Niles (eds), *Klaeber's Beowulf: Fourth Edition* (Toronto, 2008), henceforth referred to as Fulk et al. All translations are my own. 4 See F.C. Robinson, *'Beowulf' and the Appositive Style* (Knoxville, 1985), p. 28; S.B. Greenfield, 'The Authenticating Voice in *Beowulf*', *ASE* 5 (1976), 51–62. 5 See C.E. Wright, *The Cultivation of Saga in Anglo-Saxon England* (Edinburgh, 1939); R.W. Chambers, *Beowulf: an Introduction to the Study of the Poem with a Discussion of the Stories of Offa and Finn*, 3rd ed. with a supplement by C.L. Wrenn (Cambridge, 1959), pp 1–40, 401–8, 419–50.

Widsith (ll. 18, 88–92 and 111–30);[6] similarly, an allusion to the *ecghete* that will eventually burn Heorot (ll. 83b–5) anticipates the Heathobard-feud which Beowulf himself will later predict (ll. 2020–69a), also mentioned in *Widsith* (ll. 45–9).[7] But how much of the seemingly traditional material in *Beowulf* was in fact known to its Anglo-Saxon audience? To what extent can the poet be credited with originality in his reshaping of traditional materials? In this essay, I will focus on the important role assigned to [the oral poet] (OE *scop*) in *Beowulf*, in order to demonstrate that the *Beowulf*-poet draws attention to his own artistry, in particular his method of combining old tales in new ways to suit the demands of his audience. I will review biblical, classical and Germanic analogues to suggest that the story of the foundling Scyld Scefing with which the poem opens, long held to be among the poem's more traditional elements, may in fact have originated with *Beowulf*. In the absence of a consensus as to the date or provenance of composition,[8] Hugh Magennis has recently proposed that 'a more fruitful question than what was the original audience of *Beowulf* might be what could *Beowulf* have been used for in Anglo-Saxon England.'[9] By way of conclusion, I will suggest the poem might have been read as a source for the expansion of the West Saxon royal genealogy in the ninth century.

TALES OLD AND NEW

The Old English word for a poet or singer, *scop*, is related to the verb *scieppan*, 'to create, form, "shape" … make, order, destine, arrange, adjudge, assign'.[10] Following Lord and Parry's comparison of Homeric verse with the work of modern Serbo-Croatian poets, Francis Magoun, Jr, proposed that the high frequency of formulaic diction in *Beowulf* is indicative of oral composition.[11] Various theories have been advanced to account for the transition of an 'oral text' to the written page: an oral poet (or poets) may have composed in the presence of an anthologizing scribe; alternatively a poet trained in the oral tradition may have subsequently learnt the technology of writing, perhaps upon entering a monastery.[12] But lettered Anglo-Saxon writers composing in

6 See Fulk et al., p. 193.   7 See G.N. Garmonsway and J. Simpson, *'Beowulf' and Its Analogues* (London, 1968), pp 265–300.   8 See R.E. Bjork and A. Obermeier, 'Date, Provenance, Author, Audiences', in Bjork and Niles (1997), pp 13–34.   9 H. Magennis, 'Audience(s), Reception, Literacy', in P. Pulsiano and E. Treharne (eds), *A Companion to Anglo-Saxon Literature and Culture* (Oxford, 2002), pp 84–101 at 85.   10 J.R. Clark Hall, *A Concise Anglo-Saxon Dictionary*, 4th ed. (Cambridge, 1960), p. 294.   11 A.B. Lord, *The Singer of Tales* (Harvard, 1960, reprinted New York, 1976); F.P. Magoun Jr, 'The Oral-Formulaic Character of Anglo-Saxon Narrative Poetry', *Speculum* 28 (1953), 446–67. See further A. Orchard, *A Critical Companion to 'Beowulf'* (Cambridge, 2003), pp 85–91, 274–326; R.P. Creed, 'The Making of an Anglo-Saxon Poem', in D.K. Fry (ed.), *The 'Beowulf' Poet: A Collection of Critical Essays* (Englewood Cliffs, NJ, 1968), pp 141–53.   12 A.G. Brodeur, *The Art of 'Beowulf'* (Berkeley, 1959), pp 1–38; C.B. Kendall,

Latin and in Old English employed equally 'formulaic' diction,[13] and may well have consciously imitated the conventions of oral verse.[14] Indeed, as Niles has shown, the 'myth' of the oral poet exerted a powerful influence over the Anglo-Saxons, as exemplified in Bede's story of Cædmon (*Historia Ecclesiastica* iv. 24),[15] as well as the *Exeter Book* poems *Deor* and *Widsith*.

This myth lies behind several passages in *Beowulf* in which a Danish *scop* is carefully described in the act of 'shaping' old tales into a new form. One effect of the *scop*'s performances is to offer an interpretive gloss (for the audience's benefit) on the events of the main narrative. So, for example, the completion of the building of Heorot is marked by *swutol sang scopes*, 'the clear song of the poet' (l. 90a), who paraphrases Genesis I, recalling how *se ælmihtiga ... life al gesceop*, 'the Almighty ... shaped/created all life' (ll. 92a–97b). The pun on *scop/gesceop* identifies the act of poetic shaping with that of divine creation (OE *Scyppend* is a common epithet for God). But the *scop*'s ability to explain human history in terms of biblical story also aligns him with the narrator, who consistently grounds his tale in the mythical patterns of the Old Testament. For example, the allusion to the Heathobard feud mentioned above can now be understood in terms of the Great Feud between God and Fallen creation.[16] Grendel's simmering resentment of the joy in Heorot (ll. 86–9a), and his subsequent assaults on the hall, evoke the respective Falls of Lucifer and Adam and Eve.[17] His status as an exile is then explained by the narrator in terms of a genealogy which traces his ancestry to the cursed race of Cain (ll. 104–14). The *scop*'s 'Song of Creation' (ll. 89b–98) offers a Christian gloss on the account of the construction of Hrothgar's hall and the future crises that it will suffer, complementing the narrator's own use of Old Testament myth and inviting the audience to consider the joy of the Danes within the hall as an ephemeral, Edenic interlude.

Subsequent references to the performance of the *scop* cement these parallels with the role of the poet/narrator himself, both acting as mouthpieces for old tales while simultaneously modulating the audience's response to this new tale of Beowulf in Heorot. During the feasting after Beowulf's successful defence of the hall against Grendel, *Hroþgares scop* (l. 1066b) sings an abridged version of the story of the *Freswæl*, 'Frisian slaughter', itself the subject of

The Metrical Grammar of 'Beowulf' (Cambridge, 1991), pp 4–5. **13** L.D. Benson, 'The Literary Character of Anglo-Saxon Formulaic Poetry', in T.M. Andersson and S.A. Barney (eds), *Contradictions: From 'Beowulf' to Chaucer: Selected Studies of Larry D. Benson* (Aldershot, Hants, 1995), pp 15–31 at 11–12. **14** J.D. Niles, 'Locating *Beowulf* in Literary History', *Exemplaria* 5 (1993), 79–109 at 85–102. **15** J.D. Niles, 'The Myth of the Anglo-Saxon Oral Poet', *Western Folklore* 62 (2003), 7–61. See further R. Frank, 'The Anglo-Saxon Oral Poet', *Bulletin of the John Rylands University Library of Manchester* 75 (1993), 28–36. **16** See M. Osborne, 'The Great Feud: Scriptural History and Strife in *Beowulf*', *PMLA* 93 (1978), 973–81. **17** M. Godden, 'Biblical literature: the Old Testament', in M. Godden and M. Lapidge (eds), *The Cambridge Companion to Old English Literature* (Cambridge, 1986), pp 206–26 at 215.

another Old English poem, the *Finnsburh Fragment*.[18] While the *Fragment*
focuses in vivid detail on the heroic defence of Finn's hall by the Half-Danes,
the *scop* in Heorot focuses instead on themes of maternal grief and the impulse
towards revenge. What is more, the *scop*'s choice of material is prophetic, as
Grendel's mother will attack Heorot that same night. Once the news of
Beowulf's victory has been made known, a *scop* (possibly the same man, given
his identification as *cyninges þegn*, 'the king's thegn' (l. 867b)), celebrates *sið
Beowulfes*, 'Beowulf's exploits' (l. 872a) by way of allusion to two figures from
earlier poetic traditions. Before the negative *exemplum* of Heremod, he recites
a version of the tale of Sigemund:

> Hwylum cyninges þegn,
> guma gilphlæden,   gidda gemyndig,
> se ðe ealfela   ealdgesegena
> worn gemunde   word oþer fand
> soðe gebunden;   secg eft ongan
> sið Beowulfes   snyttrum styrian,
> ond on sped wrecan   spel gerade,
> wordum wrixlan;   welhwylc gecwæð,
> þæt he fram Sigemunde[s]   secgan hyrde
> ellendædum,   uncuþes fela,
> Wælsinges gewin,   wide siðas,
> þara þe gumena bearn   gearwe ne wiston   (ll. 867b–78).[19]

The unusual nature of this version of the Sigurd-Sigemund-legend is noted
by Andy Orchard, who comments that 'this is the only source which attrib-
utes a dragon-slaying to Sigemund, rather than to his son'.[20] This account of
a Danish oral poet creating a new poem from existing materials may provide
us with a useful analogue to the *Beowulf*-poet's own compositional technique.[21]
Both poets possess knowledge of old tales beyond the memories of their audi-

18 See E.G. Stanley, 'The Germanic "Heroic Lay" of Finnesburg', in his *A Collection of Papers
with Emphasis on Old English* (Toronto, 1987), pp 281–97.   19 'Sometimes the king's thane, a
man laden with songs, remembering lays, he who of a multitude of old sagas remembered many,
found other words truly bound together. The man afterwards began to skillfully recite Beowulf's
exploits and to successfully recount a tale, to mix words. He spoke a good deal that he had heard
said about Sigemund's glorious deeds, many unknown things, [about] the battles of Wael's son,
about which the sons of men did not readily know.'   20 Orchard, *Critical Companion*, p. 108.
For the analogues see Garmonsway, '*Beowulf* and Its Analogues', pp 251–64.   21 See N.E.
Eliason, 'The "Improvised Lay" in *Beowulf*', *Philological Quarterly* 31 (1952), 171–9; R.E. Kaske,
'The Sigemund-Heremod and Hama-Hygelac Passages in *Beowulf*', *PMLA* 74 (1959), 489–94;
R.P. Creed, ' "... wel-hwelc gecwæþ ...": The Singer as Architect', *Tennessee Studies in
Literature* 11 (1966), 131–43; J. Opland, 'From Horseback to Monastic Cell: The Impact on
English Literature of the Introduction of Writing', in J.D. Niles (ed.), *Old English Literature in
Context* (Cambridge, 1980), pp 30–43.

ence, and both locate their 'original' material in a traditional context by referring to what they have 'heard said' (l. 875b). The stories of Sigemund and his dragon-slaying son Sigurd appear to have been known in oral form in Anglo-Saxon England: Sigemund appears on a carving in the Old Minster, Winchester, while a scene from the Sigurd legend may be depicted on the Franks Casket. But the *scop* allows himself a degree of poetic licence in his telling of this traditional tale, as this particular song of Sigemund is one which his audience 'did not readily know' (l. 878b). Hrothgar's *scop*, or rather the *Beowulf* poet, appears, then, to have conflated the stories of Sigemund and Sigurðr (OE Sigurd) in order to establish a traditional context for the story of Beowulf's fight with the dragon.[22]

BEOWULF THE GEAT

Another story which the audience of *Beowulf* probably 'did not readily know' is that of Beowulf the Geat's three great monster-fights.[23] The late medieval Icelandic poem *Hrólfs saga kraka* records a legend of the haunting of the Skjoldung hall,[24] but the resemblances with Grendel are slight, and there are no equivalents to Grendel's mother or the story of an attack by a dragon on the royal hall of the Geats in extant Scandinavian records. Ultimately, the hero's fights with Grendel and his mother have their roots in two universal folktale-types, 'The Three Stolen Princesses' and 'The Bear's Son's Tale'.[25] But place-name evidence suggests that the name *Grendel* is derived from Anglo-Saxon, rather than Scandinavian folklore, while the dragon may owe as much to Christian saints' lives as it does to Norse mythology.[26] Beowulf himself is, if anything, even more obscure in his origins than his adversaries. Unlike other major kings in the poem he has no queen or siblings and produces no children. Neither he nor his father, Ecgtheow, appear outside the poem in historical or literary record and both their names fail to observe the pattern of alliterative name-giving which is a feature of royal families in the poem.[27] It is generally agreed, therefore, that the story of Beowulf's three great

22 See A. Bonjour, *The Digressions in 'Beowulf'* (Oxford, 1950), pp 46–7.   **23** See F. Klaeber (ed.), *'Beowulf' and the Fight at Finnsburh*, 3rd ed. (Boston, 1936), p. xlv; E.V.K. Dobbie (ed.), *'Beowulf' and 'Judith'* (New York, 1954) ASPR IV, p. xxxiv; W.W. Lawrence, *'Beowulf' and Epic Tradition* (Cambridge MA, 1928), pp 101–6; R. Frank, 'Germanic legend in Old English literature', in M. Godden and M. Lapidge (eds), *The Cambridge Companion to Old English Literature* (Cambridge, 1991), pp 88–106 at 98–101; F. Biggs, *'Beowulf'* and some fictions of the Geatish succession', *ASE* 32 (2003), 55–77 at 56–7.   **24** See J.D. Niles, 'On the Danish Origins of the *Beowulf* Story', in H. Sauer, J. Story and G. Waxenberger (eds), *Anglo-Saxon England and the Continent* (Tempe, 2011), pp 41–62.   **25** See T.M. Andersson, 'Sources and Analogues', in Bjork and Niles (1997), pp 125–48 at 133–38.   **26** See R.L. Reynolds, 'An Echo of *Beowulf* in Athelstan's Charters of 931–933 A.D.?', *Medium Aevum* 24 (1955), 101–3; C. Rauer, *'Beowulf' and the Dragon* (Cambridge, 2000).   **27** Dobbie, ASPR IV, p. xxxiv. See also K. Sisam, *The*

fights was largely the poet's innovation, allowing him to connect the stories
associated with the two main tribes of the poem, the Danes and Geats.[28]

Little is revealed of his early life before his arrival at Heorot: he is to some
extent a blank sheet onto which the poet can sketch new histories or amplify
old tales. But there are some hints about Beowulf's early youth which require
consideration. On his entrance into Heorot, the young Geat declares his reputation as the binder of five giants and an unspecified number of *niceras*, 'sea-
monsters' (ll. 420b–22). This story is soon questioned by Hrothgar's *þyle*,
Unferth, who claims to have heard tales about Beowulf losing a swimming
challenge with a Bronding chieftain named Breca (ll. 506–28). In support of
Unferth's case against Beowulf, much later we learn that the Geats had in fact
considered him lazy and cowardly (ll. 2187b–88a).[29] But the budding hero
denounces Unferth's version of events, casting himself as the greater swimmer of the two and, moreover, the brave vanquisher of no less than nine
niceras (l. 575a).[30] We see Beowulf here for the first time performing a role
equivalent to that of the traditional-narrator/*scop*, amplifying a version of his
own tale before a listening audience. These same rhetorical skills are on dis-
play again when Beowulf returns to Hygelac's court and embellishes the tale
of his adventures among the Danes by adding new details such as Grendel's
glof (ll. 2085b–91a) and Hrothgar's daughter, Freawaru, concerning whom he
indulges in a remarkable piece of prolepsis (ll. 2024b–68a). Beowulf shares
with the poet and his fictional scops a taste for auxetic embellishment, declar-
ing before Unferth that he has greater *merestrengo*, 'sea-strength', than any
other man, and in his speech to Hygelac praising the company in Heorot as
the most joyous under the heavens (ll. 2014–16a). He also possesses the poet's
eye for the details of courtly conduct and ritual, such as Freawaru's gracious
passing of a *nægled sinc*, 'nailed cup' (ll. 2020–24a), to the warriors, or the
recitation of old tales (perhaps by Hrothgar himself) to the accompaniment of
the harp (ll. 2105–14).[31]

It is interesting to note that Unferth's challenge comes immediately after
the only other reference to the practice of the *scop* in the poem:

Structure of 'Beowulf', (Oxford, 1965), p. 52; Frank, 'Germanic legend', pp 98–101; E.G. Stanley,
'*Beowulf: In the Foreground* (Cambridge, 1994), pp 14–15. The eleventh-century *Liber Vitae
Ecclesiae Dunelmensis* mentions a seventh-century monk named *Biuulf*; see P. Wormald, 'Bede,
Beowulf and the Conversion of the Anglo-Saxon Aristocracy', in his *The Times of Bede: Studies
in Early English Christian Society and Its Historian*, ed. S. Baxter (Oxford, 2006), pp 30–105 at
71–81.   **28** A.E. DuBois, 'The Unity of *Beowulf*', *PMLA* 49 (1934), 374–405 at 392–3, argues
that the poet invented Beowulf to represent the national strength of the Geats and its inevitable
decline.   **29** This echo of the folktale motif of the 'unpromising youth', who exceeds expectations and makes a name for himself in adolescence, connects Beowulf with another hero mentioned in the poem, Offa. See my article 'The Poetic Purpose of the Offa Digression in *Beowulf*',
RES 60 (2009), 538–60 at 552–3.   **30** See Bonjour, *Digressions*, pp 17–25; M. Puhvel, 'The
Aquatic Contest in *Hálfdanar saga Brönufóstra* and Beowulf's Adventure with Breca: Any
Connection?', *NM* 99 (1998), 131–8.   **31** See Fulk et al., pp 233–4.

                Scop hwilum sang
hador on Heorote.   Þær wæs hæleða dream,
duguð unlytel   Dena ond Wedera.
Unferð mæþelode,   Ecglafes bearn,
þe æt fotum sæt   frean Scyldinga,
onband beadurune.   Wæs him Beowulfes sið,
modges mereferan,   micel æfþunca   (ll. 496b–502).[32]

Though on this occasion we are not told the contents of his song, it is tempt-
ing to speculate that the *scop* may have marked the arrival of the Geatish party
by praising (and thereby no doubt exaggerating) their leader's exploits. As
Breca is mentioned in *Widsith* as a ruler of the Brondings (l. 21a), Larry
Benson proposes that 'Beowulf himself may have played some part in the tales
of the Brondings (where, by the rule of alliteration within families, he seems
to belong)'.[33] Perhaps, then, the poet chose Beowulf as the hero of this poem
because he had a reputation as a great swimmer and killer of sea-monsters,
qualities that will be required to overcome Grendel and his mother in their
water-hall. Benson suggests that the poet may have 'amplified' an existing lay
centred on the Breca-story, 'building his narrative by carefully expanding the
simple kernel of tradition from which he began' and thereby producing 'an
original work of art, based on a variety of traditional materials brought
together in a new way for new and more sophisticated purposes'.[34] The
Unferth-exchange is typically read as an opportunity for the hero to establish
his credentials against the foil of the cowardly Unferth. But given Unferth's
respected position within Heorot and subsequent rehabilitation as Beowulf's
trusted companion, there are clearly difficulties with this view. Although most
critics have readily accepted the veracity of Beowulf's version of the swimming contest, Gernot Wieland has recently argued persuasively that Unferth's
version of events should in fact be given more credence: the hero, as yet
unproven, may be telling tall tales about himself.[35] If the audience did know
something of a Beowulf-Breca story, in which Beowulf was the loser, the
Unferth-exchange may be read in a new light as a comment on the problems

32 'The scop sometimes sang brightly in Heorot. There was joy among the warriors, a large
troop of Danes and Weders. Unferth spoke, Ecglaf's son, who sat at the feet of the lord of the
Scyldings, unbound hostile thoughts. The journey of Beowulf, brave seafarer, was a great insult
to him.'   33 L.D. Benson, 'The Originality of *Beowulf*', in M.W. Bloomfield (ed.), *The
Interpretation of Narrative: Theory and Practice*, Harvard English Studies 1, (Cambridge MA,
1970), pp 1–43; reprinted in T.M. Andersson and S.A. Barney (eds), *Contradictions: From
'Beowulf' to Chaucer: Selected Studies of Larry D. Benson* (Aldershot, 1995), pp 32–69 at 48–50.
34 Benson, 'The Originality of *Beowulf*', p. 69.   35 G.R. Wieland, 'The Unferth Engima: The
þyle between the Hero and the Poet', in R. Bauer and U. Krischke (eds), *Fact and Fiction: From
the Middle Ages to Modern Times, Essays Presented to Hans Sauer on the Occasion his 65th Birthday
– Part II*, Münchner Universitätsschriften, vol. 37 (Frankfurt, 2011), pp 35–46.

that might arise when a poet tells an old tale in a new way. Unferth and
Beowulf argue over the true version of the Breca story: the poet leaves it to
his audience to decide which they would rather believe. I would suggest that
in the Unferth-exchange, as in the account of the *scop*'s song of Beowulf,
Sigemund and Heremod, the *Beowulf*-poet invites his audience to consider the
complex role of oral poets (in this case, Beowulf himself) as mediators of stories which they must reshape with each new performance. Of course, *Beowulf*
is not in its present form an oral poem, but a written text, whatever its origins may have been. After the Conversion, Anglo-Saxon England underwent
the transition from what Walter Ong has called a state of primary orality,
where the technology of the word was as yet unknown, to one of residual orality, where literacy was the preserve of an educated elite.[36] Stories about
Hrothgar and Hygelac must have originally circulated in oral form, given the
illiterate nature of southern Scandinavia. It is likely that these stories were
also the subject of oral poems in early Anglo-Saxon England. But as these
tales encountered the literate culture of Christianity they came to be copied
into manuscripts. In these passages from *Beowulf* we can observe an Anglo-
Saxon poet engaging in an instructive discourse about the inherently unstable
nature of oral storytelling. It is impossible to say whether this interest was
inspired by the poet's first-hand experience of the performance of scops, or
by his sensitivity to the challenges facing this ancient art with the emergence
of the relatively fixed medium of the written word.[37]

SCYLD SCEFING

It is generally assumed that a version of the story of Scyld Scefing and Beow[38]
Scyldinga, with which the poem begins, was part of the traditional material
known to the poem's original intended audience.[39] The story can be summa-
rized thus: Scyld arrives among the Danes as a child in a boat; he becomes
king and subjugates the neighbouring tribes; his son generously distributes
treasures among the Danes; and his death is marked by a splendid ship
funeral. The allusive style adopted throughout the Scyld-passage has encour-

---

36 W.J. Ong, *Orality and Literacy: The Technologizing of the Word* (London, 1982).   37 On the
instability of Old English written texts, see K. O'Brien O'Keeffe, *Visible Song: Transitional
Literacy in Old English Verse* (Cambridge, 1990).   38 The manuscript reads *Beowulf* but most
editors agree that at some stage in the text's transmission a scribe altered the name of Scyld's
son from Beo/Beow to Beowulf, confusing Scyld's son with the hero of the poem. See
Chambers, *Beowulf*, pp 41–7, 87–8, 291–304; K. Sisam, 'Anglo-Saxon Royal Genealogies',
Proceedings of the British Academy 39 (1953), 287–346 at 317–20 and 339–45.   39 See, for example, J.D. Niles, '*Beowulf*: the Poem and Its Tradition* (Cambridge MA, 1983), p. 207. For a general discussion of this aspect of the poet's style see D. Whitelock, *The Audience of 'Beowulf*
(Oxford, 1951), pp 34–44.

aged scholars to infer that some version of the story was already in circulation before the poem. For example, Judy King has recently commented that this passage constitutes 'less a portrait of Scyld than the poet's summary of what is known about him from poetry or song.'[40] However, there are good reasons to suspect that Scyld Scefing and Beow Scyldinga as they appear in *Beowulf* were not originally part of Danish dynastic tradition.

In the following lines, Beow Scyldinga fathers a son, Healfdene, who succeeds him as ruler of the *glæde Scyldingas* (l. 58b). Healfdene has four children, Heorogar, Hrothgar, Halga and a daughter whose name has been lost due to scribal error. Later in the poem we learn that another king of the Danes, Heremod, was exiled on account of his failure to distribute rings (ll. 901–15 and 1709–22a). Most commentators therefore place Scyld Scefing's arrival among the Danes during the interregnum that followed Heremod's deposition. But just as Beowulf the Geat and his father Ecgtheow stand apart from the Hrethlings and Wægmundings by virtue of their un-alliterating names, Scyld Scefing and Beow Scyldinga are the only male members of the Danish royal family in *Beowulf* whose names do not alliterate on *H*:[41]

Heremod
|
Scyld Scefing
↓
Beow Scyldinga
↓
Healfdene
↙ ↓ ↘
Heorogar Hrothgar Halga
↙ ↓ ↘
Heoroweard   Hrethric & Hrothmund   Hrothulf

Stories concerning Heremod (ON Hermóðr), Healfdene (ON Hálfdan), Hrothgar (ON Hróarr), Halga (ON Helgi), Hrothulf (ON Hrólfr Kraki), Heoroweard (ON Hjorvarðr) and Hrethric (ON Hrœrekr), are preserved in the later Norse records and the Old English poem *Widsith*.[42] Scyld (ON Skjold), by contrast, is conspicuously absent from the king-lists in *Widsith*, though a ruler of the Lombards named Sceafa (l. 32b) is mentioned in a list

---

40 J. King, 'Launching the Hero: the Case of Scyld and Beowulf', *Neophilologus* 87 (2003), 453–71 at 457. See also D. Clark, 'Relaunching the Hero: the Case of Scyld and Beowulf Re-opened', *Neophilologus* 90 (2006), 621–42.   **41** In addition the names of the so-called 'Half-Danes' also begin with *H*: Hoc, his son Hnæf and daughter Hildeburh, and his thane, Hengest. For the suggestion that Hengest was a Jute, see Orchard, *Critical Companion*, p. 183.   **42** For translations of the texts discussed below, see Garmonsway, *'Beowulf' and Its Analogues*, pp 124–211.

which also contains Breca, Finn, Hnæf and Ongentheow. This list in *Widsith* is placed immediately before the longer references to Offa and Hrothgar and Hrothulf, suggesting that this Lombard Sceafa he may have been part of traditions related to those which lie behind *Beowulf*. According to Paul the Deacon, the Lombards came from the island of *Scadinavia*,[43] though he does not mention Sceafa or any other ruler of the Lombards with a similar name. It is not, therefore, possible to identify the Lombard Sceafa with the Anglo-Saxon tradition of a Danish foundling named Scef. Some post-Viking age traditions about an early king of the Danes named Skjold survive in Norse records. For example, the sixteenth-century Latin abstract of the now-lost *Skjoldunga saga* (*c*.1200) states that Sciouldus, son of Odinus (ON Othin), was the first king of the Danes. Ruling from Lejre, he subdued and took possession of Jutland and it was from him that Danish kings took the title of 'Skiolldung'.[44] The story of Heremod's demise is echoed by the account of Lother and Skyoldus in Saxo Grammaticus.[45] The *Skioldung* genealogy given in Sven Aageson's late-twelfth century *History of the Kings of Denmark* is close in parts to the Scylding genealogy at the beginning of *Beowulf*, but there are some differences in detail. While in *Beowulf* Scyld has only one son, Beow Scyldinga, who is succeeded by Healfdene and Hrothgar, Sven states that Skiold had two sons Halfdan (OE Healfdene) and Frothi (the dragon slayer), who fought over the succession: Halfdan killed Frothi and took the kingdom; his son Helghi (OE Halga) succeeded him, and became famed for piracy; Helghi was succeeded by Rolf (OE Hroþulf) Kraki, who was killed at the royal residence at Lejre; Rolf was then succeeded by Rokil Slagenback and then Frothi the Bold. There is no trace of Scyld Scefing's arrival as a foundling or his ship funeral in Norse sources. Neither is Scyld/Skjold associated with the heroic traditions of Hroarr (OE Hrothgar) and Hrolfr Bjarki (OE Hrothulf), or with fertility figures equivalent to Scef, 'sheaf' and Beow, 'barley'.[46] In *Langfeðgatal* we find the generations: Magi–Seskef/Sescef–Bedvig–Athra–Itermann–Heremotr–Scealdna–Beaf–Eat–Godulfi–Finn–Frealaf–Voden. But this section of the Scandinavian royal genealogies is almost certainly dependent on West Saxon rather than authentic Scandinavian tradition: the meaningless *Seskef/Sescef* is probably a rendering of OE *se Scef*,[47] while OE Scyld/Sceldwa, Beow and Geat have also become garbled in transmission. As Chambers comments, it is unlikely that the Danes would have forgotten 'utterly so striking a story, concerning the king from whom their line derived

43 *Paul the Deacon, History of the Langobards*, trans. W.D. Foulke (Philadelphia, 1907), i, 1–7. 44 'Danasaga Arngríms Lærða', in *Danakonunga Sogur: Skjoldunga Saga, Knytlinga Saga, Ágrip Af Sogu Danakonunga*, ed. B. Guðnason, Islenzk Fornrit 35 (Reykjavik, 1982), pp 3–38.   45 See A.M. Bruce, *Scyld and Scef: Expanding the Analogues* (New York, 2002), pp 134–40.   46 See M. Fjalldal, *The Long Arm of Coincidence: the Frustrated Connection between 'Beowulf' and 'Grettis saga'* (Toronto, 1998).   47 A. Faulkes, 'Descent from the gods', *Mediaeval Scandinavia* 11 (1978–9), 92–125 at 94.

its name.'[48] If the Scyld Scefing story does not have its roots in Scandinavian royal traditions, what, then, is its provenance?

A popular theory is that the poet borrowed the foundling-story from traditions associated with the ancestors of the West Saxon royal house. The names Scyld, Scef and Beow appear in somewhat garbled forms along with other Danish legendary kings such as Heremod in the genealogy constructed for King Alfred's father, Æthelwulf, in the *Anglo-Saxon Chronicle* entry for 855. *Sceaf* is cast as the son of Noah, born in the Ark, while several generations separate him from *Sceldwa* and *Beo*. Æthelweard's late-tenth century Latin version of the *Anglo-Saxon Chronicle* provides a much closer analogue to *Beowulf*, with the generations *Scef–Scyld–Beo*.[49] In place of the story of *Sceaf*'s birth in Noah's ark, Æthelweard includes a version of the foundling story which closely resembles the account of Scyld Scefing's arrival in *Beowulf*, though here the story is attributed to *Scef* rather than *Scyld*.[50] Although Æthelweard was writing toward the end of the tenth century, it is usually assumed that he used a version of the Chronicle predating the archetype for the *Anglo-Saxon Chronicle*.[51] No literary sources have been conclusively identified for *Beowulf*: Germanic legends were likely to have been circulated principally in oral form, while allusions to the biblical stories of the Creation, Cain and Abel and the Flood may have been encountered through preaching or the liturgy rather than reading.[52] But Alistair Campbell argued that the story of Scyld Scefing's arrival in the land of the Danes is a product of bookish learning, deriving from 'an annotation to a genealogy',[53] while Audrey Meaney has argued that both *Beowulf* and Æthelweard derived the story of the foundling from a hypothetical version of the Chronicle predating that behind *Anglo-Saxon Chronicle*.[54] An alternative explanation for the partial agreement between *Beowulf* and Æthelwulf's genealogy in the *Anglo-Saxon Chronicle* is that both, as Sam Newton suggests, are dependent on 'a common Old English source, perhaps a genealogy maintained in verse'.[55] But Michael Lapidge proposes that

48 Chambers, *Beowulf*, p. 86. 49 *The Chronicle of Æthelweard*, ed. A. Campbell (London, 1962), pp 32–3. 50 Sisam, 'Genealogies', p. 320, suggests that Æthelweard may have known, and rejected, the fanciful story of Sceaf's birth in Noah's ark and descent from Adam. See also A.C. Murray, '*Beowulf*, the Danish Invasions, and Royal Genealogy', in C. Chase (ed.), *The Dating of 'Beowulf'* (Toronto, 1981), pp 101–11 at 106–07; J. Bately, *The Anglo-Saxon Chronicle: Texts and Textual Relationships* (Reading, 1991), p. 46. 51 F.M. Stenton, 'The South-Western Element in the Old English Chronicle', in D.M. Stenton (ed.), *Preparatory to Anglo-Saxon England: Being the Collected Papers of Frank Merry Stenton* (Oxford, 1970), pp 106–15 at 114; E.E. Barker, 'The Anglo-Saxon Chronicle Used by Æthelweard', *Bulletin of the Institute of Historical Research* 40 (1967), 74–91 at 77–9. 53 For reviews of the evidence see Andersson, 'Sources and Analogues', pp 138–46; and Niles, *Beowulf*, pp 66–95. 54 A. Campbell, 'The Use in *Beowulf* of Earlier Heroic Verse', in P. Clemoes and K. Hughes (eds), *England Before the Conquest: Studies in Primary Sources presented to Dorothy Whitelock* (Cambridge, 1971), pp 283–92 at 290. 55 A.L. Meaney, 'Scyld Scefing and the Dating of *Beowulf* – Again', *Bulletin of the John Rylands University Library of Manchester* 71 (1988), 7– 40 at 37. Meaney also suggests an

the West Saxon royal pedigree might in fact be indebted to 'a poem resembling (if not identical with) our *Beowulf*.[56] In the following discussion I will explore the possibility that the story of the foundling Scyld Scefing drawn on by the West Saxon genealogists may have originated with *Beowulf*.

THE ROOTS OF THE SCYLD SCEFING STORY

In the absence of any obvious precedent in Scandinavian dynastic tradition, scholars have unearthed a number of mythological parallels to the foundling story attached to Scyld Scefing in *Beowulf*. As Andy Orchard notes, the tale may have its roots in an agricultural myth: the significance of the names Scyld Scefing ('Shield with the Sheaf' or 'son of Scef'), and Beow ('Barley') would have been readily apparent to an Anglo-Saxon audience.[57] The veneration of the sheaf is an important feature of northern harvest rituals and in some instances the corn-god is represented by the figure of a boy.[58] But the closest analogue to *Beowulf*, in which we find the shield combined with the sheaf in the context of a divinely-inspired sea-journey, comes not from Scandinavian myth but from records of Anglo-Saxon monastic culture. The thirteenth-century Chronicle of Abingdon contains an account of a ritual used to settle a land-dispute during the reign of Edmund (941–6) in which a sheaf was placed on a shield and allowed to float down a river marking out territory. A miracle occurs enabling the shield to travel against the current and circle a flooded island which is then claimed as the property of the monastery.[59] Although this story survives only in a post-conquest account, the detail of the round shield suggests its authenticity, pointing to the belief in a ritualistic

account of the funeral of Saint Gildas which came to Anglo-Saxon England around 920 was the source for the account of Scyld's ship funeral. But the widespread material and documentary evidence for princely ship burial throughout the early northern world suggests that an imaginative Anglo-Saxon poet would hardly have needed to turn to a literary account of a saint's funeral for inspiration.   56 S. Newton, *The Origins of 'Beowulf' and the Pre-Viking Kingdom of East Anglia* (Cambridge, 1993), p. 76. See also Niles, 'Locating *Beowulf* in Literary History', 95.   56 M. Lapidge, '*Beowulf*, Aldhelm, the *Liber Monstrorum* and Wessex', *Studi Medievali* 3rd ser. 23 (1982), 151–92 at 187. See also R.D. Fulk, 'An Eddic Analogue to the Scyld Scefing story', *RES* 40 (1989), 313–22 at 320. For the suggestion that Æthelweard's *Chronicon*, compiled around the time of the copying of the *Beowulf*-manuscript, was influenced by the poem, see Bately, *The Anglo-Saxon Chronicle*, p. 46, n. 315; C. Tolley, '*Beowulf*'s Scyld Scefing Episode: some Norse and Finnish Analogues', *Arv: Journal of Scandinavian Folklore* 52 (1996), 7–48 at 12.   57 Orchard, *Critical Companion*, pp 102–03. See further F.C. Robinson, 'The Significance of Names in Old English Literature', *Anglia* 86 (1968), 14–85.   58 See Chambers, *Beowulf*, pp 6–8, 68–86 and 292–304; J. Harris, 'The Dossier on Byggvir, God and Hero: *Cur deus homo*', *Arv: Nordic Yearbook of Folklore* 55 (1999), 7–23; Fulk, 'An Eddic Analogue to the Scyld Scefing Story'.   59 For the text see *Chronicon Monasterii de Abingdon*, ed. J. Stevenson (London, 1858), vol. 1, p. 89; transl. in Orchard, *Critical Companion*, pp 102–03.

association of the shield and the sheaf in tenth-century Wessex, itself probably derived from much earlier West Saxon folk-traditions.

The pairing of shield and sheaf in the name of the dynastic founder figure
Scyld Scefing echoes the Indo-European motif of the 'divine twins'. In a royal
context, the name is suggestive of the protective and regenerative properties
of the ideal king. Germanic foundation legends are often focused on a pair of
war-leaders with alliterating names,[60] while in Anglo-Saxon tradition, this story
is combined with the theme of 'The Arrival of the Hero in the Ship', as
Mercedes Salvador-Bello has noted.[61] The Kentish royal house claimed
descent from Hengest, 'stallion', and Horsa, 'horse', according to Bede (*Historia Ecclesiastica* i. 15) the first Germanic mercenaries to arrive from the
Continent; while Wessex traced its dynasty back to the arrival of Cerdic and
Cynric.[62] The names of the Anglo-Saxon dynastic founders appear to have
been manipulated in the course of oral traditions to bring them into line with
place names: hence Hengest and Horsa's at *Heopwines fleot* and Cerdic and
Cynric's arrival at *Cerdicesora*.[63]

These Anglo-Saxon royal foundation myths may themselves owe something to the classical model of Romulus and Remus. Rome occupied a central
place in the Anglo-Saxon imagination,[65] and the legend of its foundation is
well attested in early Anglo-Saxon art.[65] Indeed, the pair seems to have
enjoyed special popularity during the eighth century, when they appear on
the Franks Casket juxtaposed with scenes from biblical and Germanic lore, as
well as on a bone plaque found in Norfolk and coins issued by rulers with
imperial pretensions.[66] The Romulus and Remus story certainly bears close

---

60 See D. Ward, *The Divine Twins: An Indo-European Myth in Germanic Tradition* (Berkeley
and Los Angeles, 1968); E. Polomé, 'Germanic Religion', in M. Eliade (ed.), *Encyclopedia of
Religions*, vol. 5, (New York, 1987), pp 520–36 at 531–32. So, for example, Paul the Deacon preserves the story of Ibor and Aio, ancestors of the Lombards, who opposed the aggression of the
Vandal kings Ambri and Assi; see Foulke, I, 7, pp 11–15.   61 M. Salvador-Bello, 'The Arrival
of the Hero in a Ship: A Common Leitmotif in Old English Regnal Tables and the Story of
Scyld Scefing in *Beowulf*', *SELIM – Journal of the Spanish Society for Medieval English Language
and Literature* 8 (1998), 205–21.   62 Newton, *The Origins of 'Beowulf'*, pp 77–81, suggests that
Hroðmund and Hryp, two names contained in the genealogy of King Ælfwald of East Anglia
(*c*.713–49), were thought of as alliterating dynastic founder figures for East Anglia during the
reign of Ælfwald.   63 Plummer, I, pp 12–16; Salvador-Bello, 'The Arrival of the Hero in a
Ship', p. 208.   64 See N. Howe, *Writing the Map of Anglo-Saxon England: Essays in Cultural
Geography* (New Haven, CT, 2008), pp 101–24.   65 M. Hunter, 'Germanic and Roman antiq-
uity and the sense of the past in Anglo-Saxon England', *ASE* 3 (1974), 29–50 at 32 and 38–40;
C.L. Neuman de Vergar, 'The Travelling Twins: Romulus and Remus in Anglo-Saxon
England', in J. Hawkes and S. Mills (eds), *Northumbria's Golden Age* (Stroud, 1999), pp 256–67
at 239–41.   66 L. Webster, 'The iconographic programme of the Franks Casket', in Hawkes
and Mills (1999), pp 227–46 at 239–41; B. Green, 'An Anglo-Saxon Bone Plaque from Larling,
Norfolk', *The Antiquaries Journal* 51 (1971), 321–3; D.M. Metcalf, 'Monetary Circulation in
Southern England in the First Half of the Eighth Century', in D. Hill and D.M. Metcalf (eds),
Sceatta in England and on the Continent, BAR, British Series, 128 (Oxford, 1984), pp 27–69, fig.

comparison with *Beowulf*'s sketched outline of Scyld Scefing's early career: according to Livy and Plutarch, the twins were placed on the bank of the flooding Tiber in a trough; after rescue they were suckled by a she-wolf, and then brought up among herdsmen, prospering by seizing plunder from brigands which they then distribute in return for loyalty.[67]

Of course, the Scyld Scefing story differs from these tales in that the founder figure in *Beowulf* is an individual rather than a set of twins. But the story of the individual foundling does have another counterpart in popular Anglo-Saxon tradition. As Gale Owen-Crocker notes, a Christian Anglo-Saxon audience hearing a story involving the recovery of an infant from the water who becomes a tribal saviour would inevitably have thought of Moses.[68] Nicholas Howe has shown that the Exodus provided the Anglo-Saxons with a mythical template which helped them to understand tales of their own migration in terms of Christian history.[69] The influence of the Old Testament and related apocrypha in shaping the *Beowulf*-poet's understanding of the past is widely recognized,[70] and Wieland has noted parallels between the characterization of Moses in the Old English *Exodus* and Beowulf.[71] Given the recognition that Scyld's career acts as a template for that of the Geatish hero,[72] it is worth considering that the parallels between Scyld and Moses extend beyond the obvious similarity in the circumstances of their arrival among a troubled people to the accounts of their funerals. While Scyld journeys into the keeping of the Lord *felahror*, 'very strong' (l. 27a), Moses dies with 'his eye undimmed, his vigour unimpaired' (Deuteronomy 34:7). The mourning of the Israelites at Moses' passing and their ignorance of his final location (Deuteronomy 34:5–9) is echoed by the Danes' uncomprehending sorrow at Scyld's departure. In both cases the sorrow of the mourners is offset by the presence of a successor who will continue to lead the tribe. Moses, like Scyld, is not only a foundling but also an instrument of divine intervention in the history of an afflicted people (Cf. Exodus: 2:1–10; 3:7–10) and the statement that God *fyrenðearfe ongeat*, 'recognized the dire need', (l. 14b) of the Danes echoes phraseology in Exodus describing God's recognition of the suffering of the Israelites (Exodus 2:23–25; 3:7–9; 3:16).

16.   **67** See *Lempriere's Classical Dictionary* (London, 1984), pp 146 and 592; E. M. Meletinsky, *The Poetics of Myth* (New York and London, 1998), pp 57 and 183–96.   **68** G.R. Owen-Crocker, *The Four Funerals in 'Beowulf' and the Structure of the Poem* (Manchester, 2000), p. 18.   **69** N. Howe, *Migration and Mythmaking in Anglo-Saxon England* (New Haven, 1989), p. 177.   **70** See Orchard, *Critical Companion*, pp 130–68; Godden, 'Old Testament'; D. Anlezark, *Water and Fire: The Myth of the Flood in Anglo-Saxon England* (Manchester, 2006), pp 291–67.   **71** G.R. Wieland, '*Manna mildost*: Moses and Beowulf', *Pacific Coast Philology* 23 (1988), 86–93. See also Owen-Crocker, *Four Funerals*, pp 18–19 and 103–04; T.D. Hill, 'Scyld Scefing and the *Stirps Regia*': Pagan Myth and Christian Kingship in *Beowulf*, in A. Groos (ed.), *Magister Regis: Studies in Honor of Robert Earl Kaske* (New York, 1986), pp 37–47 at 43.   **72** See Bonjour, *Digressions*, pp 1–11.

CONCLUSION

The interplay of biblical, Germanic and pagan classical elements is a defining characteristic of Anglo-Saxon culture. Artefacts like the Franks Casket, which juxtaposes scenes including Weland's revenge, Christ's nativity, the discovery of Romulus, and a tale involving Sigurd, demonstrate a tendency to allow the various disparate strands of the Anglo-Saxon cultural inheritance to comment on and complement each other. The same impulse is well attested in literary record, such as vernacular heroic poems on Christian themes, saints' lives and philosophical and sapiential works, all of which accommodate aspects of the new learning that became available to the Anglo-Saxons following their entrance into the Roman-Christian world, while still retaining distinctive elements of the old continental culture. *Beowulf* is the most sophisticated surviving literary example of this process of cultural negotiation, in which legends brought over from the Anglo-Saxon 'continental homeland'[73] are reconciled with biblical myth through the startling originality of the poet. This is achieved principally through the creation of a new hero, perhaps amplified from earlier traditions, who wins praise as much for his mildness, generosity and kindness to his subjects as for his eagerness for fame (ll. 3180–82). The Scyld Scefing story which opens the narrative may be another innovation of the poet, harmonizing Germanic and biblical conceptions of good kingship with Anglo-Saxon folk traditions involving the association of the shield and the sheaf. The poet knew that the Danish royal family (and tribe) were known as Scyldings and that their court was located in Scedeland. He also found in Danish royal tradition a convenient gap in the history of their ruling dynasty between the reigns of Heremod and Healfdende. I am not proposing that the poet invented Scyld, or Scef: the names appear to reflect early English traditions. Rather I suggest that by drawing together some, if not all, of the sources and imagery discussed above, the author of *Beowulf* reshaped these traditions to create the story of the Danish royal founder figure Scyld Scefing. He was telling an old tale (or several old tales) in a new way. By inserting this story into the gap between Heremod and Healfdene, he furnished his poem with a mythical introduction which demonstrates that royal power is a precious gift from God, while emphasizing the importance of the kingly acquisition of plunder and its generous distribution among the warrior class.

The continuing popularity of vernacular heroic verse in the late Anglo-Saxon period is suggested by topical poems such as *Brunanburh*, *Maldon* and *The Death of Edgar*, and it has been argued that *Beowulf* might have had some political significance during this period.[74] But the compilers of the Nowell

---

73 The phrase is borrowed from Howe, *Migration and Mythmaking*. **74** See R.L. Kellogg, 'The Context for Epic in Later Anglo-Saxon England', in H. Damico and J. Leyerle (eds), *Heroic Poetry in the Anglo-Saxon Period: Studies in Honor of Jess B. Bessinger, Jr* (Kalamazoo, 1993), pp

Codex appear to have valued *Beowulf* chiefly for its exotic blend of the monstrous and the antique.[75] Moreover, palaeographical and orthographical evidence strongly suggest that the poem had already passed through several stages of transmission, and therefore different 'interpretive communities',[76] prior to its final copying.[77] As most scriptoria were attached to religious houses, it is likely that the poem was read in monastic circles at some stage during the Anglo-Saxon period. Alcuin's famous castigation of the monks of Lindisfarne for their enjoyment of stories about Ingeld points to the cultivation of pagan Germanic legend within monastery walls, despite the efforts of some to suppress it. Considering the poem's aristocratic setting and pronounced concern with royal history, it would be surprising if *Beowulf* did not also attract the interest of court circles in Anglo-Saxon England. By the late ninth century, the kings of Wessex extended their dominion over the Danes living in England. It had become fashionable by this time for Anglo-Saxon kings to claim descent from legendary Germanic kings by means of elaborate genealogies, now widely recognized as the products of clerical culture rather than accurate reflections of ancient oral traditions.[78] To conclude I will return to Hugh Magennis' question concerning the use of *Beowulf* in Anglo-Saxon England with which this essay began. In reply, I would suggest that the *Beowulf*-poet was so successful in presenting Scyld Scefing as an authentic part of Danish royal tradition that some elements of the story were used as source for the remote stage of the West Saxon royal genealogy.

139–56; L. Viljoen, 'The *Beowulf* manuscript reconsidered: Reading *Beowulf* in late Anglo-Saxon England', *Literator* 24:2 (2003), 39–49; K. Powell, 'Meditating on Men and Monsters: A Reconsideration of the Thematic Unity of the *Beowulf* Manuscript', *Review of English Studies* 57 (2006), 1–15; H.L.C. Tristram, 'What's the Point of Dating *Beowulf*?', in H.L.C. Tristram (ed.), *Medieval Insular Literature Between the Oral and the Written II: Continuity of Transmission*, ScriptOralia 97 (Tübingen, 1997), pp 65–80; L. Neidorf, '*VII Æthelred* and the Genesis of the *Beowulf* Manuscript', *Philological Quarterly* 89 (2010), 119–39.   **75** See K. Sisam, *Studies in the History of Old English Literature* (Oxford, 1953; reprinted 1998), pp 65–94; A. Orchard, *Pride and Prodigies: Studies in the Monsters of the 'Beowulf' Manuscript* (Cambridge, 1995); S.B. Greenfield, 'A Touch of the Monstrous in the Hero or Beowulf Re-Marvellized', in his *Hero and Exile: The Art of Old English poetry*, ed. G.H. Brown (London and Ronceverte, 1989), pp 75–92.   **76** S. Fish, 'Interpreting the Variorum', *Critical Inquiry* 2 (1976), 465–85.   **77** M. Lapidge, 'The Archetype of *Beowulf*', *ASE* 29 (2000), 5–41.   **78** See Sisam, 'Genealogies'; D. Dumville, 'Kingship, Genealogies and Regnal Lists', in P.H. Sawyer and I.N. Wood (eds), *Early Medieval Kingship* (Leeds, 1977), pp 72–104.

Three twelfth-century kings and their successors in some Middle English chronicles

ERIK KOOPER

1120: This year the king of England and that of France became reconciled. ... Then after this the king Henry disposed his castles and his land in Normandy according to his wishes, and so went to [England] before Advent.

And on the journey the king's two sons William and Richard were drowned – and Richard earl of Chester and Ottuel his brother, and very many of the king's court: stewards, and chamberlains, and cup-bearers, and various officials, and countless very distinguished people along with them. To their friends the death of these was a double grief: one that they lost this life so suddenly, the other that few of their bodies were found anywhere afterwards.[1]

Under the year 1120 we find, in the Peterborough continuation of the *Anglo-Saxon Chronicle*, a brief account of what was one of the greatest tragedies of twelfth-century England: the wreck of the White Ship. In this naval disaster perished the king's one legitimate son, William, his (illegitimate) half-brother Richard, and many another scion of the most noble families of England and Normandy. It bereft Henry I of his son, and left the kingdom without an heir. For Geoffrey of Monmouth, according to Chris Given-Wilson, 'the single most potent reason why there were times when war and chaos descended was the failure of a king to leave an acceptable heir'.[2] This then was the situation in which Henry I found himself in 1120, and one that, as we shall see, played a major role during the rest of his reign.

The twelfth century in England is almost entirely spanned by three kings: Henry I (1100–35), Stephen (1135–54) and Henry II (1154–89). The two Henrys are usually reckoned among the greatest kings of English history, Stephen as one of the worst. Nevertheless they had a number of features in common. To secure their territories, each had to fight with (a) the king of France, (b) the rulers of Scotland and/or Wales and (c) their own relatives. All three made their barons and clergy swear oaths of fealty to their heirs. And all three saw these heirs die an untimely death before they had any offspring of their own. Apart from the problems they had in common, each had his individual cares as well: Henry I's daughter Matilda was not acknowledged as a legal heir to the throne; Stephen

---

1 M.J. Swanton, ed. and trans., *The Anglo-Saxon Chronicle* (London, 1996), E, p. 249. I am much indebted to Thea Summerfield and Sarah Peverley for their comments on an earlier draft of this paper.   2 Chris Given-Wilson, *Chronicles: The Writing of History in Medieval England* (London, 2004), p. 198.

was considered a usurper; and Henry II gave preferential treatment to his youngest son, John, infuriating the other three. In other words, each of the three lived and reigned in a complicated, explosive political situation with a delicate balance of power, all the more so because each of them also had problems with the Church: the conflict with Archbishop Anselm in the case of Henry I, the opposition from the English prelates for Stephen, and Henry II's powerplay with Thomas Becket, leading eventually to the latter's murder (to mention only the most important issues). However, it is not the purpose of this paper to summarize the lapses and triumphs of these three English kings. Rather, it addresses the relationship between them and their heirs in twelfth-century England, investigating in particular how the historiographers writing in Middle English deal with the way in which both private and political decisions and changes in policy affected the handing-on of power from generation to generation.

When, in the late thirteenth century, authors writing in the vernacular entered the field of historiography, they had many precursors relating the history of pre- and post-Conquest England in Latin and Anglo-Norman.[3] The following authors and chronicles will be considered in this paper: Robert of Gloucester (1290–1300), Thomas Castleford (*c.*1327), Robert Mannyng (1338), Ranulph Higden/John Trevisa (1387), the Prose *Brut* (*c.*1400), John Hardyng (1440–64), and John Capgrave (1462–65).

HENRY I

Dates and events[4]

1100:   William Rufus, king of England, dies. His father, William the Conqueror, had divided his bipartite kingdom between his two eldest sons, with Robert Curthose, the firstborn, receiving Normandy, while William Rufus (William's favourite) became king of England.[5] The youngest, Henry, was merely given a considerable sum of money, but had received the best education, earning him the epithet 'Beauclerc'. When William Rufus died his brother Robert was on his way back from crusade, and Henry was quick to seize the opportunity and have himself crowned within a few days of William's death. During the crusade Robert had acquired a great reputation as a warrior, and upon his return he claimed the throne.

---

3 The works of William of Malmesbury (*c.*1125; *c.*1140), Geoffrey of Monmouth (*c.*1136), Henry of Huntingdon (*c.*1130–54), Orderic Vitalis (*c.*1114–41), Gaimar (*c.*1140), Wace (*c.*1155) and the anonymous author of the Anglo-Norman Prose *Brut* (a.1300) appear to be their most important sources. 4 It goes without saying that the choice of events is limited and determined by the topic of this essay, and in no way represents the complexities of the course of history. 5 William's second son, Richard, had at an early age been killed during a hunting party; William Rufus would be killed in the same way. Henry I died following a meal of lampreys while he was staying in a hunting lodge.

1106: The Battle of Tinchebray. It is one of the ironies of history that this time Henry, now king of England, crossed the Channel, defeated Robert Curthose at Tinchebray and conquered the duchy of Normandy, the patrimonial estate. With his father imprisoned by Henry, William Clito, incited by the French king and rebellious Norman barons, repeatedly challenged Henry's lordship of Normandy.

1115: As a reaction against this continuous pressure on the stability of the Norman dynasty, Henry makes his barons swear fealty to his son, William.

1120: The tragedy of the White Ship. To secure the hereditary succession of his line after William drowned, Henry took a number of precautionary measures: within two months he married the much younger Adeliza of Louvain (he was 53, she 17), and, when the German emperor Henry V, husband of his daughter Matilda, died in 1125, he called her back to England, and made the barons renew their oath, now in favour of Matilda.

1127: Under pressure from her father, Matilda marries Geoffrey, heir of Anjou.

1131: Henry forces the nobles to repeat their oath to Matilda, as the first had been nullified due to her marriage. They did so, if grudgingly, including Stephen.

1135: Death of Henry I. Matilda's right of succession was immediately contested by Stephen and most of the other barons.

THE ACCOUNTS IN THE CHRONICLES

(a) The wreck of the White Ship and its aftermath
In his voluminous *Historia ecclesiastica*, Ordericus Vitalis (1075–1142), an English monk in the monastery of St Évroult in Normandy, gives a lengthy and dramatic account of what happened on the fateful night of 25 November 1120, including the sort of details that demonstrate that he made quite an effort to acquaint himself with the facts. Thus, he informs us how much wine the drunken crew had been given to drink, and that Stephen (the future king) and some others disembarked 'because they realized that there was too great a crowd of wild and headstrong young men on board'.[6] All in all there are seven more or less contemporary versions of the shipwreck, but, as R.M. Thomson says: 'For what happened after the ship struck the rock all the detailed accounts were ultimately dependent upon the report of the single survivor, a butcher of Rouen'.[7] Unlike most others, Henry of Huntingdon is very

6 Marjorie Chibnall, ed. and trans., *The Ecclesiastical History of Orderic Vitalis*, VI (Oxford, 1978), p. 297.   7 William of Malmesbury, *Gesta Regum Anglorum: The History of the English Kings*, II, General Introduction and Commentary by R. M. Thomson, in collaboration with M.

brief on the disaster (only a few lines), because, as he said: 'All of them, or nearly all, were said to be tainted with sodomy and they were snared and caught.' He considered it to be the 'glittering vengeance' of what to us appears a very Old Testamental God.[8] Robert of Gloucester is even more outspoken in his censure:

> In þe tuentiþe ȝer of is kinedom þis dede was ydo,
> Ac wreche of god & sunne hom broȝte þer to,
> Vor mid þe vile sunne of sodomye yproued hii were echon.
> Þeruore þoru wreche of god þer nas ybured non,
> Ne miȝte be founde in þe se of al þat hii were isoȝt,
> Vor god nolde þat such sunne were vnder erþe ybroȝt.   (9036–41)[9]

Also Higden/Trevisa follow Henry of Huntingdon closely here, while Capgrave has it that those who drowned were 'grete slaundered [disgraced]' in the sin of sodomy.[10] Castleford only mentions the death by drowning of William and Richard, without any comment on the ship or the travellers, let alone their possible sinfulness. Mannyng, the Prose *Brut* and Hardyng have a similarly detached account, but mention the grief it caused Henry.[11] Different from what one might expect with such a dramatic event, the chroniclers deal with it very cautiously and with great restraint. Evidently they were uneasy about the accusations of sodomy.

With his only legitimate son dead and his daughter married to the German emperor, the harsh reality for Henry was that he had no heir. Consequently, as William of Malmesbury says, he 'abandoned the celibate life … looking impatiently for fresh heirs from a new wife',[12] and very soon, as we saw, he married the young and attractive Adelize of Louvain, not so much to find comfort of his 'mornynge', as Hardyng thinks,[13] as for dynastic considerations. Robert of Gloucester and John Capgrave give no reasons why

---

Winterbottom (Oxford, 1999), p. 382.   8 Henry, Archdeacon of Huntingdon, *Historia Anglorum: The History of the English People*, ed. and trans. Diana Greenway (Oxford, 1996), vii.32, p. 467. Both Orderic and Henry include a poem to express the emotional impact of the disaster.   9 William Aldis Wright (ed.), *The Metrical Chronicle of Robert of Gloucester*, Rolls Series 86, 2 vols (London, 1887).   10 Peter J. Lucas, ed., *John Capgrave's Abbreuiacion of Cronicles*, EETS OS 285 (Oxford, 1983), p. 105, l. 20.   11 After listing some of the people who drowned, the Prose *Brut* continues: 'When Kyng Henry and oþere lordes arryued were in Engeland, and harde þise tidyngus, þai made sorwe ynow ; & al her merþe & ioye was turnede þo into sorwe & care'; *The Brut or The Chronicles of England*, 2 vols, EETS OS 131, 136 (London: 1906, 1908. Repr. Millwood: Kraus Reprint, 1987), I, p. 143, ll. 15–17.   12 *Gesta Regum Anglorum*, Bk.V.419 8, p. 763. Yet, as Judith Green rightly remarks, even if he 'remarried and fathered a son, he would be old before that son reached manhood'; see her *Henry I: King of England and Duke of Normandy* (Cambridge, 2006), p. 168.   13 John Hardyng, *Chronicle*, Second Version (MS Arch. Selden B.10), l. 7369. Sarah Peverley, who is preparing a new edition of this version, very kindly allowed me to use her transcription of the text.

Henry might have decided to marry Adelize, they merely refer to her remarkable beauty, of which 'was mech spech and mech wryting',[14] and the Prose *Brut* skips the marriage altogether. The most interesting item is that in Mannyng's *Chronicle*, for according to him it was the girl's father who took the initiative and offered his daughter's hand to Henry.[15] But 'Nane childre on her he gate, men saiden' (Castleford, l. 32,978), and so again Henry had to change course.[16] However, this time fortune came to his rescue because Matilda's emperor husband died, and as a result Henry could push her forward as his successor.

(b) The succession of Henry I
The most reliable information on the problems surrounding Henry's succession is found in William of Malmesbury's *Historia Novella*. Henry was under pressure from nephews on two sides: the son of his elder brother Robert Curthose, William Clito (who died childless in 1128), and Stephen, count of Blois, the second son of his younger sister Adela, who played a much more prominent role than his elder brother Theobald. William presents at length Henry's arguments that Matilda is the legitimate heir.[17] He also explains that the barons felt that Matilda's marriage 'outside' the kingdom, that is, to Geoffrey of Anjou, had freed them of their oath (Bk I, 452, pp 4–5). For this reason Henry made the barons repeat this oath (Bk I, 455, p. 10).

None of the chronicles in English makes mention of the barons' pledge of fealty to Henry's son William. This is not surprising, considering their interest was basically genealogical: since he was never king of England, William is to the chroniclers no more than a footnote in the country's line of succession. Matters are quite different with Matilda (popularly known as 'Empress Maud'), as there was a direct link between, on the one hand, the strength of her position as heir of Henry I and her claim to the throne, and, on the other, the oath taken by the barons. Here most texts refer to at least one oath to Matilda (usually the second, which makes Matilda's claim more convincing), and many mention that Stephen took it along with the other nobles.

Thomas Castleford is quite exceptional in that he explains why Henry made Matilda marry Geoffrey of Anjou (with the hope that they might produce an heir), and why, at the end of his life, he made the barons swear fealty again: Matilda still had no child. When Henry died, the barons felt not bound

---

14 Capgrave, *Abbreuiacion of Cronicles*, p. 105, l. 24. **15** Robert Mannyng of Brunne, *The Chronicle*, ed. Idelle Sullens, Medieval and Renaissance Texts and Studies 153 (Binghamton, 1996), Part II, ll. 2582–6. **16** Since Henry had, apart from his two legitimate children, at least 19 illegitimate ones, he had good reason to suspect that Adelize was barren (in fact she was not: after Henry's death she remarried and had at least seven children). For Henry's offspring, see, for example, David C. Douglas and George W. Greenaway (eds), *English Historical Documents*, II, 2nd edn., Tables II, 4. **17** William of Malmesbury, *The Historia Novella*, trans. K.R. Potter (London, 1955), Bk I, 451, pp 3–4.

by it, because Matilda had no male heir, and a woman on the throne was acceptable only if she had a son to succeed her. As a consequence they elected Stephen.[18] This account comes very close to the historical facts as we know them. It stands in stark contrast with that of Robert of Gloucester, who presents a rather distorted view of events. He first tells of Matilda's marriage and the birth of her son, 'þat was suþþe oure king' (l. 9091), then continues with a number of completely unrelated events, to finish his account thirty lines later with the king's sombre ruminations on the future of England: if he would leave the country to Stephen there would never be peace, as he was not the rightful heir, and if he left it to the rightful heir, his grandson Henry, not yet three years old, the child would soon be robbed of it, in spite of the oath that had been sworn by 'al Engelond & Steuene þe Bleis also' (ll. 9126–27). Robert makes no secret of where his sympathies lie.

Robert Mannyng shares the view of Robert of Gloucester that after William had drowned Matilda was Henry's heir by right. But when Henry died, he says, there was great uncertainty about the succession:

> On bere lay Kyng Henry, on bere beyond þe se,
> þat non wist certeynly who his heyr suld be.
> Of Mald som had þe speyre*, þe erle wif of Aniowe,   * hope
> hir son Henry, & heyre of him, was maste to trowe.
> So long he lay on bere for doute of his lynage,
> tille men þe soth mot here who suld haf þe heritage,
> els I ne wote for wham his biriyng suld men schonne,
> tille Steven of Plesance cam, þat was his sister sonne.   (II, 2620–7)

STEPHEN

Dates and events

1135:   Henry I dies. When Henry died he left all his possessions to his daughter, Matilda. But, as Frank Barlow put it, 'Had either Geoffrey or Matilda been acceptable to the baronage there would have been no crisis.'[19] As it was, Matilda's arrogance and Geoffrey of Anjou's general unpopularity led the barons, after lengthy discussions, to recognize Theobald IV of Blois, the oldest grandson of William the Conqueror and a cousin and ally of Henry, as duke of Normandy.[20] However, his younger brother Stephen did not await the outcome of the barons' deliberations, and sailed for England where, with the

---

18 *Castleford's Chronicle or The Boke of Brut*, 2 vols, ed. Caroline Eckhardt, EETS OS 305, 306 (Oxford, 1996), II, ll. 33,009–22; 33,033–60. 19 Frank Barlow, *The Feudal Kingdom of England 1042–1216*, 3rd edn. (London, 1972), pp 201–2. 20 Ibid., p. 202

help of his brother Henry, bishop of Winchester, and the support of the city of London, he was crowned at Westminster by the archbishop of Canterbury. Naturally, because Stephen had twice sworn fealty to Matilda, she considered him a usurper, and with his coronation the seed for a civil war had been sown.

1137: Stephen has his son Eustace do homage for Normandy to the French king, Louis VI.

1139: Stephen loses the support of the Church, even of his own brother, bishop Henry.[21] Contemporaries like William of Malmesbury do not give Stephen as bad a press as do modern historians, at least not for the initial period of his reign. That changed when he turned against the Church, but even then William of Malmesbury blamed his counsellors rather than the king himself.[22] On the other hand Matilda – however just her claim to the throne – managed through her haughty behaviour to antagonize even her most loyal supporters.

1140: After the death of Louis VI, Stephen arranged a marriage between Eustace and Constance, the sister of the young Louis VII, as a result of anxiety about the succession caused by Matilda's opposition. (According to Higden/Trevisa, Stephen 'bought' the bride with money he had confiscated.)[23]

1150: In this year, after a number of initial successes, prospects for Matilda's cause were unfavourable: she had withdrawn to Normandy, and although her son Henry had inherited his father's dukedom, Anjou, in 1151, and had acquired, through his marriage a year later, the duchy of his wife, Eleanor of Aquitaine, he was as yet too much engaged by these new responsibilities to recommence the war on Stephen.

1152: For Stephen it seemed the right moment to secure his succession, and so he tried to push through the coronation of his son Eustace. The attempt failed because, by order of the pope, the archbishop refused on the grounds that Stephen had broken his oath to Henry I and Matilda. This setback signalled a sudden and complete reversal of the situation.

1153: The loss in 1152 of Stephen's beloved wife (also called Matilda) was followed in 1153 by the death of his son Eustace. In the same year Henry was carrying out a successful invasion, and, as Barlow has it,

---

21 Austin Lane Poole, *From Domesday Book to Magna Carta, 1087–1216*, The Oxford History of England, 2nd ed. (Oxford, 1955), p. 136. **22** *Historia Novella*, Bk I. 465, p. 20. **23** Churchill Babington and Joseph R. Lumby (eds), *Polychronicon Ranulphi Higden Monachi Cestrensis; together with the English translation of John Trevisa and of an unknown writer of the fifteenth century*, VII, Rolls Series, 41 (London, 1879; repr. Millwood: Kraus Reprint, 1964), Lib. VII, pp 484–5.

'[b]roken at last by these calamities',[24] Stephen was ready to negoti-
ate a settlement with Matilda and Henry. On the condition that he
would remain king until his death, Stephen gave up his kingdom to
Henry, while his remaining son, William, was bought off with the
assurance that he would inherit all the family property.

The accounts in the chronicles
Not a single chronicler fails to mention Stephen's breach of oath toward
Matilda; Castleford explains, however, that by 'regale custum' (that is, because
at the time of the oath Matilda had no male heir), the barons were not bound
by it and consequently Stephen could be elected.

Although their entries on Stephen are far from short, Gloucester and
Castleford make no mention at all of Eustace, nor do the Prose *Brut* or John
Capgrave. Castleford even goes so far as to say that Stephen died childless
because he remained chaste. Simplification comes at a price. The only chronicler to give Eustace a prominent role is Hardyng; in the later, revised version of his *Chronicle* (Oxford, Arch. Selden MS B.10), the first two stanzas
on Stephen's reign run as follows:

> Stevyn of Bloys, his suster sone, was crownde,
> A manly man was than of grete powere,
> And kynge was made of Englond in that stounde,
> Withouten stryff or eny maner werre.
> To Normandie he wente and saised alle there,
> And gaff hit to his sone, Sir Eustas,
> And made hym duke there of with grete solace.
>
> This Eustas than, duke of Normandie,
> To Parice went to Kynge Lewis of Fraunce
> His homage made for his londe on hye,
> And putt oute than, with grete contrariaunce,
> The officers that did to Mawde pleasaunce,
> And other made to hir grete anoysaunce,
> And wedded the suster of Kynge Lewis to wyff
> For suppwelle of hit withouten stryff.   (7419–33)

Here Stephen's accession seems unproblematic, and it is Eustace who clears
Normandy of the nobles who sided with Matilda. There is a striking difference between the wording in this text and that in the copy that Hardyng had
presented to King Henry VI in 1457, which is highly critical of the way in
which Stephen became king:

24 Barlow, *The Feudal Kingdom of England*, p. 233

> agayne his own fewté
> Whiche he had made to Mawde afore that date
> And eche baroun had done in his estate
> Who toke none hede of thaire foule perjury
> Bot oonly than obeyed his tyrany.　　　　(Bk IV, 724–9)[25]

In addition it also lays the shameful act of bundling Matilda's followers out of Normandy with Stephen himself. Eustace then receives Normandy from his father, and pays homage for that to King Louis, but nothing is said about the marriage with the French king's daughter (or sister). In spite of these and other divergences, the two versions agree on one thing: no more is heard of Eustace after his appearance at the beginning of Stephen's reign. One gets the impression that his role was simply to emphasize Stephen's malign behaviour towards Matilda.

HENRY II

Dates and events

1154: Stephen dies, and thanks to the arrangement with Matilda,[26] Henry's succession is unproblematic. Henry had vast territories in France, but many of them, or at least their boundaries, were contested. But he was a cunning schemer and plotter, and Louis VII was no match for him. By means of a shrewd strategy of marriage contracts for his children he managed to build a network of alliances around the kingdom of France and thus to strengthen his position vis-à-vis Louis.

1158: Henry got Louis to accept a betrothal between Henry the Young King and Margaret, Louis' daughter with his second wife, Constance of Castile. Henry was three years old, his bride not yet a year. In 1160 (when Henry was five and Margaret two), permission for a marriage was sought from the pope, Alexander III, and obtained because the pope needed Henry's support in the schism which had just erupted. As soon as the marriage had been consecrated, Henry demanded the dowry, the Vexin castles, crucial Norman border strongholds.

25 John Hardyng, *Chronicle*, First Version (BL MS Lansdowne 204). I am very grateful to Sarah Peverley and James Simpson, who are jointly preparing a new edition of this version, for allowing me to use their transcription of the text. As Sarah Peverley has pointed out, 'perhaps Hardyng changed his text because he intended this new version for Richard duke of York and his son Edward IV, who had taken Henry VI's throne. The issue of feudal loyalty is a tricky debate for Hardyng to be entering into where the monarchy is concerned' (private communication). 26 It is postulated that Stephen's second son would inherit 'all that his father had held before he became King'. W.L. Warren, *Henry II* (London, 1973), p. 67.

1166:   (a) Henry arranged the betrothal of his fourth son, Geoffrey (7), to
         Constance (5), heiress of Brittany (the marriage did not take place
         before 1181). Henry forced Constance's father into retirement, and
         claimed the duchy for himself.[27] His daughter Maud (12) he mar-
         ried off to Henry the Lion, duke of Saxony (39), Eleanor (8) was
         betrothed to Alfonso VIII of Castile (15), and Joan (12) married
         King William of Sicily (24). The minimum age at which girls were
         allowed to marry was 12, for boys 16.[28] As far as can be ascertained,
         however, neither the marriages themselves, nor the ages at which the
         children had to marry, appear to lie at the root of the problems
         between them and their father. These were rather of a financial char-
         acter, or had to do with power, influence and status.
         (b) Birth of the last child, John. From this year on, Henry and
         Eleanor live separately.

1170:   (a) Henry arranged the coronation of his son Henry (15), in imita-
         tion of the practice of the Capetians,[29] and possibly also of what had
         happened in Germany a year earlier with the Emperor Frederick and
         his son Henry. But although at the coronation Henry had given his
         son a kingdom, he withheld access to the financial means he needed
         to live as a king.
         (b) Henry's conflict with Thomas Becket came to a disastrous cul-
         mination when Thomas was murdered by four of Henry's knights
         on 29 December, while celebrating mass in Canterbury Cathedral.

1173–74: The great rebellion. As a result of their dissatisfaction with Henry,
         his sons could be manipulated, and Louis was able to get Henry the
         Young King, his son-in-law, on his side, followed by Richard (who
         had received Aquitaine, his mother's homeland, and was encouraged
         by her) and Geoffrey (John was too young to take part). In 1173,
         assisted by Louis of France, the count of Flanders and the king of
         Scotland, all three rose against Henry. But even though the odds
         seemed stacked against him, Henry once again outwitted his oppo-
         nents, and in the end was reconciled with his sons. Because she had
         supported her sons, Eleanor was confined to Winchester Castle (and,
         following that, a number of other places) for the rest of Henry's reign.

1183:   Death of Henry, the Young King.

1188–9: At the instigation of his mother, Richard revolts, supported by John
         and Philip of France.

1189:   Henry dies, and is buried at Fontevraud.

---

27 David Carpenter, *The Struggle for Mastery: Britain 1066–1284*, The Penguin History of
Britain (London, 2004), p. 195.   28 Shulamith Shahar, *Childhood in the Middle Ages*, trans.
Chaya Galai (London, 1990), p. 224. However, the average age was higher, around 17.   29
Warren, *Henry II*, p. 111.

The accounts in the chronicles

From a dynastic angle the death of Young Henry was less catastrophic than that of the sons of Henry I or Stephen, as he had three brothers, two of whom, Richard and John, survived their father and became king after him. Moreover, the continuation of the dynasty was secure not only through these potential successors but also because Henry's kingship in itself was uncontested. The real drama was in the ill-fated combination of the shifting historical circumstances at the time of his reign and the bewildering complexities of the king's character,[30] as well as in his failure to build a lasting relationship with his wife, his sons, or anyone else around him. At the end of his life he had to leave his kingdom not to his preferred successor, Young Henry, but to Richard, the son who was the protégé of his wife and had shown himself his most fierce opponent.[31]

Most space in the chronicles goes to Henry's conflict with Thomas Becket, though for Capgrave and Hardyng the whole struggle is of minor importance: a mere 10 per cent of their total account of Henry II, with no specifics given, not even the cause of the rupture. Mannyng, after spending about 75 lines (approx 20 per cent of his narrative) on the subject, breaks off at the death of Thomas and refers the reader to his (Thomas') book, 'for þer in ere þei writen/meruailes grete plente þat fele of vs ne witen' (II, 3221–2). Gloucester, in a total of 320 lines on Henry's reign, throws in at least 200 lines from the legend of St Thomas in the contemporary *South English Legendary*, mostly quoted verbatim; and Castleford takes as many as 360 lines to recount the events (in a total of 1,700 lines, that is, also approx. 20 per cent). Most of them make mention, and often provide details, of the notorious Statutes of Clarendon, the articles issued by Henry in 1164 on the relation between Church and State, which were rejected by Thomas.

Practically all the chronicles include the child marriage of Young Henry and Margaret (with the exception of the Prose *Brut*), but none offers any comment on their ages. Mannyng is idiosyncratic in more ways than one here: he has Henry the Young King marry after his coronation, and with the sister of Louis VII.[32] Since of the others only Capgrave gives both the names and the ages of the couple, it would seem that to him (Capgrave) there was something extraordinary in the affair. On the other hand, what puzzles the modern reader is that Capgrave mentions neither the coronation nor the death of Young Henry.

---

30 For a contemporary's characterization of Henry II, see William of Newburgh, *Historia rerum anglicarum* (Bk 3, ch. 26; I, 280–3). For a modern historian's, see for instance Warren, *Henry II*, p. 630.   31 True as these remarks may be, Carpenter reminds us that Henry was an extraordinarily successful king, who 'restored royal authority in England and fashioned the common law. He subjected Scotland and conquered Ireland. Across the Channel he rebuilt ducal power in Normandy and established lordship over Brittany'; see his *The Struggle for Mastery*, p. 191. 32 In the older MS, Lansdowne 204, Hardyng also makes the same error, but corrects it in the later version.

Moreover, after Henry II's death he has him succeeded by his *brother* Richard
– apparently Capgrave got confused by the identical names of father and son.

The various revolts by Henry's sons tend to be handled in a fairly
detached manner. Of course Henry has much to be blamed for, such as the
murder of Thomas Becket, but in the end he proves himself stronger than his
rebellious sons, and that is a feat much appreciated by the authors. Mannyng
is again different in that he plays down the quarrels and presents Henry as a
great peacemaker, to whom his sons and even the Scottish kings swore oaths
of loyalty. Hardyng reduces the revolts to one by Young Henry alone, who
is, after his defeat, reconciled with his father. Most extraordinary is the twist
given to Young Henry's rebellion by Castleford: after Henry had done
penance for the murder of Thomas, in which he was joined by his son,

> In England ras ful gret distance,
> Sua þat þe kyng Henrik, þe fadre,
> Ful gret power bigan to gadre
> Wiþ strenþ and fors againes his son,
> Fra him for to tak þe coron.   (34,992–6)

No cause for this discord is given, it is just presented as a historical fact. In the
ensuing battles, Young Henry has the upper hand, but whenever he has to face
his father in the field, he takes his shield and goes 'to his innes' (35,020). The
fighting continues for two years, in the course of which Young Henry even goes
north to defeat the invading Scottish king and his army (in reality honour for
this feat is due to Richard de Lucy, the justiciar). The pope and the king of
France send their wisest diplomats 'betuix þe kynges þe pes to schape' (35,100).
They finally succeed in arranging a meeting in London (in reality this took
place near Tours, in France), in which Young Henry 'dide reuerens' (35,111)
to his father, who agreed henceforth to live and stay in Normandy, while Young
Henry was confirmed as king of England and Ireland.

More than any of the other chroniclers Robert of Gloucester has an eye
for the personal tragedy that developed during Henry's reign. Because he
wanted to surround himself with good counsellors, Gloucester says, Henry
appointed Thomas Becket as his chancellor. No one is trusted more by Henry,
or nearer to him, than Thomas. He makes him the teacher of Young Henry,
and leaves his son with him when he himself goes to France:

> To him þe king truste mest ne þer nas non so hey
> 9605 Þat so muche wuste is priuite ne þat him were so ney.
> So muche he truste on him þat in is warde he let do
> Henri is eldoste sone & is eir al so,
> Þat he were his wardein & al is ordeinour,
> To is wille to wissi him & to þe kinges honour.

9610 Þe king wende to Normandie to soiorni þere
    & mid sein Tomas dude is sone þat he is wardein were
    Ðo Tebaud þe erchebissop suþþe ded was
    Þe king & monekes ek chose seint Tomas.
    Ðo he was erchebissop he huld yut in is hond
9615 Þat child uort þat* þe king come into Engelond.   *until
    Þe child louede him inou more nas neuere iseye,
    Ne he nadde of no man more loue ne eye.*   *respect
    Ðo þe king to londe com sein Tomas nom is sone
    & vel vawe ayen him wende to Souþhamtone
9620 Þer was ioye & blisse inou þo hii to gadere come
    Hii custe hom & bi clupte & herede god ilome.
    ...
9635 Þe wule is children yonge were al þis was ido,
    Noman ne miyte þenche þe loue þat þer was
    Bituene þe king Henri & þe gode man sein Tomas.
    Þe deuel adde enuie þer to & sed bituene hom seu.
    Alas, alas, þulke stounde, vor al to wel it greu. (9604–39)

As Gloucester has it, the devil became envious of this happy community and came between Henry and Thomas. After Thomas was murdered, Henry went into deep mourning, realizing that this could never be set right. His life became even more complicated when his sons rebelled again. Gloucester presents this new rebellion as instigated by Young Henry's father-in-law, Louis; but Henry himself, he says, thinks it is a punishment from God for the martyrdom of Thomas. Therefore, instead of going to the head of his army, Henry goes to mass, and while he is praying, begging Thomas for mercy, his troops win the battle that is fought outside. Thanks to Thomas another reconciliation between father and son is effected. But the Young Henry's heart continued to oppose his father, often aided by his brothers (who also regularly were at loggerheads among themselves), until his death in 1183. His father seized the crown again, but he held the kingdom with 'contek muchedel', due to the 'unkindness' (that is, unnatural behaviour) of his sons, and his own sinful life, for even when he was still living with the queen he had a mistress, Rosamond, a juicy detail mentioned only by Gloucester and Higden/Trevisa.[33]

When Henry refuses to go on crusade himself and only promises generous financial support, God is displeased, and Henry has to face another war with the king of France, now Philip, and also his son Richard:

33 Gloucester, *Chronicle*, ll. 9854–59. The *Polychronicon* has a short description of her living-quarters in Woodstock, reminiscent of the underground 'boudoir' of Estrildis, the mistress of king Locrinus, the eldest son of Brutus; see vol. VIII (London, 1882; repr. Millwood: Kraus Reprint, 1964), Lib. VII, pp 52–5.

Þerwiþ nas noȝt God ipaid, oþer þing he gan hom sende,
& worre hom bituene, vor þe king of Fraunce
Cudde vpe þe king of Engelond gret destourbance.
9890   & Richard þe kinges sone, þat so god kniyt was,
Ayen is fader turnde, & to þe king of France alas,
& dude him omage anon – alas, alas, þe stounde –
& fondede mid worre to bringe is fader to grounde.
Þe olde man in Normandie worrede ayen hom vaste,
9895   & slou & barnde vp is fon þe wule is lif ilaste.
Ac he deide in þe worre sone in anguisse & in pine,
As endleue hundred yer of grace & eiyteti & nine.
Þe sixte day of Iul he deide, & mid gret onour & prute
At Founte Ebraud he was ibured, as he liþ yute.   (9887–99)

From the moment of Young Henry's coronation his father is frequently referred to as the 'old' king, no doubt to distinguish him from his son, but in the light of the phrase 'Þe olde man' in this final passage the word achieves an additional, more emotional value. Robert of Gloucester clearly feels pity for the great king who met with such a dramatic end.

CONCLUSIONS

In his comprehensive analysis of the writing of history in medieval England, Given-Wilson concludes: 'By the mid-twelfth century ... historical writing in England ... had become essentially king-centred. Reigns were becoming the "natural" divisions into which material was partitioned, and that material was becoming increasingly secular'.[34] A hundred-and-fifty years later, when histories in Middle English began to be produced, this tendency had developed into standard practice: the basic facts of a king's birth, marriage, coronation and death were sprinkled with a wide range of additional events which could vary considerably from chronicle to chronicle. But as Mannyng says, having reached the end of his chronicle (II, 8354), the core was in the matter of kings' lives, and hence the story of the wreck of the White Ship, or of Young Henry's untimely death, fascinating as they may be, are no more than ornamentation, for they are not about kings. As Hardyng put it when Young Henry had died:

And but foure yere[35] [Henry's] son regned, sothe to seyne;
Wherfore he is among kynges certayne
Noght accompted by no croniclere,
For his fadir was kyng afore and aftir clere. (Arch. Selden, 7671–4)

34 *Chronicles*, p. 164.   35 This is Hardyng's error; it should be thirteen years.

The choice of the extra material was not only determined by the impact of events on national history, but also by the stance, not to say bias, of the chronicler. In his ground-breaking study, *Politics and Poetry in the Fifteenth Century*, John Scattergood demonstrated the influence of contemporary events on the work of writers such as John Hardyng.[36] A similar conclusion regarding the author's perspective on national history was drawn for Robert of Gloucester and Robert Mannyng by Thorlac Turville-Petre.[37] For all the writers of history dealt with in this paper, John Scattergood's conclusion for fifteenth-century verse holds true:

> When a writer chooses to comment on contemporary political events or social conditions he is almost always concerned to express his own feelings, his attitudes and opinions, his hopes and fears. Frequently he intends his poem to influence others to feel the same way.[38]

The comparison of half-a-dozen history writers presented above has shown that they do indeed make very personal choices. What we need next are more detailed studies of the individual texts to obtain a better insight into the motives underlying their decisions.[39]

36 *Politics and Poetry in the Fifteenth Century*, Blandford History Series (London, 1971), pp 173–6.   37 *England the Nation: Language, Literature, and Identity, 1290–1340* (Oxford, 1996), p. 80. For Gloucester, he argues, it is, in general, the history of Christianity in Britain (p. 89), or, for post-Conquest history, the restoration of ancient liberties (p. 98); for Mannyng it is, among other things, the superiority of the English to other peoples and nations (p. 87). Both medieval authors share a clear anti-Norman sentiment.   38 *Politics and Poetry*, p. 11.   39 A good example of such a study is Thea Summerfield, *The Matter of Kings' Lives: Design of Past and Present in the Early Fourteenth-Century Verse Chronicles by Pierre de Langtoft and Robert Mannyng*, Costerus New Series 113 (Amsterdam, 1998). To this may be added the series of articles on John Hardyng and his chronicle by Sarah Peverley; see, for example, her 'Genealogy and John Hardyng's Verse Chronicle', in *Broken Lines: Genealogical Literature in Late-Medieval Britain and France*, ed. Raluca L. Radulescu and Edward Donald Kennedy, Medieval Texts and Cultures of Northern Europe 16 (Turnhout, 2008), pp 259–82, and 'Political Consciousness and the Literary Mind in Late Medieval England: Men "Brought up of Nought" in Vale, Hardyng, *Mankind*, and Malory', *Studies in Philology* 105 (2008), 1–29.

Ex chequer art. by Henry I

Culture and dispute in *Dialogus de Scaccario*

BRENDAN O'CONNELL

Surgens ergo sede ex aduerso et de his que te offendunt interroga.
Quod siquid inauditum proposueris non erubesco dicere 'Nescio, set
conueniamus ambo discretiores.'

[Come and sit here, across from me, and ask me questions as they
occur to you. If you ask me something I don't know, I'm not embar-
rassed to say, 'I don't know, but let's consult those who are wiser.']¹

a. Ka... FitzNeal

Sitting at a tower-window overlooking the Thames in the twenty-third year
of Henry II, royal treasurer Richard FitzNigel is approached by a colleague
who beseeches him to write an account of contemporary Exchequer proce-
dure.² FitzNigel reluctantly agrees, and proposes a dialogue in which he will
perform the role of *magister*, while his colleague, as *discipulus*, asks a series of
questions. The resulting work, *Dialogus de Scaccario*, or *Dialogue of the
Exchequer*, is one of the most valuable historical documents of the twelfth century and, along with such works as John of Salisbury's *Policraticus* and the
legal treatise known as *Glanvill*, one of the most distinguished products of 'the
intellectual stimulus provided by the work of government in the time of Henry
II'.³ M.T. Clanchy gives considerable prominence to the work in his study of
the emergence of lay literacy in the period 1066–1307. This is unsurprising,
given the dialogue's use of Latin to record bureaucratic procedures, as well as
its consistent characterization of the Norman Conquest as the pivotal moment
of transition from oral to written culture.⁴ The text is of further interest to
Clanchy because it represents itself not only as an attempt to codify in writing practices that had previously been transmitted orally, but also as the transcription of a spoken dialogue between teacher and student.

1 Richard FitzNigel, *Dialogus de Scaccario*, or *The Dialogue of the Exchequer*, ed. and trans. Emilie
Amt, in *Dialogus de Scaccario and Constitutio Domus Regis*, ed. Emilie Amt and S.D. Church
(Oxford, 2007), p. 8/9. All references are to this edition, unless otherwise indicated; page num-
bers cite both the original and the facing page translation. I was first introduced to the *Dialogus*
by the supervisor of my doctoral thesis, John Scattergood, who highlighted not only the importance of the text as a source for medieval economic theory and practice, but also suggested that
its form deserved greater attention from literary scholars. 2 *Dialogus*, p. 6/7. The twenty-third
year of Henry's reign lasted from 19 December 1176 to 18 December 1177. 3 R.W. Southern,
Medieval Humanism and Other Studies (Oxford, 1970), p. 176. Cited in M.T. Clanchy, *From
Memory to Written Record: England 1066–1307*, 2nd ed. (Oxford, 1993), p. 18. 4 See, for example, Clanchy's treatment of FitzNigel's representation of Domesday book, pp 19, 32, 151.

In some respects, the choice of the dialogue form seems entirely natural: the twelfth century was, after all, an age in which scholastic disputation flourished, and which produced numerous important philosophical and theological dialogues. Indeed, Alex Novikoff has written persuasively of the 'culture of disputation' in the period.[5] All the more striking, then, that no close analogues exist for FitzNigel's entirely secular and non-philosophical dialogue. The most comparable texts of which I am aware are Conrad of Hirsau's *Dialogus super auctores* (*Dialogue on the Authors*) and Adelard of Bath's *De Cura Accipitrum* (*On the Care of Falcons*), but neither bears extensive comparison with the present work. Neither of the works most intimately related to the *Dialogus* employ the form, though the author of one of them, *Glanvill*, shows familiarity with FitzNigel's work, while the other, *Constitutio Domus Regis*, shows some formal similarity to the *Dialogus*, and was probably written by or for FitzNigel's father.[6] This essay argues that FitzNigel's choice of the dialogue form is influenced not only by contemporary intellectual trends, but also by the turbulent political background against which he is writing. Notably, FitzNigel builds on a suggestive congruence between the fortunes of his family and those of Henry II to develop a provocative analogy between legitimate monarchic succession and the steady transmission of knowledge from generation to generation. Conscious, moreover, of the fraught nature of political succession in the period, and in particular of difficult relationships between rulers and their heirs, FitzNigel builds into his dialogue a dynamic relationship between master and student, in which the transmission of learning is enhanced by the desire of each generation to rival and surpass its forebears. This relationship offers a paradigm through which to better understand processes of intellectual transmission, not only in the twelfth century, but throughout the later Middle Ages.

FitzNigel asserts that he began writing his dialogue in the twenty-third year of the reign of King Henry II (that is, between 19 December 1176 and 18 December 1177). There is little reason to doubt this claim, though there is some question over when the work was brought to completion: Emilie Amt speculates that FitzNigel may have continued writing his work, or at least revising it, into the early days of Richard's reign.[7] Whatever the case, it is

---

5 Alex Novikoff offers an indispensable account of the dialogue form from 1050 to 1350 in his unpublished doctoral thesis, 'Dialogue and Disputation in Medieval Thought and Society, 1050–1350' (University of Pennsylvania, 2007). The title of this article owes an obvious debt to Novikoff's account of a 'culture of disputation', and I am extremely grateful to him for his generous response to my queries about the *Dialogus* and its analogues.   6 On the probability that Glanvill was influenced by the *Dialogus*, see *The Treatise on the Laws and Customs of England Commonly Called Glanvill*, ed. and trans. C.D.G. Hall (Oxford, 1993), p. xxxvi. On the tradition that associates the *Constitutio* with Nigel, bishop of Ely, see S.D. Church's introduction in *Dialogus de Scaccario and Constitutio Domus Regis*, ed. Emilie Amt and S.D. Church (Oxford, 2007), p. xli.   7 *Dialogus*, Introduction, pp xviii–xx.

clear that FitzNigel began writing during a period in which Henry, having
taken many steps to stabilize a kingdom long disturbed by civil war (and,
indeed, his own corrosive conflict with the church, culminating in 1170 with
the murder of Thomas Becket), saw his authority startlingly challenged by the
great rebellion of 1173–4, in which his sons, with the support of their mother,
rose against him. The absence of direct references to subsequent calamities in
the kingdom (such as the death of Henry the Young King in 1183 and
Richard's rebellion) cannot provide a definitive *terminus ad quem* for the
Dialogus, but there can be no doubt that FitzNigel's work is witness to a
period of almost unparalleled instability in the affairs of English kings, as
charted elsewhere in this volume by Erik Kooper.

The author of the *Dialogus* was a member of a family that rose to a position of unrivalled influence and prestige under the first king Henry. As Emilie
Amt notes: 'The family fortunes were founded by Roger, bishop of Salisbury
(d. 1139) who was Henry I's right-hand man in all matters administrative.
Roger brought his nephews Alexander, bishop of Lincoln (d. 1148), and Nigel,
bishop of Ely (d. 1169) into Henry I's inner circle.'[8] Nigel, the father of the
Dialogus-author, became the king's treasurer in the 1120s, and was a highly
regarded administrative official. When Henry I died, the fortunes of the family
seemed secure: in spite of having vowed loyalty to Matilda, Roger of Salisbury
was a strident opponent of the Empress and sided with Stephen, preserving
the family's considerable royal influence. There was widespread resentment of
the influence of the bishops, however, and in 1139 they fell spectacularly from
grace when they were arrested by Stephen. It is widely accepted that, in
depriving himself of the considerable expertise of these individuals, Stephen
did the financial administration of his kingdom a serious disservice.[9] Roger died
in the king's custody in 1139, and Nigel switched allegiance to Matilda and
Henry, though he was eventually reconciled with Stephen (the young Richard,
Amt notes, was twice held hostage for his father's good behaviour). In spite of
this eventful history, Nigel effected a relatively smooth transition into the
favour of Henry II, who asked him to come out of retirement and restore the
Exchequer to its former efficiency. By 1160, Richard FitzNigel was treasurer;
it appears that Nigel paid £400 for his son's advancement to this position.

As this summary makes clear, there is a marked (though by no means
uncomplicated) correspondence between the monarchic succession from Henry
I, via Stephen, to Henry II and the remarkable fortunes of Richard FitzNigel's
family. One of the most peculiar digressions in the *Dialogus*, indeed, betrays

---

8 *Dialogus*, Introduction, p. xiv. The historical account presented in this paragraph is drawn
from Amt's concise summary of events, but see also H.G. Richardson, 'Richard fitz Neal and
the *Dialogus de Scaccario*', *English Historical Review* 43 (1928), 161–71 and 321–40.   9 *Dialogus*,
Introduction, p. xiv. Graeme J. White acknowledges the negative impact of the loss of this
expertise, but feels that it has traditionally been overstated. *Restoration and Reform, 1153–1165:
Recovery from Civil War in England* (Cambridge, 2000), pp 23, 29–30.

FitzNigel's deep fascination with the workings of the capricious goddess Fortune. Reflecting on the practice of using pennies as counters at the Exchequer table (meaning that a single penny, used as a counter, can at different times represent a shilling, a pound or a thousand pounds) the pupil offers an extraordinary digression on the sudden reversals of fortune that assail men, allowing them to rise to great esteem in the world before plummeting down again. No matter what heights he may reach, a man is always just a man, as a penny remains a penny no matter what it comes to represent as it moves around the Exchequer table.[10] The author may here be alluding to the dramatic fluctuations in his own family's fortunes, as well as those of the royal family. Indeed, FitzNigel takes a number of steps to heighten the sense of correspondence between the fortunes of crown and family. He does this not only to advance his own reputation and that of his kinsmen, but also to suggest both a critical analogy and a causal relationship between legitimate monarchic succession and the stable transmission of knowledge.

FitzNigel makes no explicit reference to his induction into the world of financial administration (probably as a clerk), and certainly never alludes to the considerable sum of money that changed hands to secure his place at the Exchequer. He is everywhere at pains, rather, to emphasize his blood connections to his esteemed relatives. Nowhere is this more evident than in the striking account of the rise to prominence of Roger, bishop of Salisbury, who came to the Exchequer unknown, but not ignoble ('ignotus non tamen ignobilis'):

> Hic igitur, succrescente in eum principis ac cleri populique fauore, Saresberiensis episcopus factus, maximis in regno fungebatur officiis et honoribus et de scaccario plurimam habuit scientiam, adeo ut non sit ambiguum set ex ipsis rotulis manifestum plurimum sub eo floruisse. De cuius stillicidiis nos quoque modicum id quod habemus *per traducem* accepimus.

> [Growing in favour with prince and church and people, he was made bishop of Salisbury; he discharged the highest duties and honours in the realm, and he excelled in the knowledge of the exchequer, so that it is utterly clear from the rolls of that time that it flourished greatly under him. From the overflowing of his knowledge have I received, *as an inheritance*, the little that I know.] (p. 64/65, *emphasis added*)

This is a more remarkable passage than it seems on first reading. FitzNigel claims to have received his knowledge of the Exchequer from Roger *per traducem*, perhaps implying, as Amt notes, that he learned financial administra-

---

10 *Dialogus*, p. 38/39. The Exchequer, FitzNigel tells us, takes its name from the chequered cloth spread on the counting table, in which different columns represent different monetary denominations. The very name of the Exchequer means 'chessboard'; see pp 8–11/9–12.

tion from his kinsmen.[11] The bishop of Salisbury died when his great-nephew was only nine years old, however, making it unlikely that FitzNigel is alluding to direct instruction; rather, he implies that knowledge of the Exchequer is, so to speak, 'in his blood'.[12] His phrasing evokes not merely intellectual kinship, but direct intellectual inheritance. It is striking that, though he is not the direct descendant of the bishop of Salisbury, FitzNigel here implies a closer 'genealogical' connection with his great-uncle than he ever explicitly claims in respect of his own father, the bishop of Ely.

When he does turn to speak of his father, however, another crucial theme comes to the fore, as FitzNigel insists on the relationship between proper monarchic succession and the preservation of knowledge. Noting that his father, who had been treasurer under Henry I, had fallen out of favour under Stephen, he triumphantly connects the restoration of legitimate monarchy under Henry II with the restoration of his own family's fortunes and the renewal of financial stability and true learning, grandly comparing his father's achievements with Ezra's role in re-establishing the Hebrew law after the Babylonian captivity:

> Hic etiam, ab illustri rege Henrico secundo frequenter rogatus, scaccarii scientam continuata per multos annos bellica tempestate pene prorsus abolitam reformauit, et totius descriptionis eius formam uelut alter Esdras bibliothece sedulus raparator, renouauit.

> [He also, when the illustrious King Henry II had repeatedly asked him, restored the knowledge of the exchequer that had been almost entirely lost during the many years of civil war, and revived the whole order of its procedure, like another Ezra, the careful restorer of Scripture.] (p. 76/77)

The picture painted here is far from complete: recent historians have recognized the extent to which the traditional view of the 'anarchy' and financial mayhem of Stephen's reign was shaped by the biases of those writing under Henry, and Graeme White has directly questioned FitzNigel's assertions here about both the extent of the Exchequer's decline under Stephen and the success of his father in restoring it.[13] Yet more is at stake in this passage than self-promotion or family pride: FitzNigel is insisting that the interruption of legitimate monarchic succession exerts negative pressure not only on political and economic systems, but also on the processes which preserve the knowledge and expertise essential to political and economic stability.

In this context, it is important to remember that FitzNigel presents himself not only as a custodian of the processes of the Exchequer, but also as a

---

11 *Dialogus*, Introduction, pp xiv–xv. 12 FitzNigel was born around 1130, while the bishop of Salisbury died in 1139; *Dialogus*, Introduction, p. xiv. 13 White, *Restoration and Reform*, p. 29.

historian, the author of a now-lost account of the reign of Henry II, the
Tricolumpnis.[14] FitzNigel's description of himself as a historian perhaps helps
to explain his sophisticated grasp of the ideological potential of paralleling his
own (literal and intellectual) genealogy to that of the king. As Gabrielle
Spiegel has demonstrated, the filiative model implicit in genealogically determined historiography 'suggested the process of procreation and filiation as a
metaphor for historical change [...] The procreative process by which human
beings engender successive generations is the human shape of history gener-
ating events over time, events which stand in a filiative relation to one another
that mirrors the reproductive course of human life'.[15] With this in mind, we
are in a better position to appreciate FitzNigel's fascinating digression on the
great rebellion of 1173–4. The passage has been seen by some editors as an
interpolation, but it is of a piece with FitzNigel's digressive style, and clearly
echoes the staunch advocacy of the king's prerogative articulated elsewhere:
Amt is surely right to call the passage a revision, rather than an interpolation.[16] The passage begins by paying homage to the king: 'Illustris Anglorum
rex, Henricus, hoc nomine participantium regum secundus dictus est, set nulli
modernorum fuisse creditur in rebus componendis animi uirtute secundus.'
('The illustrious king of the English, Henry, is called the second of the kings
bearing this name, but he is second to no recent king in the strength of his
mind in managing his affairs.')[17] The verbal play encapsulates an idealized cor-
relation between monarchic succession and the betterment of the kingdom:
each king should surpass the achievements of those who go before him. This
leads neatly into the account of the great rebellion, in which the sons of the
king sought, against the orders of nature and justice, to usurp their father:

> Filios quidem, sue carnis immo et anime sue spem post deum unicam
> et gloriam singularem, dum paruuli essent et ratione etatis cerei supra
> modum et in omnem animi motum proni, uulpecule pertinaces consiliis
> prauis demolite sunt; et tandem in patrem tanquam in hostem sua uis-
> cera conuerterunt.

> [For certain stubborn little foxes suborned his sons, who were, after
> God, the sole hope and singular glory of his own flesh and indeed of
> his very spirit, while they were young and therefore blank slates, and
> vulnerable to every impulse of the mind; and at last they turned 'his
> own flesh' against their father as if against an enemy.] (p. 114/115)

FitzNigel treats the actions of the king's sons as an extraordinary rebellion
against natural order and an affront to established traditions of monarchic suc-

---

14 *Dialogus*, p. 116/117.   15 Gabrielle M. Spiegel, 'Genealogy: Form and Function in Medieval
Historical Narrative', *History and Theory* 22:1 (1983), 43–53 (pp 50–1).   16 *Dialogus*,
Introduction, p. xxxiii.   17 *Dialogus*, p. 112/113.

cession. He would perhaps have approved of Dante's damning indictment of the role played by Bertran de Born in fomenting this unnatural rebellion.[18] Yet he is careful not to lay too much blame at the feet of the rebellious sons: this is seen in the allusion to the 'stubborn foxes' of Song of Songs 2:15, and the reference to the proverbial impetuosity of youth as delineated by Horace in the *Ars Poetica*.[19] He heaps praise on Henry for his gentleness towards his children, and ends with a prayer for the princes:

> Viuat et proles eius ingenua, patri suo subiecta nec ei dissimilis, et quia nati sunt populis imperare, paterno simul et proprio discant exemplo quam gloriosum sit 'parcere subiectis et debellare rebelles'.

> [And long live his noble offspring, subject to their father and not unlike him, and, because they were born to rule over nations, may they learn from both their father's example and their own how glorious it is to spare the conquered and beat back the rebels.] (p. 116/17)

This careful disclaimer highlights FitzNigel's vision of succession: it is natural that one generation succeeds another, and it is right that each king aim to surpass the successes of his forebears, but this goal can never be achieved by violating the claims of nature and justice. This productive tension between continuity and conflict, between the desire to emulate and the desire to surpass, provides a model for the dialogue's distinctive representation of the relationship between *magister* and *discipulus*.

While the *Dialogus* must be sharply differentiated from both contemporary philosophical dialogue and the dynamic (and often unresolved) quarrels of later debate poetry, it is equally clear that the interaction between master and student in the text is much more complex than that found in earlier *altercationes*, in which information is simply transferred from one participant to the other.[20] The *Dialogus* transcends the concerns of simpler dialogues because it situates

---

18 Bertran de Born was the Occitan troubadour and baron of Hautefort who incited the Young King to rise against his father and took an active role in the rebellion (Henry II being, of course, his overlord). Dante's unforgettable portrait sets Bertran among the sowers of discord, holding his severed head in his hand as *contrapasso* for dividing father and son (strikingly, the troubadour's account of his punishment provides the only explicit reference to the principle of *contrapasso* in the entire *Commedia*). See Dante, *The Divine Comedy*, ed. and trans. John D. Sinclair (Oxford, 1939), *Inferno* XXVIII, 112–42.   19 See Horace, *The Art of Poetry*, in *Classical Literary Criticism*, ed. Penelope Murray (London, 2000) pp 102–3 (ll. 160ff).   20 Debate poetry is extensively analyzed in Thomas L. Reed, *Middle English Debate Poetry and the Aesthetics of Irresolution* (Columbia, MO, 1990), esp. chapters I and II. The classic discussion of the *altercatio* between *magister* and *discipulus* is *Altercatio Hadriani Augusti et Epicteti Philosophi*, ed. Lloyd William Daly and Walther Suchier (Urbana, IL, 1939). Perhaps the most famous example of this simple form of master/student dialogue is Alcuin's *Disputatio regalis et nobilissimi juvenis Pippini cum Albino scholastico*, or *Disputatio Pippini*.

itself within a wider intellectual programme that aims not only to preserve knowledge, but to encourage further inquiry and debate. The dialogue structure reinforces one of the crucial tenets of the text: knowledge can only be preserved and augmented as long as debate and dialogue continue.

This crucial principle is highlighted by a number of idiosyncrasies in the relationship between master and disciple. Of these, the most striking is the age of FitzNigel's interlocutor. The text specifies that the *discipulus* is an old man, who has worked in the Exchequer for a number of years. This assertion has encouraged the most recent editor of the text to propose, entirely reasonably, that the dialogue is modelled on an encounter with a historical individual.[21] This is quite probable, but the care with which this fact is brought to our attention suggests that the point is of some significance. While the disciple notes that he and his other colleagues require FitzNigel's deeper knowledge, he also emphasizes that they need theoretical grounding in the fundamental principles of the Exchequer.[22] To express his embarrassment at having to undergo such rudimentary instruction, the disciple borrows from Seneca: 'Licet autem turpis et ridicula res sit elementarius senex ab ipsis tamen elementis incipiam.' ('And though it may be ridiculous, or even disgraceful, for an old man to be learning the alphabet, I'll start with the ABCs.')[23] The word *senex* here implies that the pupil may be considerably older than his master, as FitzNigel was only in his late forties when composing the text. Even if the age of the disciple reflects a historical circumstance, the insistence on his need for tutelage in fundamental principles seems designed to corroborate FitzNigel's assertion about the decay of Exchequer under Stephen, as well to advance the supremacy of the knowledge transmitted to FitzNigel by his family members. The embarrassment of the old man, forced to learn his alphabet from a younger master, captures perfectly the sense of a lost intellectual generation, whose fragmentary understanding is the direct result of Stephen's unnatural and unjust usurpation of Matilda's claim to the throne and the economic and administrative chaos that ensued. Thankfully, for pupil, king and kingdom, this knowledge has survived undiminished in the bloodline of the *Dialogus*-author.

Through details such as these, FitzNigel complicates our sense of one generation transmitting information to another. Though one might hesitate to describe this dialogue between colleagues as a medieval example of 'peer-learning', the relationship of master and pupil here is certainly more equal than that in older *altercationes*, such as Alcuin's *Disputatio Pippini*. The student is consistently praised for his meticulousness and understanding, while at one point the master consciously highlights the sense of equality and parity by noting that he was equally confused when he first encountered a particular

---

21 *Dialogus*, Introduction, p. xviii. 22 *Dialogus*, p. 6/7. 23 *Dialogus*, p. 8/9. Amt notes that the quotation is from Seneca, *Epistles*, xxxvi.

problem vexing the student.[24] This strong sense of equality is most evident in
the master's willingness to let the student set the pace of learning, and even
dictate the order in which subjects are to be discussed. Thus, when they arrive
at the Exchequer's seating arrangements, the master asks:

> *Magister*: Vis prosequar de ipsis secundum gradus dignitatum an secun-
> dum dispositionem sedium?
> *Discipulus*: Secundum quod quisque ratione officii sui sedem adeptus
> est. Facile enim erit, ut credo, ex officiis perpendere dignitates.

> [*Teacher*: Do you want me to proceed by their ranks or by seating
> order?
> *Student*: By the seat each has attained because of his office – for I think
> I can judge their ranks by their responsibilities.] (p. 24/5)

Of course, there are a number of occasions on which the master resists the
student's attempts to direct the discussion, insisting on covering the basics
before moving onto questions the student finds more interesting.[25] Indeed, at
one point, when the student appears to have overreached his grasp, the master
does not hesitate to pull him sharply back to earth, criticizing his supercilious
pedantry.[26] This highlights one of the most striking features of the relationship: as the pupil's understanding improves, and the pair moves into more
challenging terrain, a strong sense of rivalry develops. Moments such as the
following, in which the master speaks of the pupil's rigorous questioning as
if it were a form of aggression, or at best a ruthless game, highlight a kernel
of conflict at the heart of the educational process:

> *Magister*: In propriam te uideor armasse perniciem; ex predictis enim
> alia coniciens armatis me uexas questionibus.

> *Teacher*: I seem to have given you weapons to defeat me, for you draw
> inferences from what has been said and attack me with an array of
> questions. (p. 144/5)[27]

This moment, in which the knowledge transmitted from master to student
rebounds against him, recalls the earlier observation about the king's sons
rebelling against the father with whose spirit and understanding they have

---

24 For the master's praise of the student, see for example, *Dialogus*, pp 10/11, 12/13. For the
master's admission that he once struggled with the same difficulties now facing the student, see
pp 76/77. 25 See, for example, pp 30/31, 34/35. 26 *Dialogus*, pp 136-8/137-9. 27 There
are a number of other moments where the master and student appear almost at loggerheads, as
the student challenges points made by the master, and the master appears almost to regret sub-
mitting himself to such a rigorous questioner. See for example, pp 148/149, 150/151, 164/165.

been imbued. But there is more to it than this. The text that has allowed so
great an equality to emerge between master and pupil here suggests that conflict is crucial to intellectual transmission and the furtherance of knowledge.
The principle is that of *zelos* or emulation, which Rita Copeland identifies as
a crucial element of Roman theory of imitation, and which applies equally well
in this case:

> Dionysius of Helicarnassus had defined emulation (*zelos*) as an 'activ-
> ity of the soul impelled towards admiration of what seems to be fine';
> and *zelos*, the desire to vie with the object of admiration, is recognized
> throughout Roman theory of imitation as a factor that ensures excel-
> lence and cultural evolution through new achievement.[28]

The desire of each successive generation to vie with the previous one, and to
stage its own intellectual inquiry as a form of both conflict and continuity, is
crucial to FitzNigel's conception of the preservation and transmission of
knowledge. FitzNigel injects a strong sense of conflict into the later stages of
the work, which propels the discussion into new territory. Indeed, at one
point, the master acknowledges his discomfort with the direction the dialogue
has taken:

> *Magister*: In pelagus me questionum impellis, nescio, deus scit, qua
> emersurum. ... Ab initio debitor tibi factus sum ex promisso hinc est
> quod nolens teneor parere petenti.

> *Teacher*: You push me into a sea of questions; God only knows how I'll
> get out. ... From the beginning I've been bound by my promise to you:
> hence I must answer your questions, whether I want to or not. (p. 164/5)

Indeed, the dialogue comes surprisingly to an end with the master's refusal
to answer a question posed by the student. Earlier, when the student had pondered the workings of Fortune, the teacher had observed that the Exchequer
contained hidden meanings, and suggested a startling system of analogies with
sacred history and the Final Judgement:

> *Magister*: Nec in his tantum que ommemoras set in tota scaccarii
> descriptione sacramentorum quedam latibula sunt. Officiorum namque
> diuersitas, iudiciarie potestatis auctoritas, regie imaginis impressio, cita-
> tionum emissio, rotulorum conscriptio, uillicationum ratio, debitorum
> exactio, reorum condempnatio uel absolutio districti examinis figura
> sunt, quod reuelabitur cum omnium libri aperti erunt et ianua clausa.

---

28 Rita Copeland, *Rhetoric, Hermeneutics, and Translation in the Middle Ages: Academic Traditions
and Vernacular Texts* (Cambridge, 1991), p. 28.

Teacher: Indeed, holy mysteries can be found hiding not only in the things you have just noticed, but in the whole account of the exchequer. For the diversity of duties, the great authority of the judiciary, the seal bearing the royal image, the sending of summonses, the writing of the rolls, the accounting for one's stewardship, the collection of debts, and the condemnation or absolution of defendants are symbols of the strict accounting that will be revealed when the books of all are opened and the door shut. (p. 38/9)

As the evening draws in, and he notices his teacher beginning to flag, the student suggests that an investigation of these hidden mysteries would constitute the perfect conclusion to their discussion:

Discipulus: Verum, licet instantis noctis crepusculum et productioris operis labor prolixior ad alia nos euocent et paululum respirare compellant, uellem tamen, si fieri posset, ut suspensam, et hactenus fluctuantem in uerbo tuo, discipuli tui mentem confirmares, ostendens quid sit, quod ab initio dixisse te recolo, totam scilicet scaccarii discriptionem quedem esse sacramentorum latibula que reuelanda sunt cum omnium libri aperti erunt et ianua clausa.
Magister: Magnum est quod queris et alterius egens inquisitionis, nec his exponendis ex promisso debitor tibi factus sum. His igitur ad presens supersedeo, in alterius diei diputationem eadam reseruans.

Student: Evening is falling, and other, more burdensome, tasks call us away, but even though we must take a rest, I am in suspense and uncertain because of your words, and I wish you would, if possible, set my mind at rest. Please explain how, as I remember you said at the beginning, the whole description of the exchequer conceals sacred truths that are to be revealed when the books of all are opened and the gates are closed.
Teacher: Your question is vast and would need a separate inquiry, and I didn't promise to explain such things. So I'll pass over them for now, saving that discussion for another day. (p. 190/1)

Near the start of the *Dialogus*, FitzNigel had made a bold claim for his mundane subject matter, arguing that it participated in a profound scheme of analogy encompassing the Final Judgement itself. Though he declines to expand on this, the close of his work reveals a similarly grand conception of the dialogue form itself, suggesting that the real dialogue is that between generations of scholars, past, present and future, in which this pair play only a small if pivotal role:

Magister: Ceterum ad singula, que tractu temporis uideri poterunt nec-
essaria, ungue tenus explananda nec uirtus hominis, nec uita forte, suf-
ficeret. Ex uariis enim et insolitis casibus uel nulla fiet uel adhuc incog-
nita disciplina; unde fit ut detractoriis linguis hinc potius exponar dum,
succedente tempore, pleraque dubia necdum audita proponi continget,
de quibus aut consimilibus cum hic nichil inuenerint, incipiant illud-
ere, dicentes, 'hic homo cepit edificare et non potuit, uel non nouit,
consummare'. His ego non dissentio, pessimum namque magistrum, me
ipsum, secutus sum.

Teacher: But as far as explaining precisely the various questions that
will come up over time, neither human strength nor even, perhaps, a
human life will suffice. For systematic instruction, at least as we know
it, cannot cover a miscellany of unusual cases; and so I will be criticized by my detractors when, over time, many doubtful and unprece-
dented questions arise. And when no answers are found here for them
or similar ones, they will begin to mock me, saying, 'This person began
to build and could not finish it', or did not know how to do so. I don't
disagree with them, for as a teacher I am the worst of the worst. (p.
190/1–192/3)

This passage sees the transformation of at least three familiar literary tropes,
each centred on the role of the author. First, we witness an allusion to the
ars longa, vita brevis trope, adapted so brilliantly by Chaucer in the fourteenth-century *Parliament of Fowls*.[29] The invocation of this trope makes it
clear that FitzNigel's text must necessarily participate in a dialogue with the
future, since a single human life can by no means cover all that must be said
on the chosen subject, especially if the workings of the Exchequer contain
the sacred mysteries alluded to. This is further developed in FitzNigel's adap-
tation of the envy *topos*, which is made to parallel the productive tension
between emulation and conflict that characterized the student's relationship
with his master.[30] Rather than pray that his work be safe from detractors, as
we might expect, FitzNigel acknowledges not only the inevitability of such
detraction, but even its desirability. His text's detractors, indeed, will not set
out finally to destroy his work, but to complete it, by asking questions never
put before. Though FitzNigel has not written the final or definitive study of
the Exchequer, he has played his part. This is emphasized in FitzNigel's
development of the final literary trope in this quotation: Geoffrey of Vinsauf's

---

29 *Parliament of Fowls*, ll. 1–7, *The Riverside Chaucer*, gen. ed. Larry D. Benson (Boston, 1987;
Oxford, 1988). In the *Parliament*, the *ars* is of course love, while the allusion to *ars longa, vita
brevis* arguably anticipates the formel's deferral of choice at the end of the poem, and the final
irresolution of the piece.   **30** For an account of the envy *topos*, see Frederick Tupper, 'The
Envy Theme in Prologues and Epilogues', *JEGP* 16 (1917), 551–72.

image of the author as master-builder, which lurks behind the allusion to Luke 14:[31]

> *Magister*: Feci tamen, te cogente, quod potui duce carens et exemplari: de intacta namque rudique silua, regiis edificiis, missa securi ligna secui, prudentioris architecti dolabro complananda. Cum, igitur, ex his regie domus structura surrexerit, is, qui dedit initia, primam, licet non precipuam, gratiam mereatur. Valeat rex illustris.

> *Teacher*: At your urging, I have done what I could without a guide or example: for I have laid my axe to wild and untouched woodland, cutting timber for royal buildings, to be planed by more skilful builders. And when a royal palace arises from that wood, he who started it shall deserve, if not the greatest thanks, at least the first. Long live our noble king. (p. 92/93)

As it draws to a close, then, the *Dialogus* remains keenly resistant to the sort of closure we might expect of such a work. This openness to further inquiry suggests something of the medieval 'aesthetics of irresolution' that Thomas Reed has detected in the rich genre of debate poems such as the *Owl and the Nightingale*, a tradition that Darragh Greene explores elsewhere in this volume in connection with the *Parlement of the Thre Ages*.[32] In the vision of intellectual and cultural transmission articulated by FitzNigel, dialogue and debate play a crucial role, not only within individual works but across the expanse of time. While Geoffrey of Vinsauf invoked the image of the master-builder to describe the careful planning required by each author before the execution of a single work, FitzNigel's *magister* understands that the voices in his dialogue, speaking by a tower-window overlooking the Thames in the twenty-third year of Henry II, are only part of the never-ending dialogue out of which the palace of knowledge must arise.

31 For a brilliant analysis of Geoffrey's concept, see Mary Carruthers, 'The Poet as Master Builder: Composition and Locational Memory in the Middle Ages', *New Literary History* 24.4 (1993), 881–904. 32 *The Owl and the Nightingale* is usually dated to a period not long after FitzNigel's work, immediately following the death of Henry II, but one of the poem's recent editors has argued that a later date, following the death of Henry III, is not beyond question. See Neil Cartlidge (ed.), *The Owl and the Nightingale* (Exeter, 2003), Introduction, pp xiii–xvi.

The *Parlement of the Thre Ages*: age, argument and allegory

DARRAGH GREENE

The Middle English alliterative dream-vision and debate poem, the *Parlement of the Thre Ages* (*c*.1353–90), has been interpreted by certain critics as a closed text, one in which the sapiential figure of Elde authoritatively addresses, answers and silences the quarrelling figures of Youthe and Medill Elde.[1] John Spiers presents the case for a closed text, thus: 'The pageant he [that is, the narrator] witnesses and the flyting he overhears in his dream produce a salutary recognition of his own mortality. The poem thus establishes a wise attitude to life – involving a recognition of death – by presenting an inclusive view of the human condition.'[2] Spiers, therefore, recognizes an integrated and positive *sentence* or deep meaning in the text that arises from the wisdom found in contemplating one's mortality; however, he does not hold that this wisdom derives solely from Elde's speech, for he contends that 'the total wisdom of the poem cannot be said to be exclusively that of Elde, though Elde sums up; for we remember that Elde is envious and wrathful, though rightly sorry for his sins'.[3] David E. Lampe, on the other hand, accepts Elde's long response to the younger debaters' quarrel as decisive.[4] John Scattergood agrees, concluding specifically that Elde resolves the question at issue in Youthe and Medill Elde's heated debate:

> Elde's magisterial intervention renders explicit the non static nature of the disputants and makes their debate redundant. He does not say he will refute them, only that he will put an end to their dispute ... And this he does by insisting on a broader perspective, in the manner of a master delivering the *determinatio* in a quodlibet. ... He demonstrates conclusively that Youthe and Medill Elde are wrong to assume that

1 Concerning the difficult question of precisely dating the poem, Ralph Hanna concludes that '*The Parliament of the Three Ages*, although it survives collocated with *Winner [and Waster]*, with which it shares the form of visionary debate, simply cannot be dated.' See 'Alliterative Poetry', *The Cambridge History of Medieval English Literature*, ed. David Wallace (Cambridge, 1999), p. 496. The concepts of 'open' and 'closed' texts are developed by Umberto Eco in *The Role of the Reader: Explorations in the Semiotics of Texts* (Bloomington, 1979). 2 John Spiers, *Medieval English Poetry: The Non-Chaucerian Tradition* (London, 1971), p. 289. Anne Kernan also identifies unavoidable mortality as the key theme of the poem in 'Theme and Structure in *The Parlement of Thre Ages*', *Neuphilologische Mitteilungen* 75 (1974), 253–4. 3 Spiers, *Medieval English* Poetry, p. 301. 4 David E. Lampe, 'The Poetic Strategy of the *Parlement of the Thre Ages*', *Chaucer Review* 7:3 (1973), 181–2.

their positions are static, or that the achievements in which they take
pride are at all lasting.[5]

This reading too closes down the field of possible meaning of the text. Lisa
Kiser also defends the effectiveness of Elde's teaching, although she accepts
that his speech is stylistically unwieldy in its length and digressiveness. She
argues that:

> A careful reading of *The Parlement* uncovers a hidden coherence to the
> dream vision proper: nearly every one of Elde's digressions is somehow
> prompted by imagery in the speeches of Youthe and Medill Elde,
> making for a more unified poem than has been recognized – and more
> of a 'debate,' since it can be shown that Elde is answering his com-
> panions' arguments in very specific ways.[6]

Although she holds that no single perspective offered by the debaters is pre-
eminent, her admittedly clever defence of Elde's teaching leads her to over-
state its effectiveness and, by corollary, the error of Youthe and Medill Elde's
approaches to life. Finally, in his excellent *Middle English Debate Poetry*,
Thomas L. Reed Jr argues that a poetics of irresolution operates among many
Middle English debate texts, but decides that while the author of the
Parlement 'seems very much aware of the experiential complexity of this world,
the closing passages of the poem move unmistakeably if implicitly beyond such
ambivalence'.[7]

There are some critics, however, who accept that the *Parlement* is not a
closed text; they argue for its indeterminacy or irresolution. Thorlac Turville-
Petre opens up the *sentence* of the poem by doubting Elde's authority:

> Is he not, like Youthe and Middle Elde, simply a spokesman for an
> extreme position, representing the views of those who have reached a
> particular period in their lives? The poem leaves us with two statements
> side by side: the world is lovely and much can be achieved in it, but
> all loveliness and achievements are futile because they are finite. The
> two statements taken together add up to the total meaning of the poem,
> and so Elde's position is just one part of the meaning. Of course, to
> say that the two statements add up overlooks the fact that they are ulti-
> mately irreconcilable, presenting the reader a dilemma rather than a

5 John Scattergood, *The Lost Tradition: Essays on Middle English Poetry* (Dublin, 2000), pp 94–
7.   6 Lisa Kiser, 'Elde and His Teaching in *The Parlement of the Thre Ages*', *Philological
Quarterly* 66 (1987), 303–14, at 305.   7 Thomas L. Reed, Jr, *Middle English Debate Poetry and
the Aesthetics of Irresolution* (Columbia, MO, 1990), p. 215 n. 72; see pp 213–18 for his unconvincing closed reading of the *Parlement*.

synthesis. The narrator of the *Parlement* does not attempt to resolve this dilemma, though no doubt he pondered the issues as he 'ferkede to-warde towwn!'[8]

David V. Harrington professes dissatisfaction with all definitive readings of the poem; he argues that debate poems like *Winner and Waster* and the *Parlement* ought to be examined 'not so much for their obvious didactic lessons as for the doubts they raise about such lessons; that is, we should notice how they challenge and dramatize the inadequacies of commonplace statements of value. In short, notice how the poets aim at a high degree of indeterminacy.'[9] Concerning the openness of the text, I align my reading with Turville-Petre's and Harrington's, but my principal aim is to clarify and extend the case against Elde's speech as cogent *determinatio* of the text's debate.

In this essay, I argue that the respective perspectives of all three personifications are thoroughly and necessarily conditioned by their allegorical natures, so they cannot meaningfully engage each other's point-of-view; this includes Elde's perspective, which is – as shall be shown – less than magisterial. In fact, when Elde intervenes in the quarrel and proposes to 'stynte [the] stryffe and stillen [the] threpe' (268), he proceeds to commit the informal fallacy known as *ignoratio elenchi*, one of the oldest known, by introducing an irrelevant thesis and missing the point under discussion; so the febrile debate remains unresolved, and, ultimately, the poem produces an open text.[10]

Aristotle was the first to identify and define the *ignoratio elenchi* fallacy in his short logical treatise, *Sophistical Refutations* (*De sophisticis elenchis*), where he delineates and analyzes it, thus:

> Those [fallacies] which arise because it has not been defined what a deduction is and what a refutation is, come about because something is left out in their definition. For to refute is to contradict one and the same attribute – not the name, but the object and one that is not synonymous but the same – and to confute it from the propositions granted, necessarily, without including in the reckoning the original point to be proved, in the same respect and relation and manner and time in which it was asserted. ... Some people, however, omit some one of the said conditions and give a merely apparent refutation.[11]

8 Thorlac Turville-Petre, 'The Ages of Man in *The Parlement of the Thre Ages*', *Medium Aevum* 46 (1977), 66–76, at 74–5.   9 David V. Harrington, 'Indeterminacy in *Winner and Waster* and *The Parliament of the Three Ages*', *Chaucer Review* 20:3 (1986), 246–58, at 246.   10 *Wynnere and Wastoure and The Parlement of the Thre Ages*, ed. Warren Ginsberg (Kalamazoo, 1992); all quotations from the poem are taken from this edition.   11 Aristotle, *Sophistical Refutations*, I.5, 167a21–9 in *The Complete Works of Aristotle: The Revised Oxford Translation* vol. I, Bollingen Series LXXI: 2, ed. Jonathan Barnes (Princeton, 1984; sixth printing with corrections, 1995). The medieval student of logic knew the *Refutations* by virtue of Boethius' translation into Latin

Characteristically, Aristotle's explanation is dense and requires elucidation itself. Douglas Walton clarifies the operation of the fallacy, thus:

> The term *ignoratio elenchi*, from Aristotle, literally means 'ignorance of refutation.' The origin of this term derives from the Greek tradition that contestive argument is like a game of dialogue where each participant has a thesis or conclusion to be proven. The argument is contestive, i.e., a dispute, if the thesis of the one participant in the dialogue is opposed to the thesis of the other. Therefore, the point of the game is for each player to refute the thesis of the other. Any argument that seems to refute the thesis of the other, but really does not, could be seen as a case of ignorance of refutation. In other words, the arguer only thought his argument refuted his opponent's thesis, but in reality he was ignorant of the fact that it did not.[12]

The *Sophistical Refutations* formed part of the *Organon*, the collection of logical works attributed to Aristotle in the Middle Ages, and studied by every student of the *trivium* subject of logic or dialectic: any medieval student of logic, therefore, would be familiar with the work and its taxonomy of fallacies, including the *ignoratio elenchi*.[13]

Would the original audience of the *Parlement*, however, have been familiar with such 'lered' or erudite matter as logical fallacies? It is impossible to know for certain the exact nature of the contemporary audience of the poem; however, the fact that the poet chooses to fashion a debate of his matter implies, at least, an ideal or model audience who would be interested in the intellectual discussion of the problem of life and living well.[14] Concerning the text's possible original audience and its competence in judging the debate, Harrington argues that even 'moderately intelligent listeners should feel competent, if not impelled, to correct, modify, or reject either or any of the positions represented by the major personifications and try to construct better solutions'.[15] Hence, if his judgement is sound, the model addressee of the text would not need to know the correct Aristotelian taxonomy for this or that fallacy, but would need to possess a keen nose for fishy arguments, especially the red herrings of *ignoratio elenchi*.

I turn now to my reading of the *Parlement*, and show how the analysis of the informal logic of its central debate sheds light on the overall status of the text's *sentence* or meaning. The poem's *fabula* or story is easy enough to tell. *The Parlement* is recounted in the first-person by a narrator-persona who is a

from the original Greek; see *Patrologiae: Cursus Completus Series Latina*, ed. J.P. Migne (Paris, 1844 –73), 64:1007–40.   **12** Douglas Walton, *Informal Logic: A Pragmatic Approach*, 2nd ed. (Cambridge, 2008), p. 81.   **13** See James J. Murphy, *Rhetoric in the Middle Ages* (Berkeley, 1974), pp 101–6 for a discussion of the basis of scholastic dialectic in the study of Aristotle's *Topics* and *Sophistical Refutations*.   **14** For the theory of model addressees and readers see Eco, *The Role of the Reader*, pp 3–44.   **15** Harrington, 'Indeterminacy', 250.

poacher; in the summer month of May, he arrives in the woods before sun-
rise in order to hunt deer. He stalks, kills and brittles his prey, a hart, then
hides it carefully, fearful that it might be discovered by wild boar, other
hunters or the forester. In this state of anxiety and mental agitation, he falls
asleep, and dreams of a heated debate or quarrel between the figures of
Youthe, Medill Elde and Elde, that is, the three Ages of Man. Youthe and
Medill Elde argue about whose is the best way of life, but Elde intervenes by
counselling them to forget their vanities, as he himself does, by remembering
and preparing for Death. The dreamer awakes; the sun is setting, the day
over, and he returns to town while offering a prayer to God and Mary. So
much, then, for the story; but what does it all mean?

The conventions of the dream-vision genre are central to the *intentio operis*
or intention of the text, not only in framing the debate and offering an account
of its existence as the product of a dream, but, crucially, in problematizing
the very interpretation of the debate that lies at the heart of the text.[16] In the
Middle Ages, the foremost authority on dreams was Macrobius, the fifth-cen-
tury Neoplatonist commentator on Cicero's *Somnium Scipionis*. He divided
dreams into two broad categories: (i) the *somnium*, that is, the true and
prophetic dream; and (ii) the *insomnium*, that is, the false and deceitful dream.
On the thirteenth-century medical authority of Petrus de Abano (*c.*1250–
*c.*1315), Macrobius' categories were further distinguished into the *somnium
coeleste*, the *somnium animale* and the *somnium naturale*.[17] The former was of
divine origin and deemed to be true, whereas the latter two were said to be
of mental and physical origins respectively, and were considered false.
Medieval poets knew of these technical distinctions among the various types
of dream, and they incorporated them into the frame and fabric of their texts,
eagerly exploiting them in order to pose questions concerning the origin,
nature and truth-value of their dream-visions. A famous example of just how
playful a medieval poet could be with the categories of dreams occurs in
Chaucer's deliberately aporematic and baffling proem to the *House of Fame*:

> God turne us every drem to goode!
> For hyt is wonder, be the roode,

---

16 I appropriate the notion of *intentio operis* from Eco, concerning which he writes: 'A text is a
device conceived in order to produce its model reader ... Since the intention of the text is basically to produce a model reader able to make conjectures about it, the initiative of the model
reader consists in figuring out a model author that is not the empirical one and that, in the end,
coincides with the intention of the text. Thus, more than a parameter to use in order to vali-
date the interpretation, the text is an object that the interpretation builds up in the course of
the circular effort of validating itself on the basis of what it makes up as its result.' Umberto
Eco, *Interpretation and Overinterpretation*, ed. Stefan Collini (Cambridge, 1992), p. 64.   17 See
A.C. Spearing, *Medieval Dream-Poetry* (Cambridge, 1976), pp 55–7; Steven Kruger, *Dreaming
in the Middle Ages* (Cambridge, 1992), pp 21–122.

> To my wyt, what causeth swevenes
> Eyther on morwes or on evenes,
> And why th'effect folweth of somme,
> And of somme hit shal never come;
> Why that is an avision
> And why this a revelacion,
> Why this a drem, why that a sweven,
> And noght to every man lyche even;
> Why this a fantome, why these oracles,
> I not; but whoso of these miracles
> The causes knoweth bet then I,
> Devyne he, for I certeinly
> Ne kan hem noght ...   (1–15)[18]

Furthermore, even a *somnium* – the supposedly true vision – is by its very nature enigmatic in mode, for, as Macrobius says, it 'conceals with strange shapes and veils with ambiguity the true meaning of the information being offered, and requires interpretation for its understanding'.[19] Medieval poets employed this ambiguity of enigmatic dreams in order to explore in their texts the boundaries between truth and falsehood; the real and the unreal; and, ultimately, *logos* and *mythos*. The ambivalence and ambiguity surrounding the origin, nature and truth-value of dream-visions, the chosen framing-device for the text in question, must therefore influence the reader's engagement with and judgement of the debate in the *Parlement*.

The poem's opening verse, 'In the monethe of Maye when mirthes bene fele' (l. 1), triggers a horizon of expectation in the literate reader familiar with the thirteenth-century *Roman de la Rose*. This, the most authoritative of vernacular dream-vision texts, sets the pattern for all subsequent dream-visions beginning in May, which it calls 'el tens enmoreus, plain de joie', 'the amorous month, when everything rejoices' (48), and, furthermore, declares that it is in May:

> lors estuet joines genz entendre
> a estre gais et amoreus
> par le tens bel et doucereus.
> Mout a dur cuer qui en may n'aime ...   (78–81)

[that young men must become gay and amorous in the sweet, lovely weather. He has a very hard heart who does not love in May].[20]

18 All quotations from Chaucer are taken from *The Riverside Chaucer*, gen. ed. Larry D. Benson (Boston, 1987; Oxford, 1988).   19 Macrobius, *Commentarium in Somnium Scipionis*, trans. William Stahl (New York, 1952; repr. 1990), i.3, pp 87–92.   20 Guillaume de Lorris and Jean de Meun, *Le Roman de la Rose*, ed. Félix Lecoy, vol. I (Paris, 1965); *The Romance of the Rose*,

The Parlement's opening, by contrast, focuses not on love but the hunting or, more accurately, poaching of deer, the season for which began in medieval France and England in May. Hunting, however, was often a metaphor for the pursuit of love, so when the narrator later falls asleep, the literate reader of the *Parlement* could still expect the poem to conform to the love-vision paradigm constructed by the *Roman de la Rose*. He could, perhaps, but it will be seen that the Middle English text, ultimately, produces a radical paradigm shift, upsetting its literate reader's expectations.[21]

Having skilfully brittled his kill, the narrator-poacher carefully hides his butchered meat, so 'That no fostere of the fee scholde fynde it theraftir' (94). Indeed, he recounts how he:

> Hid the hornes and the hede in ane hologhe oke,
> That no hunte scholde it hent ne have it in sighte.
> I foundede faste therefro for ferde to be wryghede,
> And sett me oute one a syde to see how it chevede
> To wayte it frome wylde swyne that wyse bene of nesse.   (95–9)

The narrator-poacher, thus, reveals his anxiety and fear concerning the safety and security of his catch. Equally, he fears for his own security, for if the forester were to catch him, then he would be liable for a fine or imprisonment. It is important to note his mental agitation and anxiety, for it implies that his subsequent dream may be a *somnium animale*, the type of false dream produced by excessive mental activity or stress.

In the *Parliament of Fowls*, Chaucer, closely following a passage from Claudian's *De IV consulato honorii*, writes:

> The wery huntere, slepynge in his bed,
> To wode ayeyn his mynde goth anon;
> The juge dremeth how his plees been sped;
> The cartere dremeth how his cart is gon;
> The riche, of gold; the knight fyght with his fon;
> The syke met he drynketh of the tonne;
> The lovere met he hath his lady wonne.   (99–105)

This is exactly the theory of the *somnium animale*, but the weary poacher in the *Parlement of the Thre Ages*, slumbering in a state of 'dowte' (102), does not dream once more of the woods; rather, his dream is entirely unexpected. It is neither of love nor of hunting, but of the best way to live one's life. The literate medieval reader's expectations, therefore, are utterly confounded.

trans. Charles Dahlberg, 3rd ed. (Princeton, 1995).   21 The figurative relation of the hunting to the dream is discussed below.

Indeed, further to complicate matters, there is a clue in the text that this dream may be a *somnium coeleste*, that is, a dream of divine origin, for the narrator-poacher says, 'And whate I saughe in my saule the sothe I schall telle' (103). The 'saule' was the site of divine illumination in Neoplatonic and Augustinian epistemology, so what is seen in the soul may be the result of divine illumination and therefore true. In any case, the juxtaposition between these last two lines before the account of the dream-vision proper implies two different types of *somnium*, *animale* and *coeleste*, and this produces an ambivalence and ambiguity that will further pervade the content of the dream-vision itself.

The dream opens with the vision of three figures in heated debate, as the dreamer-narrator relates:

> I seghe thre thro men threpden full yerne,
> And moted of mych-whate and maden thaym full tale.   (104–5)

What is the nature of their dispute? The dreamer-narrator characterizes their verbal activity as 'carpynge' (168), which could mean conversation, but in the ensuing context must mean debate or quarrel with a pejorative connotation of foolishness.[22] It begins when Youthe pronounces a complaint addressed to his lady, but Medill Elde replies, addressing him contemptuously as 'Felowe' (183), and further abuses him as playing the fool, 'thou fonnes full yerne,/ For alle es fantome and folly that thou with faris' (183–4). Having summarily dismissed Youthe's devotion to love, he attacks him from his own perspective, thus:

> Where es the londe and the lythe that thou arte lorde over?
> For alle thy ryalle araye renttis hase thou none,
> Ne for thi pompe and thi pride penyes bot fewe,
> For alle thi golde and thi gude gloes one thi clothes,
> And thou hafe caughte thi kaple thou cares for no fothire.   (185–9)

Medill Elde presents a decidedly one-sided assessment of Youthe, and that side is his own. He damns Youthe's way of life, and advises him to live as he (Medill Elde) does:

> Bye the stirkes with thi stede and stalles thaym make,
> Thi brydell of brent golde wolde bullokes the gete,
> The pryce of thi perrye wolde purches the londes.   (190–2)

---

22 *Middle English Dictionary*, s.v. 'carping' (ger.) 1. (a) 'Talking, speech, conversation'; (b) 'foolish talk'. See: http://quod.lib.umich.edu/cgi/m/mec/med-idx?type=id&id=MED6861. Accessed 17 September 2008.

But he does not offer any argument as to why Youthe is wrong and he is right; he merely attacks and asserts, blaming Youthe's way of life and praising his own, with no concern for a persuasive dialogue or critical discussion directed at discovering the truth of the matter.

Unsurprisingly, Medill Elde's *ad hominem* attack has 'greved full sore' (194) Youthe, who responds in kind to the personal abuse by attacking and censuring his older interlocutor's 'counsell' (195) as 'feble' (195). Youthe proceeds at length to describe and praise his own way of life, concluding, 'And this es life for to lede while I schalle lyfe here' (256), while he attacks Medill Elde, thus:

> And thou with wandrynge and woo schalte wake for thi gudes,
> And be thou dolven and dede thi dole schall be schorte,
> And he that thou leste luffes schall layke hym therewith,
> And spend that thou haste longe sparede, the devyll spede hym els!
>
> (257–60)

Medill Elde's emotional reaction is captured choicely in the verb 'rothelede' (261) which evokes the angry croaking of his response:

> Thryfte and thou have threpid this thirtene wynter;
> I seghe wele samples bene sothe that sayde bene yore:
> Fole es that with foles delys; flyte we no lengare. (262–4)

Once again, then, Medill Elde resorts to an abusive *ad hominem* attack on Youthe by suggesting that he is a fool; in his anger he decides to halt the 'flytyng', a term closer in meaning to 'quarrel' than 'debate'.

At this point, Elde enters the debate. He begins combatively by immediately branding both Youthe and Medill Elde as 'sottes' (266), an abusive *ad hominem* attack:

> Sirres, by my soule, sottes bene ye bothe!
> Bot will ye hendely me herken ane hande-while,
> And I schalle stynte your stryffe and stillen your threpe.
> I sett ensample bi myselfe and sekis it no forthire. (266–9)

Elde's request for courtesy from his two interlocutors may be read as sarcastic, since it follows so soon on the heels of an insult hurled at both of them. His boast to put an end to the quarrel smacks of pride, and he goes badly wrong by presenting himself as an example, for the problem so far has been to convince the opponent of conclusions when he does not accept the unstated presuppositions that support them. So far, both Youthe and Medill Elde have begged the question concerning the best way of life by presuming that their

own way of life is best. Now Elde is about to do the same thing again; therefore, he does not intervene from a position of superiority. By offering himself
as an *exemplum*, rather, his intervention is as bleared by the same subjective
defects as his two opponents'.

In this spirit, Elde advises Youthe and Medill Elde to take him as their
model, their mirror, as he says:

> Makes youre mirrours bi me, men, bi youre trouthe:
> This schadowe in my schewere schunte ye no while.   (290–1)

Again, one figure seeks to impose his standards, his principles, on the others.
If he were to justify this by way of offering evidence and sound argument for
his way of life being best, then, perhaps, he might have a point. He misses
the point entirely, however, when, obsessed by death, as is his nature, he
digresses on a lengthy catalogue of the Nine Worthies (330 lines long), the
point of which is to prove the inevitability of death, the vanity of the world
and the need for repentance. His argument is thorough, well supported by the
evidence of his nine examples, and actually valid, that is, it lacks logical errors.
In short, the digression on the Nine Worthies convinces the reader of the
inevitability of death, the vanity of the world and the need for repentance. Yet
what has this to do with Youthe and Medill Elde's debate?

Youthe and Medill Elde fall to debate and eventually quarrel over the *best
way to live life*. The topic is never explicitly articulated, but it is implicit in
the nature of their exchanges. Harrington recognizes and confirms this infer-
ence when he asserts: 'In *The Parliament of the Three Ages*, the unstated question turns out to be: what principles are best for guiding one's life?'[23] Elde,
however, intervenes to argue that no one can escape death:

> Sythen doughtynes when dede comes ne dare noghte habyde,
> Ne dethe wondes for no witt to wende where hym lykes,
> And therto paramours and pride puttes he full lowe,
> Ne there es reches ne rent may rawnsone your lyves,
> Ne noghte es sekire to youreselfe in certayne bot dethe,
> And he es so uncertayne that sodaynly he comes,
> Me thynke the wele of this werlde worthes to noghte.   (631–7)

The disjunction between the implicit topic of Youthe and Medill Elde's debate
and the topic of Elde's intervention is subtle. The *ignoratio elenchi* fallacy is
most seductive when the irrelevant thesis introduced appears to relate to the
thesis under discussion, and Elde's obsession with death seems to relate to the
discussion of life. Death, however, is precisely the end or termination of life,

23 Harrington, 'Indeterminacy', 248.

and the discussion of death sheds no light on exactly *how* to live well, the topic Youthe and Medill Elde have been heatedly debating. It may seem, nevertheless, that Youthe and Medill Elde have followed the red herring of the digression on the Nine Worthies, for it appears that Elde's long speech silences them; and according to the rules of the medieval debate whoever silences his opponent wins.[24] It *may* seem so, but there is no evidence in the text to confirm it; for when Elde concludes his speech ('Dethe dynges one my dore, I dare no lengare byde', 654), the very next line of the text returns to the narrator-poacher waking from his slumber, and he makes no judgement on what he has witnessed in his dream.

How is the reader to interpret this? Does Elde really offer a magisterial response in the form of a *determinatio* to Youthe and Medill Elde's disputation, or does the debate, having descended to the level of a quarrel, end in a state of *aporia*, or confusion? It must be conceded that a close reading of the whole debate reveals that it is sorely lacking in logical or dialectical merit. Youthe and Medill Elde argue at cross-purposes, and neither works to convince the other of his conclusions on the basis of propositions assented to by the particular interlocutor being debated or by reasonable people in general. In effect, each figure praises his own way of life and blames the other's without offering evidence or sound argument to substantiate the praise and blame. Elde, equally, attacks the other two from the prejudice of his own perspective, going so far as to offer his own life as an *exemplum*. Furthermore, his long digression on the Nine Worthies, by way of proving the inevitability of death, something for which the one-hundred-year-old Elde has especial concern, has nothing to do with the way a young or middle-aged person ought to live their life in the best manner possible. Elde's whole speech, therefore, amounts to a glorious *non sequitur*, for his thesis is utterly irrelevant to the topic under debate. What do Youthe and Medill Elde think of his speech? We simply do not know, but I think the introduction to the dream perhaps implies that they were dissatisfied by Elde's intervention, for we may recall that the narrator-poacher rendered a general summary of his vision first before going into detail:

> I seghe thre thro men threpden full yerne,
> And moted of mych-whate and maden thaym full tale.   (104–5)

This implies nothing concerning an authoritative conclusion to their debate; rather, the reader may infer further disputation and argument than is

---

24 In *The Lost Tradition*, Scattergood affirms that 'in medieval debates, whoever argued his opponent or opponents into silence was held to be the victor, and to Elde's authoritative exposition there is no reply' (p. 97). He follows E.G. Stanley who writes of medieval debate: 'Whoever silenced his opponent, by forcing him into a position that he cannot argue himself out of, gains victory in the debate'; *The Owl and the Nightingale*, ed. E.G. Stanley (London, 1960), p. 27.

recounted in the body of the text. There is no diegetic statement between lines 654 and 655, between the end of Elde's speech and the dreamer-narrator's awakening from his visionary slumber that affirms that Elde's speech silenced the other two figures. Perhaps, indeed, the debate was endless, each figure convinced of the correctness of his own, prejudiced perspective.

It is not really surprising that personifications in an allegory should be conditioned by their respective abstract universals. In this vein, Harrington observes of the debating personifications: 'They give us nothing but one-sided, self-serving defenses of extreme positions, making no concessions, offering no compromises, and recognizing no need for the co-existence of conflicting values. The inadequacy of the debaters relates directly to what they represent as personifications.'[25] In this instance, when the personifications figure forth the Ages of Man, it is especially important to note that a key aspect of this division of life into salient periods in the Middle Ages was the notion that each age or period had certain activities or habits appropriate to it. In the *Convivio*, Dante, following Cicero's *De Senectute*, puts it thus:

> Dov'è da sapere che la nostra buona e diritta natura ragionevolmente procede in noi, sì come vedemo procedere la natura de la piante in quelle; e però altri costumi e altri portamenti sono ragionevoli ad una etade più che ad altra, ne li quali l'anima nobilitata ordinatamente procede per una semplice via, usando li suoi atti ne li loro tempi ed etadi sì come a l'ultimo suo frutto sono ordinati.

> [(O)ur nature, when it is good and upright, develops in us by following a fitting sequence (just as we observe the nature of plants developing in them), and so different customs and different kinds of behaviour are fitting at one stage which are not so at another. In these the ennobled soul develops in an ordered way guided by a single criterion: it brings its activities into play at the times and stages suited to producing its various fruit.][26]

It is fitting, therefore, that Youthe should be a lover, and it is seemly that Medill Elde should be concerned with his property, and it is just that Elde should be concerned with impending death. What would be inappropriate, however, would be for any of these figures to engage in or practice the specific activities of any of the other two. In so far as Youthe, Medill Elde and Elde embody and express the appropriate activities and habits of their respective ages, their ways of life are just and, above all, in accordance with reason and the natural order. Youthe, Medill Elde and Elde as personifications, then,

25 Harrington, 'Indeterminacy', 253. 26 Dante Alighieri, *Il Convivio*, ed. Maria Simonelli (Bologna, 1966), IV, xxiv, 8; Dante Alighieri, *The Banquet*, trans. and intro. Christopher Ryan (Saratoga, 1989).

as figures in the allegory, can never understand this, that is, they can never accept the point-of-view of anyone other than themselves; but the careful reader, trained in allegoresis, can uncover the *sentence* or covert meaning of the text in terms of an hermeneutical dialectic that he practises, first, in conjunction with and, then, beyond the text itself. It falls not to Elde to decide the debate; rather, it falls to the reader, and his decision will be made or deferred outside the text. Neither, indeed, does the dreamer when woken offer a moralization of his vision. This doubly confirms that the interpretation of the whole vision belongs to the reader who must critically engage and grapple with its *aporia* beyond the text, by embarking on his own journey of dialectic in search of the 'sothe' of his own 'saule'.

Although the above reading of the poem emphasizes the openness of the text, there remains one puzzle that might be amenable to solution: how does the hunting and brittling of the hart at the beginning of the text relate to the dream-vision that follows? If the hunting is no longer tenable as a metaphor of hunting love, how might it relate thematically to this new interpretation of the dream-vision debate? In Chaucer's *Book of the Duchess*, hunting frames the dreamer-narrator's encounter with the grieving Man in Black; it is not a metaphor for the hunting of love in that text; rather, it is a metaphor for the searching dialectic between the dreamer-narrator and the Man in Black concerning the nature and ultimate resolution of his grief. In the *Parlement*, too, hunting is a metaphor for the pursuit of and search for truth, and the technical account of the careful brittling of the hart is a fitting metaphor for the careful, critical assessment required on the part of the reader in order properly to interpret the subsequent dream-vision debate.[27] Only by attending closely to the logic of the debate, the propositions and consequents, will the truth be uncovered, and, in particular, the false trail represented by the Nine Worthies avoided.

In conclusion, then, the *Parlement* is a multi-faceted, polysemous text composed of diverse disjunctions of matter, genre and theme that confound convention and explode expectation. The text produces a puzzle that it resolutely refuses to solve. Interpretation and judgement, therefore, are deferred, but the alert, attentive and attuned reader, like the poacher on his hunt, will move beyond the deliberate *aporia* of the poem's curt conclusion to a careful, critical engagement, by way of active dialectic, with the perennial ethical problem that constitutes the heart of the debate, the *sentence* or deep meaning of the text, that is, the old Socratic question: how ought I to live well?

---

27 For an exploration of some figurative uses of hunting in poetic texts, see Ad Putter, 'The Ways and Words of the Hunt: Notes on *Sir Gawain and the Green Knight*, *The Master of Game*, *Sir Tristrem*, *Pearl* and *Saint Erkenwald*', *Chaucer Review* 40:4 (2006), 372–80.

Reinterpreting the later life of Isabelle of France
(*c*.1295–1358)

NIAMH PATTWELL

Often referred to as the 'She-Wolf of France', Isabelle (*c*.1295–1358), queen consort to Edward II of England (1284–1327), is best known for her adulterous relationship with Roger Mortimer, with whom she plotted against her husband.[1] In 1325, Isabelle had fled to France and the home of her brother, Charles IV, where her son, the future Edward III, later joined her. With Edward, Mortimer and other disaffected nobles, she returned to England in 1326 where they overcame the Despensers, and other apparently unsavoury companions of Edward II, with the military backing of the French Hainaults. When, however, her son came to the throne in 1330, Isabelle was declared a traitor and her lands were confiscated.[2] Popular belief suggests that for the rest of her life Isabelle was a prisoner and lived in relative obscurity and poverty, removed from the courtly circles of the mid-fourteenth century. This understanding of Isabelle's life after Mortimer persisted for a long time, despite scholarly evidence to the contrary. In recent years the rediscovery of a much-neglected manuscript, British Library Cotton Galba E XIV, has revised this popular view of Isabelle's life after her fall from power. The manuscript details the financial transactions of the house of Isabelle from October 1357 to December 1358, thereby providing a textured picture of the daily life of an aristocratic household in the mid-fourteenth century.

I first came to the manuscript in search of further information on a wayward medieval cleric, William de Walcote, following the advice of John Scattergood, who was supervising my doctoral thesis. I was working on a pastoral manual of religious education and was interested in the 'typical reading' of the clergy of the late Middle Ages. Professor Scattergood directed me to a

1 The portrayal of Isabelle as the scheming wife of a weak-willed monarch probably gained currency through Christopher Marlowe's play *The Troublesome Reign and Lamentable Death of Edward the Second, King of England, with the Tragical Fall of Proud Mortimer* (*c*.1592). Sophie Menache offers a brief overview of the representation of Isabelle in contemporary and later literature. She concludes: 'it appears that one can clearly distinguish between two Isabelles: the one of contemporary reality and image and the other, no less prevalent, of later plays, literature and historical research.' Sophie Menache, 'Isabelle of France, Queen of England – a Reconsideration', *Journal of Medieval History* 10 (1984), 107–24 (120).   2 For a discussion of the nature and place of Isabelle's imprisonment, see Edward Bond, 'Notices of the Last Days of Isabella, Queen of Edward the Second, Drawn from an Account of the Expenses of her Household', *Archaeologia* 35 (1854), 453–69.   3 V.J. Scattergood, 'Two Medieval Book Lists', *The Library*, 5th series, 23:3 (1968), 236–9.

book list he published in 1968, which was an inventory of William de Walcote, keeper of the queen's wardrobe, who, through unknown circumstances, had fallen into bad debt and whose effects were the subject of an inventory still surviving in the Public Record Office.[3] Among de Walcote's goods was a size-able collection of books with the names of buyers attached. In the interest of examining the circulation of books among the clergy, I made an effort to iden-tify the buyers of de Walcote's books, and soon discovered that many of them were clerics employed at Isabelle's house.[4] Stumbling on a reference to BL Cotton Galba E XIV, I searched the manuscript for further information on the clergy of the queen mother's household, finding therein a wealth of detail on her expenses that year, including her travels, visitors, entertainment, house-hold composition and coterie of friends and acquaintances – particularly from France. The manuscript not only provides invaluable insight into court life in the period, but also offers strong evidence for a reinterpretation of Isabelle's later life.

Several papers appearing before and after the turn of the twentieth cen-tury argued that Isabelle led a more salubrious existence in her later years than is commonly assumed. The renowned historian T.F. Tout, for example, com-mented on Edward III's treatment of Isabelle after the demise of her and Mortimer's interregnum, writing that Edward made every effort

> to make relations pleasant and easy. Isabella came out well from her failure. Although she renounced the greater part of her swollen dower, she kept possessions of the sample revenue of £3000 a year. Henceforth somewhat apart from politics, she yet retained the dignified position of queen mother.[5]

Hilda Johnstone also offered a nuanced view of Isabelle's life after Edward III's ascendancy, arguing that Isabelle's disgrace and impoverishment were short-lived:

> The tales that used to be told of her disgrace, imprisonment and impoverishment have been proved by modern research to be completely untrue, except for a brief period following immediately upon Edward III's assertion of his rights. Step by step, her position improved, until by 1337 she was in possession of revenues equivalent in value to those assigned to her when queen consort.[6]

4 I am currently preparing an article on this material, intended for circulation in the *The Library*.
5 Thomas F. Tout, chapters in the *Administrative History of Medieval England*, 6 vols (Manchester, 1925–33), vol. 3, pp 33–4. 6 Hilda Johnstone, 'The She-wolf of France', *History* 21 (1936), 208–18, p. 213. Johnstone is clearly sympathetic to the difficulties Isabelle faced in her marriage to the troubled Edward II and suggests that Edward's lack of culture and

It is possible that Tout and Johnstone based their understanding on a paper, delivered to the Society of London Antiquaries in 1854, in which Edward Bond proposed that Isabelle in her final years led a more fulfilled and active political life than perhaps in her 'middle years'.[7] In fact, Bond's paper is frequently cited by book and art historians writing on Isabelle's books.[8] While Tout mentions the Cotton Galba manuscript, there is little evidence to suggest that he had actually studied it. He does not make direct reference to the contents of the account book; although, in his appraisal of books belonging to the queen, he describes the 'script so minute that it can hardly be read without a magnifying glass, yet of exquisite finish and clearness.'[9]

Written in Latin in a fourteenth-century secretary script, MS BL Cotton Galba E XIV details the financial transactions of the queen mother's household for the period of September 1357 to December 1358, including details for the queen's funeral, which took place in November 1358.[10] It is difficult to know why this particular manuscript remained undisturbed by scholars. One could speculate that the damage it incurred during the infamous fire of 1731, which charred some pages and caused others to shrink, makes it a daunting and time-consuming source for any scholar. Historian Michael Bennett, however, is probably closest to the truth when he deduces that the absence of this manuscript from the British Library catalogue most likely kept it one of the hidden treasures of the medieval world.[11]

In his rediscovery of BL Galba E XIV, Bennett has deconstructed the myth that Isabelle lived as a virtual prisoner at the hands of her son and has illustrated the weighty role that she played in the politics of France and England during the beginning of the Hundred Years War.[12] Bennett laments the absence of the manuscript from 'recent studies of Edward III and the late medieval household', suggesting that this manuscript and 'three other sets of household accounts from this time' offer 'rare insights on court life in the 1350s.' For Bennett, the accounts indicate that Isabelle was interested in pol-

---

refinement was the motivation for Isabelle's betrayal. Coincidentally, this change of heart towards Isabelle is in line with Brecht's 1923 *The Life of Edward II*, which is essentially a re-interpretation of Marlowe's play.   7 See n. 2 above.   8 At least 45 manuscripts, 11 extant, have been linked with Isabelle. These manuscripts include romances, bibles, books of hours and books of advice to princes. See Suzanne Lewis, 'The Apocalypse of Isabelle of France: Paris Bibl. Nat. MS Fr. 13096', *The Art Bulletin*, 72:2 (1990), 224–60 and Anne Rudolff Stanton, 'Isabelle of France and Her Manuscripts, 1308–58', in *Capetian Women*, ed. Kathleen Nolan (London, 2003), pp 225–52.   9 Tout, *Administrative History*, vol. 5, p. 285.   10 According to a note on fol. 31v of MS BL Cotton Galba E XIV, she died on 22 August 1358.   11 Bennett, acknowledging the work done by Bond in 1853, posits a theory that 'Bond had the manuscript in his possession at the time that some assistant put together the catalogue' and that consequently the manuscript remained unrecorded and unknown. Michael Bennett, 'Isabelle of France, Anglo-French Diplomacy and Cultural Exchange in the late 1350s', in J.S. Bothwell (ed.), *The Age of Edward III* (York, 2001), pp 215–23 (p. 216).   12 Bennett, 'Isabelle of France', pp 215–25.

itics and diplomacy on both sides of the Channel. He notes, for example, the payments made to messengers bringing news of the escape of Charles of Navarre, Isabelle's grand-nephew and 'a thorn in the side of the French Government.'[13] There are several references to Isabelle's role as hostess and 'intermediary' in the relations of England and France.[14] Moreover, Bennett details many of the references which exhibit the role Isabelle played in the 'cultural patronage' of fourteenth-century England, including the presence of other women in her intimate circle who were also given to literary patronage.[15]

The tenacity of Marlowe's 'She-Wolf' label, up to and including the twentieth century, seems perverse, all the more as Isabelle seems to have enjoyed some admiration in her own lifetime. According to Menache, there are many contemporary references to her beauty by French chroniclers, to her fecundity by the English and, in both English and French sources, to her distress at the hands of a tyrannical husband as an excuse for her actions.[16] Menache's concluding remarks illustrate the injustice of dwelling on Isabelle's moral life as a measure of her success as Queen: 'If the Kings of England are not measured according to their morality alone, then Isabelle of France should not be denied this privilege either.'[17] The evidence of the Cotton Galba manuscript suggests that Isabelle was a diplomat, a patron of the arts and a devout and pious lady. Indeed, she might be better described as the 'gide and lady sovereine' of her time, inspiring and enriching the courtly circle of her adopted land with the circulation and copying of 'old stories' from her native France.[18]

Like a real 'sovereine', Isabelle enjoyed a busy and active life in these final years. The accounts open with details of a pilgrimage she undertook to Canterbury from her residence in Hertford during October and November 1357. She attended great feasts, including the Great Feast of the Garter in April 1358.[19] The marginalia of the opening section of the manuscript, which lists the day-to-day expenses of the household, contains the names of people who attended the court of the queen mother. These include such dignitaries as the keeper of the Privy Seal, John Wynewyck, and her son King Edward III. There are several records of letters being passed between her and the countess of Pembroke, who was in regular attendance on the queen mother at Hertford Castle and visited her often.[20] The countess of Pembroke, best known as the founder of Pembroke College, Cambridge in 1347, was the

---

13 Bennett, 'Isabelle of France', p. 222.   14 Ibid., pp 220–1.   15 Ibid., pp 223–4 and 219.   16 Menache, 'Isabelle of France, Queen of England', 117–19.   17 Ibid., 122.   18 Geoffrey Chaucer, *Legend of Good Women*, F 94, 98. *The Riverside Chaucer*, 3rd ed., gen. ed. Larry D. Benson (Oxford, 2008).   19 On fol. 15r, the scribe has noted the places in which the court spent the night while away from the queen's permanent residence at Hertford Castle with phrases such as 'apud London' and 'apud Totenham'.   20 For example, on the 4th April money was paid to a messenger bringing a letter from the Countess of Pembroke (fols 51v and 52r); the Countess attended the queen mother on 1, 2 and 3 December and again on 15 (fol. 6r); on 10 and 11 January (fol. 8r).

daughter of Guy de Chatillon, count of St Pol and Butler of France. Following the sudden death of her husband, Aymer de Valence, in 1324, she lived out her life between England and France. Alison Weir notes that Isabelle and the Countess Pembroke were cousins and were also related through the Countess' sister, Matilda, who married one of Isabelle's uncles, Charles of Valois.[21] She was a lifelong companion to Isabelle and the inventory at her death reveals that she too was a bibliophile.[22] Isabelle gave her a breviary in 1357, which corrects, I think, the Rouses' assumption that the breviary the countess bequeathed to her confessor, William Morin OFM, was a gift from Queen Philippa: the gift was from Isabelle.[23]

On fol. 24r, there is a note in the margins noting that the countess of Ulster had attended the Queen Mother the night before she died. The countess of Ulster was Isabelle's granddaughter-in-law. She married Prince Lionel, son of Edward III, and their daughter Philippa was just three years of age at the time of Isabelle's death. Intriguingly, this Philippa later married Edmund, the great-grandson of Mortimer, Isabelle's former lover, who would have been six or seven at the time of Isabelle's death. It may be somewhat fanciful to imagine that Isabelle plotted, or at least instigated, the betrothal of her great-granddaughter and Mortimer's great-grandson in those final years of her life. Yet, despite the perpetuation of 1368 as the date of Philippa's and Edmund's marriage, W.M. Ormrod has demonstrated that the betrothal had taken place by December 1358. It seems likely, therefore, that Isabelle would, at the very least, have known of, if not participated in the arrangements.[24]

Interest in the countess of Ulster is further heightened by our knowledge that Geoffrey Chaucer was a page in her household and may therefore have had first-hand contact with this circle of cultural patronage at a young age.[25] The famous entries in the countess of Ulster's household accounts indicate

21 Alison Weir, *Isabella: She-Wolf of France, Queen of England* (London, 2006), p. 131.   22 For a synopsis of the Countess' life and details on the extant manuscripts that can be identified as hers, see Richard and Mary Rouse, 'Marie de St-Pol and Cambridge University Library, MS Dd. 5.5', Stella Panayotova (ed.), *The Cambridge Illuminations: The Conference Papers* (London, 2007), pp 187–91.   23 The Rouses are correcting the assumption by previous historians that the term *my queen* refers to the Queen of France. They state clearly that this is an incorrect assumption, arguing that 'when Marie says 'the king' she demonstrably meant the King of England, and the same should hold for 'the queen', p. 190 n. 19.   24 W.M. Ormrod, 'Edward III and His Family', *The Journal of British Studies*, 26:4 (1987), 398–422. Ormrod takes pains to point out 'that there has been much misunderstanding over the dates of these weddings' on the grounds of 'an ambiguous reference' in the Patent Rolls for 1367–70 (p. 410, n. 46). Ormrod dates the wedding to pre-December 1358 on the basis of a reference in exchequer documents specifically, *Issues of the Exchequer, Henry III to Henry VI* ed. Frederick Devon (London, 1847), p. 172.   25 Derek Pearsall acknowledges the influence of the French court on Chaucer during his time as an esquire. See *The Life of Geoffrey Chaucer: A Critical Biography* (Oxford, 1992), p. 62. Perhaps Chaucer's somewhat inauspicious beginnings as a page boy, in and out of the world of the French lady patrons, also played a contributory part.

that Chaucer was attired in the livery of the household in time for certain feasts and celebrations, a number of which would have been attended by Isabelle and her coterie.[26] On 20 December 1357 he receives 2s. 6d. for Christmas clothes to be celebrated at the royal residence of Hatfield, a few miles northeast of Doncaster, in the keeping of Queen Philippa. The household attended the Great Tournament of 1358 and the funeral of Isabelle in December of the same year.[27] We can assume that, as a humble page boy, Chaucer would have had occasion to mingle with, and listen to, the French attendants of Isabelle's circle of friends and may have had ample opportunity to watch unnoticed the entertainments and festivities of the royal circle.

Isabelle seems to have remained constant in her love of things French. We know, for example, that she was in a position to lend books to John II of France during his stay in England. To this end, on 10 December, money was paid to a French man who returned two French romances from King John in London.[28] In earlier accounts she was given a selection of French books from the Royal Library by the keeper of the wardrobe.[29] The books listed in the inventory at the time of her death include religious books typical for a lady of her rank such as Books of Hours, an Apocalypse and bibles, but also include French romances.[30] Isabelle maintained her retinue as French, orchestrated the marriage of her son Edward III to Philippa of Hainault (also known for her patronage of high courtly culture) and her closest companions in these last years were French nobles.[31] It is evident, in fact, that Isabelle ended her life as she began it: deeply immersed in French culture.

Even the many references to minstrels in her accounts reveal a number of French entertainers. It is not always clear what exactly is intended by the entertainment, except that these minstrels were part of the celebrations of particular feast days. On 14 May, we note the gift of 40s. to a 'Iohan Maille', a minstrel of the French queen, and on the same day two other minstrels of the queen received the much smaller sum of 6s. 7d. Minstrels from the house of the duke of Brabant performed on the feast of Corpus Christi and received 16s. for their efforts, while another group received 21s. and 8d. On fol. 49v, we read that the minstrels of the king visited and performed on 1 November

---

26 Pearsall gives the details of purchases made by or on behalf of Chaucer at this time. Chaucer's page suit was bought between 4 and 9 April 1357 (Easter was 9 April) and consisted of a short cloak or cassock (4s.) and a pair of black and red hose and shoes (3s.). Again on 20 May 1357 he was paid 2s. for expenses incurred in dressing for Pentecost at Woodstock (Pearsall, *Life of Geoffrey Chaucer*, p. 35). 27 Ibid., p. 35. 28 The books were the *Holy Grail* and *Sir Lancelot* (fol. 4r). 29 The romances borrowed by Isabelle in 1327 included 'Arthurian romance ("de gestis Arthuri", "de Tristram et Isolda", "de Perceual et Gauwayn"), *chanson de geste* such as "Emery et [sic] Nerbon" and "de duce Basyns", a volume relating to the Trojan war ("de bello troiano") and another "de Baudrous".' (Juliet Vale, *Edward III and Chivalry: Chivalric Society and Its Context, 1270–1350* (Suffolk, 1982), p. 50. 30 Vale, *Edward III*, p. 52. 31 For a brief introduction to Philippa's interest in art and literature see Vale, *Edward III*, pp 44–7.

for the Feast of All Saints. Two pipers from London received 10s. over the
Easter period, as did two minstrels of the countess of Ulster. During the Feast
of Pentecost, a group of pipers received 20s. and another lot of minstrels got
24s.; minstrels played again at Midsummer on the Feast of John the Baptist.
Occasionally, rather than the identity of patrons, the names of individuals are
offered, such as a Robert and a Gerard who played for the court while it
resided in Leeds.³² Minstrels obviously vied for space at the households of the
great royals, despite the fact that royals had minstrels of their own:

> We know, however, that minstrels regularly performed at ordinary
> meals in such a court as that of Edward III, and often played for indi-
> vidual members of the household, who frequently had their own per-
> sonal musicians. Janettus le Sautreour, who was the minstrel of Isabella,
> the King's mother, is an example.³³

Some attention has been given to Walter Hert, a viol-player mentioned in
Isabelle's household book for 22 February and the last day of March 1358.³⁴
On his return from a school of music in London during Lent, he received 4s.,
although he also received a separate sum of 13s. 4d.³⁵ Schools of music were
common practice on the Continent.³⁶ Maricarmen Gómez describes them as
'annual meetings attended by minstrels of different nationalities' and lists
'Paris, Malines, Tournais, Beauvais, Lille, Douai, Bruges and Cambrai among
the cities listed as sites for these schools'.³⁷ Lent, when all revelry, including
music, was forbidden, was an opportune time for minstrels to travel to centres of learning. The precise nature of the activities at such schools is not
clear, but it is generally believed that they were informal gatherings where
musicians could swap material or share new techniques, and that only the
wealthy could afford to send minstrels to school. It is not clear who hosted or
even organized these events, and the reference to a London School of Music
is particularly mysterious because there are no other references to a School of
Music in London during the fourteenth century. Edward III gave permission
to two bagpipers to attend a Continental School of Music in the eighth year
of his reign.³⁸ Given the lack of evidence of a regular London School of
Music, this may have been a once-off event in response to the circumstances

32 Fols 49v–52r.   33 Claire C. Olson, 'The Minstrels at the Court of Edward III', *PMLA* 56:3
(1941), 601–12, p. 610. Olson is referring to Thomas Rymer, *Foedera* (London: Record
Commission, 1821) II, Part 2, p. 738.   34 Fol. 51v. See Edith Rickerts, 'Chaucer at School',
Modern Philology, 29:3 (1932), 258–74, p. 272.   35 Fol. 51v. Perhaps it is coincidental, but Olson
notes that 13s. 4d. was the standard annual payment to a yeoman of the house of King Edward
at this time (p. 606).   36 Olson makes the point that they were 'commonly held on the
Continent' (p. 606).   37 Maricarmen Gómez, 'Minstrel Schools in the Late Middle Ages,' *Early
Music* 18:2 (1990), 213–16. URL: http://www.jstor.org/stable/3127809. Accessed 26 August
2008.   38 Olson, 'Minstrels at the Court of Edward III', p. 603.

in which many exiled French aristocrats and their retinue found themselves. The months of 1357–8 were full of colour and courtly entertainment, including the night-time tournament of Bristol for the New Year in 1358 and the Feast of the Garter in April of the same year.[39] It would have been an opportune time for Isabelle and her French friends to organize a school in London to facilitate the presence of so many talented musicians in England.

It is difficult to be absolutely certain of the identity of an individual in the Middle Ages. In the case of Walter Hert, there are two entries in the official records, but only one of these Walters had a connection with Isabelle, making him the likelier candidate. In one entry, there is mention of a Walter Hert, a cleric of the diocese of Norwich, who received permission to choose a confessor in a number of indults sought in January and granted in March 1361.[40] The other Walter Hert is the subject of letters patent, from the house of Queen Isabelle, written in French on 18 July 1357, in which he received twenty-five acres of land in reward for his service to the queen:

> Inspeximus and confirmation of letters patent (in French) of Queen Isabel, dated at Hertford Castle, 18 July, 27 Edward III, granting to her yeoman and watchman (geyte) Walter Hert, for long service, and to Isabel, his wife, and Peter, their son, 25 acres in land in Wotton by La Fasterne, Co Wilts, which Ralph Bolle of Seint Botulf then held for life of Hugh le Despenser, to hold after the death of Ralph for life, rendering yearly the rent and services due.[41]

It is even more poignant that these lands were once in the possession of one of Isabelle's most hated enemies, Hugh Despenser.

If Walter Hert were both yeoman and minstrel, it adds strength to the thesis of another student of John Scattergood's, Clifton Hoyt, who explored the records of several medieval households in search of information on minstrels of the late Middle Ages. He concluded that references to money paid to minstrels did not indicate that this was the full-time employment of that person, but merely that the money was the reward for a talent or entertainment offered to the household and patron, and he therefore argues for an *ad hoc* approach to defining minstrel status.[42] Hoyt also claims that the minstrel belongs in the category of general servant.[43] Further to this, we must consider that in the medieval household, the viol, unlike the viola, cello or violin, is not a 'professional's instrument', played with a focus on the player's technique and skill, but is used rather to accompany singers or dancers at an informal

39 Vale, *Edward III*, pp 69 and 141 n.172.   40 *Calendar of Papal Letters 1358–61*, p. 565 and *Calendar of Papal Letters 1342–62*, p. 501.   41 *Calendar of Patent Rolls 1354–58*, p. 588.   42 Clifton L. Hoyt, 'Professional Minstrelsy and Amateur Performance in Medieval England' (PhD thesis, University of Dublin, 1994), p. 90.   43 Hoyt, p. 78.

gathering.[44] It is quite possible that a medieval yeoman (in this case one responsible for tending the queen mother's goats) would have had time to develop his skills on such an instrument and gain a reputation for entertainment that was appreciated equally in and out of the court. Walter Hert was not the only non-professional minstrel in a royal house. Olson notes that a minstrel named Nicholas de Prage in Edward III's house may also have been a sergeant-at-arms.[45]

In light of the significant number of books linked to Isabelle, it is no surprise to discover several references to book production in the household accounts. In March 1358, 2s. was paid out for 2lbs of wax, two skins for 'mura per diversis libris regine'.[46] On 26 of October 1357, we read that a William de Taterford was paid 3s. 4d. for six vellum skins, 'pellibus vellumis', and two aborted skins, 'pellibus aborcinis', bought by him for the books of the queen and written in his own hand, 'per ipsum emptor pro libris regine scribend per manus propter'.[47] It is impossible to be sure that the vellum was intended for literary purposes, but on the same date there is another entry for a Richard Painter who was paid 3s. 4d. for azure; it is probable that both entries refer to the same activity, and unlikely that a household book would be decorated. Lewis suggests a link between an unfinished Book of Hours in Isabelle's inventory of books and the activities of de Taterford and Richard Painter. It is plausible that 'Isabella had commissioned an illuminated book that was not yet finished at her death,' but without further evidence this remains speculative.[48]

The scribe William de Taterford, whose name appears regularly throughout the household book, is easier to identify. Apart from money received in October for 'scripta' and parchment, he received a further sum of money on 18 November to buy shoes, hosiery, a robe and a tunic of wool, indicating that he was regular member of the Queen's household.[49] In fact, on fol.37r, he is referred to as 'scriptori regine' and paid 14s. for writing the queen's books. William de Taterford, according to the official records, was a notary of the queen; he was a married cleric of the diocese of Norwich. He and his wife are

---

44'During the first decades of its rising popularity in Europe, viol consorts did not have a specific repertoire, but instead were used to play general instrumental dances, as well as music written for vocal ensembles. Viol consorts lent themselves exceedingly well to vocal music, due to the viol's ability to imitate the expressiveness of the human voice.' Emily Peppers, 'Moving Music: Travelling Music and the Introduction of the Viol into James V's Scotland', *eSharp* 4 (2005), p. 4. See also Ian Woodfield, *The Early History of the Viol* (Cambridge, 1984); Mary Remnant, 'Rebec, Fiddle and Crowd in England', *Proceedings of the Royal Music Association*, 95th session (1968–9), pp 15–28. 45 Olson, 'Minstrels at the Court of Edward III', p. 607. 46 Fol. 38v. 47 Fol. 37r. 48 Lewis, 'The Apocalypse of Isabelle of France', 234 n. 65. Vale, in her comments on Queen Philippa's household accounts, makes reference to a payment sought by the queen to the wife ('nostre bien aimee Johanne qui fuist la femme') of an illuminator ('Robert nostre elumynour') stressing the rarity of detail pertaining to the personal interests of the royal personage. She describes the entry as 'a rare survival' adding that most household accounts 'are concerned with rents and land-management rather than personal expenses' (p. 47). 49 fol. 37r.

listed in a set of indults in relation to confessors granted in July 1353.[50] It is no coincidence that William de Taterford bears the name of a town in Norfolk granted to the Bohuns after the conquest.[51] The sixth earl of Bohun was renowned for his patronage of literature and culture, practically running a workshop of scribes and painters for the production of 'a remarkable series of handsomely illuminated psalters'.[52] Perhaps William was trained in the Bohun household, from whence he came to Isabelle's court.

The possible connection between William de Taterford and the Bohun household is especially provocative because it may contribute another piece to the puzzle concerning the origins of the popular medieval work, *Mandeville's Travels*.[53] Addressing the argument made by Josephine Bennett for an Anglo-Norman rather than French origin for the *Travels*, Michael Bennett draws attention to the reference in Cotton Galba E XIV to a gift of venison brought by John Mandeville in December 1357.[54] Mandeville brought game on at least two more occasions that December.[55] Bennett explains that most recent scholarly opinion favours the French origins of this pastiche of encyclopaedic works based on

> the growing appreciation of the sources used by 'Mandeville'. M.C. Seymour, the leading Mandeville scholar in England, claims that the *Travels* was written in a major monastic library in Northern France.[56]

Bennett is correct, I think, when he asserts that Seymour is overstating his case for the author's dependence on a monastic library. Anglo-Norman relations in the fourteenth century lent themselves to book exchange, either as gifts of peace or trophies of war. Moreover, as stated above, French nobles moving between England and France had ample opportunity to acquire and to circulate books of high literary merit. Bennett mentions that the countess

50 *Calendar of Papal Letters 1342–62*, p. 501.   **51** Melville M. Bigelow, 'The Bohun Wills', *American Historical Review* 1:3 (1896), 414–35 (p. 414).   **52** Michael Bennett, '*Mandeville's Travels* and the Anglo-French Moment', *Medium Aevum* 75:2 (2006), 272–92 (p. 279).   **53** My original paper for the Scattergood symposium held in September 2006 made a great deal more of the Mandeville references in the Cotton Galba E XIV manuscript. In light of Michael Bennett's *Medium Aevum* article on Mandeville, however, I include here only material that adds strength to his case for a re-examination of the insular Mandeville tradition.   **54** BL Cotton Galba E XIV, fol. 50r.   **55** See fols 49r, 49v and 51r.   **56** Michael Bennett, '*Mandeville's Travels*', p. 274. Later, Bennett explains Seymour's hypothesis: 'More recently M.C. Seymour has broadened the case for French provenance by reference to the library required for the composition of the *Travels*. 'Mandeville' drew on a wide range of relatively rare books, including an anthology of travel literature translated into French around 1351 by Jean le Long, monk of Saint-Bertin at Saint-Omer. On the assumption that such books were more likely to be found in a monastery in France than in England, Seymour has concluded that the author of the *Travels* was a French monk or cleric, someone not unlike Jean le Long himself' (Bennett, p. 276). See also, J.W. Bennett, *The Rediscovery of Sir John Mandeville* (New York, 1954).

owned a copy of *Godefroy de Bouillon*, and both Josephine and Michael Bennett make a strong case for the Bohun connection to *Mandeville's Travels*.[57] The references in the Cotton Galba manuscript to William de Taterford provide a possible link between the literary Bohun household and the court of Isabelle, where the exchange of books and ideas was commonplace, and may lend further support to the argument for the Anglo-Norman origins of *Mandeville's Travels*. There is certainly a strong case for re-examining the circulation of the insular manuscripts, including the extant Hiberno-manuscripts of the fifteenth century.

My interest in Isabelle and her household began with a reference provided by John Scattergood in a conversation about the distribution of clerical books. Moving beyond the list of books for clergy, I discovered a set of household accounts which portrayed a royal house that played host to a wide cultural circle, encouraged by the presence of the French nobility during their enforced exile in England in the mid-fourteenth century. Isabelle's contributions to England, indeed, may have been more than diplomatic. Discrete articles have appeared on the books in Isabelle's possession at the time of her death, but a comprehensive study of the noble patrons moving around Isabelle at this crucial time in Anglo-French history would be invaluable to our understanding of the development and distribution of literature, both English and French.[58] Isabelle was part of a strong coterie of cultural exchange in England. Raised in her native France, she brought with her, surrounded herself with and invested in the best of European art, music and literature throughout her life.

57 Michael Bennett, '*Mandeville's Travels*', pp 278–80. In particular, Bennett comments on the Brabant-Bohun political connection, but the presence of minstrels at Isabelle's court suggests that there was also a cultural connection.   58 See n. 8 and n. 22 above. See also Bennett, 'Isabelle of France', p. 217, n. 10.

The Franklin's Tale: the Generous Father and the Spendthrift Son

CLÍODHNA CARNEY

[T]he behaviour of human beings shows differences, which ethics, disregarding the fact that such differences are determined, classifies as "good" or "bad". So long as these undeniable differences have not been removed, obedience to high ethical demands entails damage to the aims of civilisation, for it puts a positive premium on being bad.[1]

It is hard to find the *mot juste* to describe the Franklin's behaviour towards the Squire in the Squire–Franklin link, just before the Franklin begins his tale. Perhaps there is not a word for it. *Patronize* comes close, but only if one labours the word's etymology, its roots in Latin *pater*. The part-friendly, part-authoritarian, part-maddening attitude of the father towards his maturing son (and in the case of the Squire, the son-substitute) is a familiar enough idea. Freud described the 'primal horde' of sons long overshadowed by an authoritarian father who monopolizes all the women, leaving the sons to plot against and eventually overcome him.[2] These sons feel both love and hatred for their father. In their hatred they kill him, but in their remorse for their deed, their filial love 'comes to the fore'.[3] Their remorse causes them to re-make the father they destroyed, in the form of their own super-ego 'identification with the father'.[4] At the same time, they pull up the ladder, to prevent their own sons from murdering them.

The Franklin begins his performance in the *Canterbury Tales* with a tonally puzzling commendation of another man's son, a commendation which quickly segues into a lament for his own son's shortcomings:

> 'In feith, Squier, thow hast thee wel yquit
> And gentilly. I preise wel thy wit,'
> Quod the Frankeleyn, 'considerynge thy yowthe,
> So feelyngly thou spekest, sire, I allow the!
> As to my doom, ther is noon that is heere
> Of eloquence that shal be thy peere,
> If that thou lyve; God yeve thee good chaunce,
> And in vertu sende thee continuaunce,

---

1 Sigmund Freud, *Civilisation and Its Discontents*, trans. James Strachey ([1961]; New York, 1962), p. 58. 2 Ibid., pp 47–8. 3 Ibid., p. 79. 4 Ibid.

> For of thy speche I have greet deyntee.
> I have a sone, and by the Trinitee,
> I hadde levere than twenty pound worth lond,
> Though it right now were fallen in myn hond,
> He were a man of swich discrecioun
> As that ye been! Fy on possessioun,
> But if a man be vertuous withal!
> I have my sone snybbed, and yet shal,
> For he to vertu listeth nat entende;
> But for to pleye at dees, and to despende
> And lese al that he hath is his usage.
> And he hath levere talken with a page
> Than to comune with any gentil wight
> Where he myghte lerne gentillesse aright.'   (V, 673–94)[5]

What is the Franklin up to here?[6] Has he just interrupted the Squire? And if so, is it because he wants to spare himself and the pilgrims the tedium of a long-winded tale, or to let its poor teller off the hook of an embarrassing social performance? Or does he like to have things both ways: to do someone a mischief and at the same time claim the credit for kindness? The tale the Franklin goes on to tell is certainly full of moral switchbacks.

Ostensibly, the Franklin is depreciating himself and his own son relative to the Squire, and by implication, the Squire's father, the Knight. The Franklin's son is apparently a recidivist spendthrift, resistant to his father's advice and authority. The Squire, on the other hand, according to the Franklin, is enviably *gentil*, in spite of his youth. In an address of age to youth, then, is framed an address of age to youth: the old Franklin tells the young Squire about his, the old Franklin's attempt to correct his young son. So far, so medieval. Youth and age are often in debate, as Chaucer writes elsewhere.[7] And when age does talk to youth, what does it talk about? Age and youth, of course. So far, so modern.

Another complication arises, however, with the question of the Franklin's rank. Is he gentle or is he not?[8] The point was debated several times over sev-

---

5 All quotations from Chaucer are taken from *The Riverside Chaucer*, gen. ed. Larry D. Benson (Boston, 1987; Oxford, 1988).   6 It is impossible to say for certain whether the 'Squire's Tale' is unfinished for the extrinsic reason that Chaucer gave up on it, or for the intrinsic, fictive reason that the Franklin interrupts it. Not that either one of the two alternatives precludes the other. Chaucer might well have given up on the 'Squire's Tale', only to see in its unfinished condition the perfect cue for the entrance of the Franklin into the *Tales*, in which case the whole Squire-Franklin link would be a piece of inspired opportunism.   7 'For youthe and elde is often at debaat', 'Miller's Tale', (3230).   8 The Franklin's rank has been the object of sustained interest over many decades of scholarship. G.H. Gerould's article on the subject appeared in 1926: 'The Social Status of Chaucer's Franklin', *PMLA* 41 (1926), 262–79. In 1981, Henrik Specht

eral decades, and if the extrinsic matter of the rank of historical franklins now seems to be resolved in favour of their gentility, the preoccupation of Chaucer's own Franklin with the nuances of rank cannot be so easily smoothed away.[9]

The Franklin begins by recommending a kind of *gentilesse* that is not dependent upon 'possessioun', a *gentilesse* that instead stems from 'virtue', but no sooner has he done so than he finds fault with his son for his profligacy, laziness, and tendency to socialize with 'a page' rather than with a 'gentil wight/ Where he myght lerne gentilesse aright'. The pure Christian *gentilesse* that does not rely upon *possessioun* is that *generositas virtus, non sanguis*, which has become a common trope by the time Chaucer comes to write the *Canterbury Tales*.[10] There are several uses of the word 'page' in the *Tales*, and rarely if ever is the word associated with villainy or churlishness; rather it is variously associated with one or more of the following: masculinity, servility, service, poverty, ignorance (in the strict sense of lack of knowledge or education, rather than boorishness).[11] Social and financial lowliness, rather than any unpleasant personal traits, seem to be the distinguishing features of the page as he appears in Chaucer's work. According to the philosophy of *generositas virtus, non sanguis*, which the Franklin is expounding here, the page's lack of wealth and social position should be no impediment to his being truly *gentil*. But the Franklin's exposition of true *gentilesse* is nothing if not illogical.

The logical contradiction aside, there is also the question of the tonal ambiguity that I mentioned above. The Franklin, congratulating the Squire's virtue, manages, by way of apparently running himself down, to demonstrate, first, his own internalization of the principle of *generositas virtus, non sanguis* – in

published his *Chaucer's Franklin in 'The Canterbury Tales'* (Copenhagen, 1981), and the same year saw the publication of Mary Carruthers' 'The Gentilesse of Chaucer's Franklin', *Criticism* 23 (1981), 283–300. See also R.J. Pearcy, 'Chaucer's Franklin and the Literary Vavasour', *Chaucer Review* 8 (1973), 33–59. 9 Specht provides a holistic account, drawing on manorial, legal and literary evidence of late-medieval franklins, concluding that the franklins of the fourteenth century, in contradistinction to their 'servile neighbours holding in villeinage', were *free* (p. 179), *gentle* (p. 180), and, usually, *wealthy* (p. 180). 10 Chaucer's other direct treatments of *virtus, non sanguis* occur in the 'Wife of Bath's Tale', (1109–76); the 'Clerk's Tale'(155–61) and in the short poem *Gentilesse*. The topic is treated by Dante in the canzone that precedes *Il Convivio* 4 and also in *Il Convivio* 4.3, 10, 14, 15, and in *Le Roman de la Rose* (6579–92) and (607–896), and in *De Consolatione Philosophiae* II, pr. vi; III, pr. iii-met. iii; III, pr. vi and III, met. vi. (A. J. Minnis argues that the *locus classicus* of the distinction between 'nobility of soul' and 'nobility by ancestry and rank' is Book III, pr. iii-met. iii of the *Consolation*; A.J. Minnis and A.B. Scott (eds), *Medieval Literary Theory and Criticism c.1100–c.1375* (1988; rev. with corrections and additions, Oxford, 1991), p. 381. G.M. Vogt, 'Gleanings for the History of a Sentiment: *Generositas virtus, non sanguis*', *Journal of English and Germanic Philology* 24 (1925), 102–24. 11 'Knight's Tale', (142), (303); 'Miller's Tale' (33); 'Reeve's Tale' (397); 'Summoner's Tale' (21); 'Merchant's Tale' (14); 'Squire's Tale' (692); 'Pardoner's Prologue' (449); 'Pardoner's Tale' (6); 'Shipman's Tale' (4) that he would forego twenty pounds worth of land were his son to achieve the 'discrecioun' displayed by the Squire – and second, his incidental possession of considerable wealth. Unlike the virtuous but shabby-genteel Knight's son, and irrespective of the difference in degree between Knight and Franklin, the Franklin and his son appear to be in possession. The very behaviour which the Franklin decries – his son's profligacy – hints that there is something to be lost. The dice-playing in which his son indulges, involves his 'despending' and losing 'al that he hath'. We know already, from the portrait in the 'General Prologue', that the Franklin is a man of substance, whose defining characteristics are hospitality and largesse. Is the Franklin really disappointed in his son, or is the son just the more youthful image of his father, profligate where his father is generous?

In the Freudian paradigm of the primal horde, the rebellious son in time becomes the conservative father. The Franklin is old.[12] His beard is white, his complexion ruddy from the consolatory wining and dining that is typical of his time of life.[13] In several respects, however, he is youthful. The old Reeve in his prologue describes his agedness in terms of the four 'gleedes' or embers in the old ashes of decrepitude: boasting, lying, anger and avarice.[14] The Franklin in the Squire–Franklin link is almost directly the opposite. As one reader after another has noted, he is modest, self-deprecating, gentle, and says that nobility is not based on wealth or rank. When the Host speaks rudely to him, he responds politely. He is also energetic, holding down several positions at once. He oversees the order of his household with gusto. And his official line on the subject of worldly goods and nobility is the one already associated in Chaucer's day with social ferment, with youth rather than age, with the dispossessed rather than with the ruling classes: true nobility has nothing whatever to do with inheritance, pedigree or wealth.[15] The portrait of the Franklin, like most of Chaucer's portraits, is psychologically convincing: he may be old, but he wants to seem and feel young; likewise, he reproves his son in public, but are (the very things he reproves, and in which he rightly sees a challenge to himself, also the seeds of the son's love, and filial imitation of the father?

---

12 That is not to try to attach a particular age to the Franklin. At times in medieval literature there is a concern with precise calibrations of the ages of man. But at others, as here, there is just the binary distinction between youth and age.   13 It might be objected here that in the detail of the Franklin's sanguine complexion Chaucer is referring to the theory of the four humours. He undoubtedly is, but he is clearly using that theory to make a joke about the Franklin's taste for wine, as the rich rhyme between *sangwyn* and *wyn* suggests.   14 'Reeve's Prologue' (3881–5).   15 In the B-text of *Piers Plowman*, when the Knight makes the radical suggestion to Piers that he would like to be taught to plough the earth, even Piers rows back from the implications, urging the Knight instead to stick to his traditional pursuits of hunting and fighting, but to do so under the auspices of Truth. William Langland, *Piers Plowman: A Critical Edition of the B-text based on Trinity College Cambridge MS B.15.17*, ed. A.V.C. Schmidt (London, 1995), VI, (21–32). See also (45–9).

The tale that the Franklin goes on to tell appears to follow naturally from the topic broached in the Squire–Franklin link. Ostensibly it extols the virtue of 'fredom' or generosity, by the performance of which the moral deadlock of the tale is broken. It is the knight Arveragus' *gentil* deed and the imitation of it first by the squire Aurelius and then by the clerk, that demonstrate the truth of the Franklin's theory that the only true nobility is *generositas virtus, non sanguis*. As the clerk points out at the end of the tale, even a clerk 'koude doon a gentil dede' (1611).

The problem is that while some readers think the Franklin is fit to speak on the subject of *gentilesse*, some do not. Scholars have generally assumed that there is a natural connection between the high birth of the teller, and the moral loftiness of the tale he tells, and *vice-versa*. To the extent that the Franklin is a gentleman, his tale is idealized, harmonious, successful, both artistically and ethically.[16] To the extent that he is an upstart, his tale is suspect, its *gentil* message as doubtful as the Franklin's own rank.[17]

What I would like to do is look again at the resolution of the tale's problem to see if it does or does not fulfil the Franklin's publicly espoused theory of *generositas virtus, non sanguis*. This is the very theory which lies at the centre of the contention between son and father. It is not only a private matter between them, however, far from it. In both the link and his tale, the Franklin transposes his private familial relations, first onto the Squire and, by implication, the latter's father, the Knight, and then, in the fiction of the tale, onto the wider world of social order *per se*. The Franklin has already, in the

16 See, for example: G.L. Kittredge's famous article in which 'The Franklin's Tale' is seen as a harmonious resolution to the questions raised by the "marriage group" of tales, 'Chaucer's Discussion of Marriage', *Modern Philology* 9 (1911–12), 435–67; R.J. Pearcy, 'Chaucer's Franklin and the Literary Vavasour', *Chaucer Review* 8 (1973), 33–59, in which the Franklin is compared favourably with knights and vavasours; Gerald Morgan (ed.), *The Franklin's Tale* (London, 1981), pp 12–14, and his articles, 'A Defence of Dorigen's Complaint', *Medium Ævum* 46 (1977), 77–97, and 'Boccaccio's *Filocolo* and the Moral Argument of the *Franklin's Tale*', *Chaucer Review* 20 (1986), 285–306; Mary Carruthers, 'The Gentilesse of Chaucer's Franklin', *Criticism* 23 (1981), 283–300; Jill Mann, 'Chaucerian Themes and Style in the *Franklin's Tale*', *New Pelican Guide to English Literature*, vol. I *Medieval Literature, Part One: Chaucer and the Alliterative Tradition*, ed. Boris Ford (London, 1982), p. 135.   17 See, for example: R.M. Lumiansky, *Of Sondry Folk: The Dramatic Principle in 'The Canterbury Tales'* (Austin, 1955), pp 180–93; Donald R. Howard, 'The Conclusion of the Marriage Group: Chaucer and the Human Condition', *Modern Philology* 57 (1960–61), 223–32; D.W. Robertson, *A Preface to Chaucer: Studies in Medieval Perspectives* (Princeton, 1962); Alan Gaylord, 'The Promises in *The Franklin's Tale*', *ELH* 31 (1964), 331–65; Robert B. Burlin, *Chaucerian Fictions* (Princeton, 1977); Douglas Wurtele, 'Chaucer's Franklin and the Truth about *Trouthe*', *English Studies in Canada* 13 (1987): 359–74; Judson Boyce Allen, *A Distinction of Stories: The Medieval Unity of Chaucer's Fair Chain of Narratives for Canterbury* (Columbus, 1981); Judith L. Kellogg, '"Large and Fre": The Influence of Middle English Romance on Chaucer's Chivalric Language', *Allegorica* 9 (1987–8), 221–48; Susan Crane, 'The Franklin as Dorigen', *Chaucer Review* 24 (1990), 236–52; Joe Green, 'Chaucer's Genial Franklin', *Platte Valley Review* 21 (1993), 6–16.

Squire–Franklin link, produced a precedent for comparing his own son to the Squire, and by extension, himself to the Knight. What I want to focus on in the tale, therefore, is the depiction of the squire, Aurelius, and to look, in particular, at that section of the tale in which, after a protracted period of love-sickness, lassitude, insanity and raving, he behaves 'frely' or generously.

The stimulus for Aurelius' generous act is of course the generous act of Arveragus, who prefers to forfeit his own claim on happiness and on his wife's marital fidelity, than to see her break her 'trouthe' to Aurelius. This is the critical point in the tale, the original act of *fredom* and *gentilesse* that allows the wheels to turn again. But it is at this very point, at which self-interest is set aside for the sake of another's moral integrity, that a new dimension of interest begins to open up in the tale. As he altruistically comforts his wife, downplaying the seriousness of the matter, Arveragus raises the question of *outcome*: 'It may be wel, paraventure, yet to day' (1473). Without going as far as to say that Arveragus knows that things will work out well, it is the case that he offers encouragement to Dorigen that there might be a happy conclusion. Nor is Arveragus the only one to feel somewhat optimistic. The narrator, having just described Arveragus' generous and unselfish act, intervenes with a meditation of his own. We might expect him also to assert the higher value of the code that Arveragus is observing, just as earlier in the tale, he follows up his description of the marriage of Arveragus and Dorigen with a thoughtful reflection on the merits of the kind of marriage they have embarked upon. But Arveragus' statement that 'trouthe is the hyeste thyng that man may kepe' (1479) is not duplicated or seconded by the narrator. Instead, the narrator suggests that actually, self-interest may be served after all, and that we should wait until we see how things turn out, before we jump to conclusions:

> Paraventure an heep of yow, ywis,
> Wol holden hym a lewed man in this
> That he wol putte his wyf in jupartie.
> Herkneth the tale er ye upon hire crie.
> She may have bettre fortune than yow semeth;
> And whan that ye han herd the tale, demeth.   (1493–8)[18]

---

[18] The lines appear only in Ellesmere and British Library Additional MS 35286. For a recent comment on the status of British Library Additional MS 35286, see Peter Robinson, 'The History, Discoveries, and Aims of the Canterbury Tales Project', *Chaucer Review* 38 (2003), 126–39, at 130. For a more thorough discussion, and a treatment of the various editorial and critical attitudes to ll. 1493–8 in particular, see Simon Horobin, 'Editorial Assumptions and the Manuscripts of the *Canterbury Tales*', *The Canterbury Tales Project Occasional Papers*, ed. Norman Blake and Peter Robinson, vol. II (Oxford, 1997), pp 15–21, at pp 18–20. See also Horobin, 'Additional 35286 and the Order of the *Canterbury Tales*', *Chaucer Review* 31 (1997), 272–8.

So rather than being encouraged to make a moral evaluation of the situation, we are being advised to hold off from calculating the final balance until all the figures are in. Arveragus has been much criticized, especially in feminist readings of the tale, in which his supposedly unselfish deed has been seen as self-serving, competitive and even cruel.[19] But the narrator's defense of Arveragus is not concerned with the possibility that he might be seen to be cruel, selfish or vain, but with the possibility that he might be considered 'lewed' (meaning foolish, ignorant, uncouth or ill-bred), because he has placed his wife in 'jupartie'.

The narrator interrupts the narrative at this high point and tries to influence our understanding and interpretation of events. He defines the part of the audience to which he is addressing himself: 'an heep of yow'. Coming together in these few lines then, are the following elements: intrusion by the narrator at a climactic point in the narrative; heightened awareness of audience, and by implication, of the tale as performance, whether written or oral; an attempt to redirect the audience's interpretation of the unfolding events, and in particular, to postpone calling the result before the result is in. Taken together, these elements encourage us to give priority to the outcome or results of the characters' behaviour, and to consider the dilemma of the characters as a game, in which their choices are moves.

The decision to use the word *jupartie* to describe the situation in which Arveragus has placed his wife, together with the fact that we are urged not to prejudge the situation until we know the outcome of the events, and the fact that Arveragus is defended by the narrator against the charge of folly, rather than vice – these three elements seen in conjunction with each other at the crux of the tale, and at a point where the best way to interpret the tale is being raised, encourage us to go against the grain of the surface narrative and the ostensibly purely moral quality of the problem, and to read the tale as a study of tactics and game-plan. Instead of a tale concerned with individual moral choices, and their impact on others, we have instead a tale interested in a dynamic, in a social situation, organized for our pleasure, and played by its participants as a *game*.[20]

19 David Raybin considers that Arveragus fails to protect his wife, that he delivers a 'murderous threat' to her in the form of the ban on her disclosing their plight to a third party, and that 'he preserves the all-knowing male voice of absolute marital authority, but he dissipates his power in the production of empty phrases.' David Raybin, '"Wommen, of kynde, desiren libertee": Rereading Dorigen, Rereading Marriage', *Chaucer Review* 27 (1992), pp 67–9; Joseph D. Parry argues that the tale 'shows us Arveragus' strategy for sovereignty in marriage; and this becomes even more disturbingly clear when, after his comforting words to Dorigen uttered with "glad chiere, in freendly wyse," Arveragus revises his smiling manner, and tearfully forbids his wife, on pain of death, to tell anyone this terrible thing has happened.' Joseph D. Parry, 'Dorigen, Narration, and Coming Home in the *Franklin's Tale*', *Chaucer Review* 30 (1996), 262–93 (p. 283); Parry is following Susan Crane's influential article, in which she argued that Dorigen is occluded in the course of a competition between the three male protagonists; 'The Franklin as Dorigen', *Chaucer Review* 24 (1990), 236–52. 20 Richard A. Lanham has made a persuasive case for the

Jupartie, from OF *iu parti*, meaning literally 'divided game', from Latin *jocus partitus*, was originally a term used in chess and other games.[21] Chaucer uses the word on several occasions, in *Troilus and Criseyde*, in *The Romaunt of the Rose*, in the 'Canon's Yeoman's Prologue', in the 'Canon's Yeoman's Tale', and in *The Book of the Duchess*. Chaucer's is the earliest recorded deployment of the word in English.[22] Sometimes he uses it, much as it is commonly used in Modern English, to mean 'danger' or 'risk' simply; sometimes, as Jenny Adams has shown, it is associated with gambling, and therefore with the cultivation, rather than mere existence, of risk.[23] While the *OED* lists its primary meaning as 'problem', the word sometimes was simply coterminous with chess, or other games involving different sides, or with an uncertain outcome.[24] The word appears in the course of an extended chess metaphor in *The Book of the Duchess*:

> But God wolde I had oones or twyes
> Ykoud and knowe the jeupardyes
> That kowde the Grek Pictagores!   (665–7)

importance of the game in understanding Chaucer's *modus operandi* in *The Canterbury Tales*, *The Book of the Duchess*, *Troilus and Criseyde* and elsewhere. See 'Game, Play and High Seriousness in Chaucer', *English Studies* 48 (1967), 1–24; 'The Chaucerian Biogrammar and the Takeover of Culture' in Richard A. Lanham (ed.), *Literacy and the Survival of Humanism* (New Haven, 1983), pp 41–57; *The Motives of Eloquence* (New Haven, 1976). Stephen Manning builds on Lanham's work in 'Rhetoric, Game, Morality and Geoffrey Chaucer', *Studies in the Age of Chaucer* 1 (1979), 105–18, applying game theory to 'The Pardoner's Tale' and 'The Franklin's Tale'. G.D. Josipivici offers a somewhat different take on game in 'Fiction and Game in the *Canterbury Tales*', *Critical Quarterly* 7 (1965), 185–97, and more recently, Malcolm Arnold has provided an overview of the literature on Chaucer and game in 'Games', *A Companion to Chaucer*, ed. Peter Brown (Oxford, 2000), pp 167–79. Laura Kendrick's *Chaucerian Play* (Berkeley, 1988), is a full-scale study of Chaucer and play. Other studies include: Glending Olson, 'Chaucer's Idea of a Canterbury Game' in James M. Dean and Christian Zacher (ed.), *The Idea of Medieval Literature*, (Newark, 1992), 72–90; Michael Olmert, 'The Parson's Ludic Formula for Winning on the Road [to Canterbury]', *Chaucer Review* 20 (1985), 158–68; with reference to *Troilus*, Richard F. Green, 'Troilus and the Game of Love', *Chaucer Review* 13 (1979), 201–20, and Tison Pugh, 'Christian Revelation and the Cruel Game of Courtly Love in *Troilus and Criseyde*', *Chaucer Review* 39 (2005), 379–401. On the more general question of play in culture, see Johan Huizinga's classic study, *Homo Ludens: Vom Ursprung der Kultur im Spiel* (Hamburg, 1956), trans. by R.F.C. Hull as *Homo Ludens: a Study of the Play-element in Culture* (London, 1949; repr. 1998).   **21** *OED*, 2nd edn, s. v. 'jeopardy'; *MED*, s. v. 'jupartie'.   **22** Guillemette Bolens and Paul Beekman Taylor, 'The Game of Chess in Chaucer's *Book of the Duchess*', *Chaucer Review* 32 (1998), 325–34, at 330.   **23** 'Gambling on chess games by players and bystanders, a practice that lasted into the sixteenth century became so popular in the thirteenth and fourteenth centuries that players often used dice to expedite the game's conclusion'. Jenny Adams, 'Pawn Takes Knight's Queen: Playing with Chess in Chaucer's *Book of the Duchess*', *Chaucer Review* 32 (1999), 125–38, at 132. See also Adams, 'Pieces of Power: Medieval Chess and Male Homosocial Desire', *Journal of English and Germanic Philology* 103 (2004), 197–214, and Margaret Connolly, 'Chaucer and Chess', *Chaucer Review* 29 (1994), 40–4.   **24** Already in the thirteenth century '*juparti*' (jeopardy) appeared in England in courtly French as a synonym for chess.' Bolens and Beekman Taylor, 'The Game of Chess', 331.

Here, a 'jeopardy' would seem to be the equivalent of the modern chess term 'problem', which presents the player with a particular arrangement of the pieces, and requires him to achieve a specified result.[25]

Chess, whether in its distinctive medieval or modern form, requires its expert players to be able to consider simultaneously, and choose from, a wide range of possible scenarios and outcomes, and to pick the optimal tactic to arrive at the desired result. The setting and solving of chess 'problems' develops the players' ability to think ahead. While the novice might be thinking only of the move at hand, the expert weighs up his and his opponent's every move in terms of their long-term implications and his overall game-plan. The Black Knight laments the fact that he does not possess more of this long-range strategic ability that would have come from doing chess problems.

Arveragus, however, while he might seem to the majority of the audience to be doing something very foolish, by placing his beloved wife in jeopardy, at risk, is actually, as both he and the narrator intuit, doing something rather clever, and in a desperate situation. Dorigen is on the brink of destroying herself: she perceives her choices to be intolerable in every direction. There is no low-risk, sensible option that will get them out of their plight. We know the importance to both of them of honour, *trouthe* and wedded chastity. If the promise is fulfilled, and she is joined to Aurelius, she loses her honour, her chastity and her *trouthe* to her husband. If she refuses to fulfil the promise, she loses her honour (a prospect which gives Aurelius' brother some satisfaction; see lines 1163–4), and breaks her *trouthe* to Aurelius. In the face of this level of threat, Arveragus follows a high-risk strategy, and the reward is commensurate with the risk.

The element of social game-playing which is inaugurated in this the first act of *fredom* in the domino-like chain of *fre* acts that occupy the rest of the tale, suggests that the Franklin's disembodied, non-materialistic idea of *generositas virtus non sanguis*, that says 'fy on possessioun' (686), may not be all that it appears.

In his own reactive '*fre*' deed, Aurelius himself is very keen to point out that he behaves *gentilly*, and that he is giving up a great deal. He acknowledges and pays tribute to Arveragus' gesture, and it stings him into a corresponding awareness of the 'cherlyssh wrecchednesse' (1523) that his partaking of the dish offered by Arveragus would amount to. While in his release

25 *The Oxford Companion to Chess* confirms this view of the medieval meaning of *jupartie*: 'Jeopardy: in medieval times a chess position that seemed in the balance, the kind of position that appears today in newspapers and chess magazines as a mental exercise for the reader, the forerunner of the problem. The word is derived in various ways from the Old French jeu parti, literally a divided game of uncertain issue; in English this was corrupted in various ways, e.g. juperty, and eventually disappeared from chess to pass into general usage with its current meaning.' *The Oxford Companion to Chess*, ed. David Hooper and Kenneth Whyld (Oxford, 1984), pp 156–7.

of Dorigen, he speaks in formal and legal terms, removing himself from the centre of the action to the dispassionate and objective edge, ignoring entirely his own role in bringing Dorigen into the trap in the first place, he is nonetheless determined that she should carry away with her a sense of the extent of his own selflessness:

> 'I have wel levere evere to suffre wo
> Than I departe the love bitwix yow two.'   (1531–2)

His words bear comparison with the similar but rather more understated words spoken earlier by Arveragus:

> 'As I may best, I wol my wo endure – '   (1484)

What is intriguing about the attention that Aurelius draws to the scale of his own sacrifice in giving up Dorigen, is that it coincides with the vanishing of his desire for her. He is cured of his love-sickness. Up to the point at which he hears of Arveragus' *gentil* deed, the tale has given us numerous accounts of Aurelius' love-sickness and his life-threatening suffering. After this point we hear no more of his condition. It is not so much, then, that Aurelius behaves selflessly than that his powerful need for Dorigen is dissolved by the message from Arveragus. It reappears as his need to reassert his claim to *gentilesse*, and to address his dire financial situation. From this point onward in the tale, Aurelius is entirely concerned with himself and his money.

Once Aurelius has done his *gentil* deed, as we have seen, he becomes aware of his financial predicament. Why is he so appalled by the prospect of relying on others, of becoming a beggar? This may seem like a silly question – who in his right mind would not shrink from the condition of beggary? But why, on the other hand? If you have just defended the virtue of *fredom*, why not assume that *fredom* will bail you out in turn, and provide you with a living, albeit a humble one? Aurelius, it seems, though having apparently given up his self-interest for the sake of others, does not want to throw himself upon the mercy of the human species as a whole. He is not a St Francis. His faith in *fredom* extends only to the clerk. Aurelius contemplates his future, and the possibility of appealing to the clerk, as follows:

> 'Allas!' quod he. 'Allas, that I bihighte
> Of pured gold a thousand pound of wighte
> Unto this philosophre! How shal I do?
> I se namoore but that I am fordo.
> Myn heritage moot I nedes selle,
> And been a beggere; heere may I nat dwelle
> And shamen al my kynrede in this place,

> But I of hym may gete bettre grace.
> But nathelees, I wole of hym assaye,
> At certeyn dayes, yeer by yeer, to paye,
> And thanke hym of his grete curteisye.
> My trouthe wol I kepe, I wol nat lye.'   (1559–70)

Then, in the very next line, he goes to the clerk, and makes his appeal. The appeal corresponds very closely to the content of Aurelius' private considerations, and goes as follows:

> With herte soor he gooth unto his cofre,
> And broghte gold unto this philosophre,
> The value of fyve hundred pound, I gesse,
> And hym bisecheth, of his gentillesse,
> To graunte hym dayes of the remenaunt;
> And seyde, 'Maister, I dar wel make avaunt,
> I failled nevere of my trouthe as yit.
> For sikerly my dette shal be quyt
> Towardes yow, howevere that I fare
> To goon a-begged in my kirtle bare.
> But wolde ye vouche sauf, upon seuretee,
> Two yeer or thre for to respiten me,
> Thanne were I wel; for elles moot I selle
> Myn heritage; ther is namoore to telle.'   (1571–84)

The same elements appear in Aurelius' private planning of the appeal, and the appeal itself: the tribute to the *gentilesse* of the clerk; the threat of beggary for Aurelius; the dismal prospect of selling the heritage; the suggestion of a plan for staggered repayments; the declaration of his unwavering attachment to *trouthe*; the fear of becoming a beggar; the hope for grace. Aurelius has an idea, then, and carries it out rationally. Like Arveragus, like the narrator, he is optimistic, even though he is also worried.

In the original promise that Aurelius made to the Clerk, he said:

> 'This bargayn is ful dryve, for we been knyt.
> Ye shal be payed trewely, by my trouthe!'   (1230–1)

From this certain and unambiguous guarantee of unproblematic payment, Aurelius wanders away in the course of the tale, so that, when it comes to the time to pay the debt, he is able to produce only half the agreed sum, and he pleads for 'dayes of the remenaunt'; this is swiftly followed up by a request for two or three years respite.

Aurelius' modification of the timescales involved in the various pacts he has contracted is not the only instance of his skilful rhetorical sleight of hand. In the same speech to the clerk, Aurelius states his intention to pay his debt even if it entails his impoverishment, and reduction to begging in his 'kirtle bare'; a moment later, he asks (or begs?) for respite, on the basis that he would otherwise be impoverished, lose his heritage, and presumably have to beg, presumably in his 'kirtle bare'.

Like the Franklin in his prologue, who rejects the use of fancy rhetoric, Aurelius presents himself to the clerk as a simple, ingenuous, noble and vulnerable man. Aurelius' initial laying out of his situation to the clerk flatters the clerk, intimating that there is a similarity between the two men (between the clerk's *gentilesse* and Aurelius' commitment to *trouthe*). He provides very few details in his first presentation of the case, and ends, having asked the clerk to postpone for years the calling-in of the debt, with the heroic '... for elles moot I sell/ Myn heritage; ther is namoore to telle'. What a tantalizing and sparse account he has presented to his creditor of his inability to pay an enormous debt: it is surely intended as a cue for the clerk, who certainly takes it up that way, asking question after question until the full extent of Aurelius' nobility is well exposed:

> 'And right as frely as he sente hire me,
> As frely sente I hire to hym ageyn.'   (1604–5)

What is the clerk going to do? The challenge of first-rate behaviour by both the knight Arveragus and the squire Aurelius has been put to him, together with the intimation that he too is a rare creature of *gentilesse*. Aurelius has hinted at a comparison between himself and the clerk, as well as giving the clerk the rules of the game of gallant-move-and-gallant-response already under way. He is effectively prompting the clerk: 'Your move.'

The complexity of the game increases with Aurelius' subtle invitation to the clerk to act like him. Aurelius stresses the cooperation of Arveragus and Dorigen, and in response, he and the clerk form a pseudo-aristocratic coalition. The clerk gives up his own immediate self-interest (being paid) in order to express a group interest (which, ultimately, feeds into his self-interest again, in the sense that being seen to be capable of first-rate behaviour is more valuable capital than the thousand pounds he gives up).

If it seems that I am translating the morals of the tale into mere quantities, I would point out that the tale is implicitly doing this, while explicitly arguing for just the opposite. It is organized so that Arveragus' action of releasing Dorigen from her marriage obligations in order that she protect her moral integrity is made equivalent in the tale to a thousand pounds. Just as the Franklin tries in the Squire–Franklin link to express the non-monetary (*gentilesse*) by means of a monetary amount (twenty pounds worth of land), so the tale shows the interchangeableness of *gentil* deeds with money.

But because the humans in the tale are seen to be involved in a kind of giving that expects return, and a kind of altruism that furthers self-interest, it does not mean that they are not worthy of the name *gentil*. 'The Franklin's Tale' is not an *exposé* of crass materialism lurking beneath aristocratic *fredom*. It is not intended to shock, to criticize, to sting into reform. 'The Franklin's Tale' shows the cyclicity of what we like to call 'high' and 'low' motives, the admixture of egoism in selflessness and of so-called vice in so-called virtue. But, above all, it shows the complicated ways in which our self-interest overlaps with our group-interest. 'The Franklin's Tale', like its teller, is social.

The *gentilesse* that is described by *generositas virtus, non sanguis* involves the removal of virtue from all worldly and social context. It is an idealized and purified virtue that is isolated in this process, untainted by inheritance, position or prestige. The Franklin asserts his belief in this kind of *gentilesse* in his words to the Squire in the Squire–Franklin link. What his tale actually accomplishes, however, is a reversal of this isolation, purification and idealization of virtue. 'The Franklin's Tale' brings virtue back to its home, back to its complicated social context, back to the dubious friends of wealth, position and inheritance, from whom Christianity and the code of *generositas virtus, non sanguis* had encouraged it to part company. For the moment the Franklin's son is wasting his inheritance, and paradoxically, therefore, enacting a key aspect of *generositas virtus, non sanguis*. He is only missing the *virtus*. If he is his father's son he will learn in time, as Billie Holiday put it with a nod to St. Luke, 'God bless the child that's got his own'.[26]

---

26 'Mama may have, Papa may have,/ But God bless the child that's got his own', Billie Holiday and Arthur Herzog, Jr, 'God Bless the Child', 1942. In the parable of the talents, the nobleman says to the servants: 'I tell you, that to every one who has will more be given; but from him who has not, even what he has will be taken away'. Luke 19:26, Revised Standard Version.

The Heterodoxy of Sir John Clanvowe's
The Two Ways

FRANCES MCCORMACK

The Lollards adopted a remarkable variety of strategies in articulating their break with the 'new ways' of the medieval Church, as well as indicating the extent of their subscription to the 'old ways' of the apostolic Church founded of Christ in the gospels – a way that had come to be perceived as heretical. While some of these texts are clearly propagandist, others are purely devotional. Naturally, the more extreme and polemical writings have received the bulk of critical attention; yet there are less subversive texts, such as Sir John Clanvowe's *The Two Ways* (brought to scholarly attention in 1967 by John Scattergood's edition), which can be valuable in assessing the religious and political culture from which these texts emerge, and in defining the affiliations of those who produced Lollard writing.

At the heart of the Lollard movement was a group of men of the gentry and the lower nobility, serving in the court of Richard II. These men[1] – known as the Lollard Knights – were identified by name by the contemporary chroniclers Thomas Walsingham[2] and Henry Knighton.[3] Knighton refers to these men as 'the strongest promoters and most powerful protectors [of Lollardy]; ... its most effective defenders and invincible champions'.[4] He suggests, indeed, that when the Lollard Poor Priests arrived in their districts, the Lollard Knights would gather an audience of listeners, and defend the preachers with arms.[5] Apart from having given protection to Lollard preachers, though,[6] members of this group also seem to have been responsible for patronizing some of the Lollard

---

1 The named knights were Sir Thomas Latimer, Sir William Nevill, Sir John Clanvowe, Sir Lewis Clifford, Sir John Cheyne, Sir William Beauchamp, Sir Richard Sturry, Sir John Trussell, Sir Reynold Hilton and Sir John Peachey, although K.B. McFarlane argues in *Lancastrian Kings and Lollard Knights* (Oxford, 1972) that there was no case against the latter three men. Margaret Aston and Colin Richmond assert that 'K.B. McFarlane's ... main finding, that the chroniclers were right in accusing a group of prominent knights of Lollard sympathy, has stood the test of time, and seems likely to hold.' Introduction to *Lollardy and the Gentry in the Later Middle Ages* (New York, 1997), p. 1. 2 M. Thompson (ed.), *Chronicon Angliae* (London, 1874); H.T. Riley (ed.), *Historia Anglicana*, RS 1863–4, II 159–216 (under the years 1387, 1395, 1399). 3 J.R. Lumby (ed.), *Chronicon Henrici Knighton*, RS 1889–5, II 181 (under the year 1382). 4 G.H. Martin (ed. and trans.), *Knighton's Chronicle, 1337–1396* (Oxford, 1995), p. 295. 5 Ibid. 6 When the preacher, Nicholas Hereford, was arrested in 1382, Sir William Nevill petitioned for his release (McFarlane, p. 199); Sir Lewis Clifford intervened (apparently acting as an emissary for the Queen Mother) at an episcopal tribunal at Lambeth in March 1378, and forbade the bishops to pass judgement on John Wyclif who was appearing there. See Joseph H. Dahmus,

102

projects of textual production. Sir William Beauchamp, for example, is closely
associated with the production and dissemination of Lollard texts, and came
under sufficient suspicion for his connection with the movement that his manors
in Worcestershire were searched for heretical writings in the early 1400s.[7]
Beauchamp seems to be a significant sponsor and patron of Lollard textual production. Indeed, Nigel Saul holds that:

> It is possible that Beauchamp owned a small library of Lollard tracts
> and devotional pieces; certainly his cultural affinities appear to have
> been with that group of well-lettered religious radicals which centered
> on Clanvowe and Montagu.[8]

It is quite exciting, then, that one of the Lollard Knights, Sir John Clanvowe,
left behind him a religious treatise; the only piece of writing, apart from some
last wills and testaments, that we are sure has come from this group.

Unfortunately, Clanvowe has disappointed both literary critics and historians who have examined his *Two Ways* in search of clues that might provide
them with some insight into the form of Lollardy to which the Lollard
Knights subscribed. Anne Hudson, for example, asserts that:

> much time and ink has been spent in fruitless speculation on the
> authorship of Lollard texts, and it is ironic that the one early tract
> whose author is identifiable and of significant status, *The Two Ways* by
> Sir John Clanvowe, should be of virtually no interest either in its ideas
> or its contemporary reference.[9]

She writes elsewhere of *The Two Ways* that 'the text is of an insipidity that
hardly encourages others to think that further exploration in this field would
be a fruitful enterprise'.[10] It is not difficult to see how Hudson came to this

'John Wyclif and the English Government', *Speculum* 35:1 (1960), 51–68, p. 55. Aston and
Richmond assert that 'The Lollards, clerical Lollards most of all, were well aware of the importance of patrons. The patronage of John of Gaunt's patronage kept Wycliffe out of prison and
possibly kept him alive; and the patronage Sir Philip de la Vache seems likely to have exercised
on behalf of Lollard Knights is one of the "missing links" in the early history of Lollardy',
Introduction to *Lollardy and the Gentry*, p. 7.   7 Nigel Saul, *Richard II* (New Haven, 1997), p.
298.   8 Ibid., citing J.S. Roskell, L. Clark and C. Rawliffe (eds), *The History of Parliament: The
House of Commons, 1386–1421*, 4 vols (London, 1992), pp 838–40; J.I. Catto, 'Sir William
Beauchamp Between Chivalry and Lollardy', in C. Harper-Bill and R. Harvey (eds), *The Ideals
and Practice in Medieval Knighthood: Papers from the Fourth Strawberry Hill Conference*
(Woodbridge, 1990), pp 39–48.   9 Anne Hudson, *Lollards and their Books* (London, 1985), p.
54, citing H.B. Workman, *John Wyclif* (Oxford, 1926), esp. vol. I, pp 329–32; M. Deanesley,
The Lollard Bible (Cambridge, 1920), esp. pp 252ff; V.J. Scattergood (ed.), *The Works of Sir
John Clanvowe* (Cambridge, 1975), pp 57–80; K.B. McFarlane, *Lancastrian Kings and Lollard
Knights*, pp 199–206.   10 Anne Hudson, *The Premature Reformation: Wycliffite Texts and Lollard
History* (Oxford, 1988), p. 7.   11 For the Lollard use of the false prophet motif, see F.

conclusion. In his treatise, Clanvowe acknowledges that accusations of Lollardy have been made against him and his fellows, but his text does not appear to promote any of the ideas of the movement. This is not a text that sets out to censure the wolf-like false prophets[11] whom the Lollards accuse of leading the Christian flock to hell;[12] there is no questioning of the efficacy of the sacraments. Clanvowe does not make mention of the Twelve Conclusions or of the Wycliffite project of biblical translation. There is no denunciation of either war or pilgrimage in this text; Clanvowe, in fact, is associated with both – he fought in the French campaigns for example, and died near Constantinople on what is believed to be a pilgrimage undertaken with fellow Lollard Knight, Sir William Nevill.[13] *The Two Ways* appears, therefore, to be little more than an expression of personal piety which refuses to fulfil its potential to provide insight into the devotion of the Lollard Knights.

John Scattergood, however, as editor of Clanvowe's writings, has been far more sensitive to the nuances of *The Two Ways* than scholars who have analyzed it before or since. He suggests, for example, that the subtlety of the text might itself be an indication of 'the degree and nature of Clanvowe's interest in Lollardy',[14] and he promotes this treatise because of its implications for analysis of the Lollardy of the Knights in Clanvowe's circle. Scattergood does, however, acknowledge that *The Two Ways* might frustrate the reader who expects explicit endorsement of the principal tenets of the movement. He writes:

> The *Two Ways* is not so much a Lollard tract as a treatise which shows some sympathy with the Lollard position. It is not doctrinally polemical: it attacks neither the tenets nor the organization of the medieval Church. It has nothing to say about papal and priestly authority, the necessity for Church endowment, the validity of confession, or the use of pilgrimages, indulgences or images. The controversial doctrine of the real presence is never mentioned. Perhaps the most significant fact about the treatise is that the Church and its teaching is ignored.[15]

There is nothing radical about Clanvowe's treatise; it refuses to conform in the most obvious of ways to the ideas and modes of the discourse of Lollardy. Were the author not a known Lollard, and had he not mentioned in his trea-

---

McCormack, *Chaucer and the Culture of Dissent* (Dublin, 2007).   **12** The motif of the wolf being left in charge of the flock is frequently used by the Lollards as a figure for the negligent clergy. It is based on the description of the Pharisees in Matthew 7:15 ('Beware of false prophets, who come to you in the clothing of sheep but inwardly they are ravening wolves'). For more on this motif, see McCormack, esp. pp 199–201.   **13** For more on Clanvowe's life and career, see the edition of Scattergood, and McFarlane, *Lancastrian Kings and Lollard Knights*.   **14** *Works of Sir John Clanvowe*, p. 9.   **15** Ibid., pp 19–20.

tise that he had been named among the suspects, this text could quite easily be passed off as an orthodox devotional treatise. Here, however, is one of the main paradoxes of the Lollard movement: Lollardy was not a separatist movement; it did not, in fact, have its origins in a desire for schism. Rather it was fundamentally driven by an impulse to return the Church to the state in which it was born of Christ in the gospels. Many of the Lollard objections to contemporary ecclesiastical practice were objections to those 'accessories' which were not instituted by Christ – auricular confession, the fraternal orders, the doctrine of transubstantiation, the clergy's exemption from the rule of civil law, clerical celibacy: these things were not of scripture. On the whole, the policies and principles of the Lollards were shared with the organized Church in theory (although in practice the fourteenth-century Church had strayed from many of the virtues and principles that it would have claimed for itself). The Lollards, for example, asserted the primacy of scripture and the necessity of proper pastoral instruction, they condemned the materiality of contemporary life and devotion – in these details and many others Lollard doctrine seems to share some common ground with that of the orthodox Church.

To further blur the issue, Lollardy was a decentralized movement without any clearly defined structure. No member would have had access to all of the writings of the movement, and it is likely that different social groups in different parts of the country would have subscribed for different reasons, and therefore to different tenets. Many considered themselves Lollards who merely appealed against the abuses of the Church – its trappings and excesses, for example – and there were many more who held to the antimendicant, anti-sacramental view of the Lollards who would not have associated themselves in any way with the movement. On these problems of definition of the movement, J.A.F. Thomson writes:

> Any consideration of the nature of Lollardy, particularly in its earlier years, must accept that the term had a number of different connotations. The modern perception of it, predominantly as a doctrinal movement which owed its origins to the teaching of Wycliffe, is not necessarily the same as the view that was held of it by chroniclers such as Knighton and Walsingham, who denounced various knights as Lollards and enemies of the church ... Even when personal ties existed among them, these may have been prompted by shared pious sympathies and a general community of outlook, and it is not necessary to assume that they were identical in all their views. Early Lollardy was complex and individualistic, and each supporter of it was probably drawn to favour it for his or her own particular reasons.[16]

16 J.A.F. Thomson, 'Knightly Piety and the Margins of Lollardy', in Aston and Richmond (eds), *Lollardy and the Gentry in the Later Middle Ages*, pp 95–111 (pp 106–7).

Not only, then, did different subscribers to the movement have different inter-
pretations of the meaning of their subscription, but these subscriptions would
vary depending upon the areas in which the subscribers lived and the circles
in which they moved.

It is clear from various sources – from polemical tracts, from the English
sermon cycle, and from accounts of the movement (whether contemporary or
modern) – that those who supported the Lollards differed in the extent of
their subscription. John of Gaunt, for example, supported Wyclif while the
latter called for clerical disendowment, but he withdrew his protection when
Wyclif began to question the doctrine of transubstantiation.[17] Many Lollards
disapproved of Oldcastle's revolt; the Lollard Knights appeared to have continued their military service despite the exhortation against such in the *Twelve
Conclusions* (which, incidentally, were addressed to 'þe lordis and þe
comunys'), and Richard Wyche twice made the concession that oral confession was necessary for salvation.[18] Margaret Aston and Colin Richmond attribute such inconsistencies to a tension created by these men's positions:

> ... in 1395 as at other times, sanctity and politics made awkward if not
> incompatible bedfellows, and for those of knightly status, there was
> another kind of tension: that between Lollardy and chivalry.[19]

It is likely, however, that there may have been some overlap in the reasons
for, and therefore type of, subscription to the movement by the Lollard
Knights. These men were of a similar status and background, and it is likely
that their interest in the movement would have been political, focussing on
those tenets of the movement by which they were directly affected, and perhaps seeing Lollardy as providing a solution to the crises of the court that
were threatening their position in those later years of the fourteenth century.[20]
Nonetheless, Thomson warns against a homogeneous understanding of the
culture of the Lollard Knights:

> The piety of these individuals showed considerable variety. They
> cannot be seen as a sect, but rather as a group of individuals, whose
> doctrinal views were by no means homogeneous. Personal associations
> among them undoubtedly existed, which may well have led to similar-

17 Cf. Dahmus, 'John Wyclif and the English Government'.   18 Christina von Nolcken,
'Richard Wyche, a Certain Knight and the Beginning of the End', in Aston and Richmond (eds),
Lollardy and the Gentry, pp 127–54 (p. 33).   19 Introduction to *Lollardy and the Gentry*, p. 11,
citing Catto, 'Sir William Beauchamp', pp 39–48; Michael Wilks, 'Wyclif and the Great
Persecution', *SCH*, Subsidia 10 (1994), 39–63 (p. 62).   20 In fact, it seems likely that the sixth
of the *Twelve Conclusions* 'petitioned for the end of clerical employment in secular government,'
might be thought to have strong appeal to the gentry.' See Aston and Richmond, 'Introduction'
to *Lollardy and the Gentry*, pp 5–6.

ities in their views, but it would be erroneous to see these as identical. Even more important is the fact that some of these views might be radical but were not necessarily heretical, for the margin between orthodoxy and heresy was by no means clear-cut, and individuals who held some unorthodox views, were not necessarily opposed to the church's teaching in every respect. Indeed, it is often by no means certain what precisely all their views were, for much of the evidence which has survived is purely circumstantial.[21]

This programme, however, is barely visible in *The Two Ways*, which provides little evidence about the level and type of Clanvowe's interest in the movement. In fact, it is difficult to locate the heterodox elements of this treatise. Knowing, as we do, that Clanvowe was a Lollard, and that he acknowledges this, does not make it any easier for the reader to categorize what precisely is heterodox about *The Two Ways*. Even Clanvowe's 'admission' of subscription is somewhat ambiguous:

> And also swiche folke þat wolden fayne lyuen meekeliche in þis world and ben out offe swich forseid riot, noise, and stryf, and lyuen symplely, and vsen to eten and drynken in mesure, and to clooþen hem meekely, and suffren paciently wroonges þat ooþere folk doon and seyn to hem, and hoolden hem apayed with lytel good of þis world, and desiren noo greet naame of þis world, ne no pris ther of, swiche folke þe world scoorneth and hooldeþ hem lolleris and loselis, foolis and schameful wrecches.[22]

The term 'loller' itself is a problematic one, likely to have originated from a Dutch word meaning 'to mumble',[23] and is found in various texts with the generally pejorative meaning of 'idler'.[24] It is its collocation with the word 'losel', however, that cements the meaning of 'loller' as an accusation of heresy. This word, 'losel', is also used in a generally pejorative sense meaning 'rogue' or 'rascal',[25] but in collocation with the word 'loller' it is intensi-

---

21 Thomson, 'Knightly Piety', p. 96.   22 Sir John Clanvowe, *The Two Ways*, in Scattergood (ed.), *The Works of Sir John Clanvowe*, p. 70, ll. 504–13.   23 Anne Hudson, Introduction to *Selections from English Wycliffite Writings* (Cambridge, 1978), p. 8.   24 The C-Text of *Piers Plowman* contains a number of problematic occurrences of the word 'loller'. For a discussion of these, see Wendy Scase, *Piers Plowman and the New Anticlericalism* (Cambridge, 1989); see also Paul J. Patterson, 'Reforming Chaucer: Margins and Religion in an Apocryphal *Canterbury Tale*', *Book History* 8 (205), 11–36.   25 Cf. *Middle English Dictionary*. Often, however, the sense of 'theological deviant' is also implied. See, for example, *Pierce the Ploughman's Creed*, l. 96–7:'leue nought on tho losels but let hem forth pasen, /For thei ben fals in her feith and fele mo othere', Helen Barr (ed.), *The Piers Plowman Tradition* (London: 1993). *The Testimony of William Thorpe* makes ample use of the word 'losel', which Archbishop Thomas Arundel uses in reference to the company kept by Thorpe (cf. *The Testimony of William Thorpe*, in Anne Hudson (ed.), *Two*

fied, often to censure the heretics. References to 'lollers and losels' abound in texts that make reference to these heretics, whether written by the heretics themselves or their opponents. The *Middle English Dictionary* cites a number of examples, including one example by John Drury ('For ho be ... out þe feyth he is a renegat, a lollard, a loosel')[26] and one by Langland ('Ich shal fynde hem fode ... Saf ... frere faytour and folke of [þat] ordre, þat lollers and loseles for leel men halden').[27] It is quite likely, then, that Clanvowe's use of the collocation was performed with this context in mind.

Nonetheless, *The Two Ways* is, on the whole, moderate in terms of its subscription to Lollardy. It is clearly an evangelical text, in which personal piety and the authority of the gospels are emphasised above all else. Thomson sees this as an attribute of Clanvowe's circle:

> There is no doubt that within the landed class of the late fourteenth and early fifteenth centuries, there were men who were attracted to an evangelical style of religion and who were concerned with the pursuit of personal salvation by means beyond the routine practices of confession and regular receipt of the sacraments which the Church required.[28]

Not only does *The Two Ways* manifest this type of personal piety, but it also propounds a salvation that depends on faith in atonement. It bypasses the Church in its formulation of a soteriological plan, emphasizing implicitly that the gospels are sufficient to mediate between Christ and humankind, thus excluding the necessity for a clerical intermediary. In fact, Clanvowe's excision of the Church from his discussion of salvation is, in many ways, more subversive than a condemnation of its pastoral failure would have been. Condemnation affords at least some significance to that which is being censured; excision, by necessity, denies it.

According to Clanvowe, then, personal salvation is not something that requires the pomp and circumstance of ritual, frequent participation in the sacraments, the purchase of aids to salvation, and so on. He emphasizes, rather, that 'þer nys noon oothere wey to heuene but by keeping of Goddis hestes.'[29] His scheme promotes, above all, the importance of the Decalogue in the life of the individual. In fact, the Lollards were renowned for their exposition of the Decalogue, and, by the later fourteenth century, preaching of the Ten Commandments often brought the preacher under suspicion of heresy. Hudson provides the example of Thomas Taylor of Newbury, who was accused for the

Wycliffite Texts (Oxford, 1993), ll. 519, 538, 650, 740, 887, 891, 1103, 1144, 1156, 1179, 1332, 1364, 1517, 1562, 1573. **26** John Drury's *Works* in Cambridge University Library, Additional 2830, 77/86. **27** William Langland, *The Vision of William Concerning Piers the Plowman*, ed. Walter W. Skeat, EETS OS 54 (London, 1979). **28** Thomson, 'Knightly Piety', p. 97. **29** Clanvowe, *The Two Ways*, ll. 102–3.

simple reason of his ownership of 'one suspecte boke of commaundementis', emphasizing that there were many more brought under suspicion for similar reasons.[30] Clanvowe's entire treatise revolves around his endorsement of these ordinances and their role in the salvation of every individual; in fact, the two ways revealed by Clanvowe – the narrow way to heaven, and the broad way to hell – are the keeping of the commandments and their breaking respectively.[31] These commandments, he asserts, are the only path to heaven. Of course, there is nothing explicitly subversive about this, apart from, of course, the context in which it occurs: namely in a treatise written by a knight who admits to having been accused of Lollardy, and at a time when preaching such as the kind manifested in this treatise provoked suspicion.

Some contemporary Lollard expositions of the Decalogue were glossed in such a way that they showed the Church's failure to adhere to them. They categorized simony as a breaking of the commandment against theft, religious images and icons as a form of idolatry, and so on. Anne Hudson writes that:

> A *suspect book of commandments* is very frequently mentioned; presumably one reason why commentaries on the commandments were so often incriminated was that the prohibition on the making of graven images offered in such an obvious place, and obvious hunting place, for Lollard views, whilst the order to honour father and mother led often at best to the omission of exhortation to honour spiritual father, at worst to indictment of the contemporary shortcomings of such spiritual directors.[32]

Clanvowe's discussion of the Ten Commandments can be read in this way, with his exhortation against 'fals byleeue' or 'ydolatrie' (listed under the first commandment) being read as a typical Lollard censuring of the earthly Church.[33] The fourth commandment, similarly, excises references to the earthly Church, employing a typically Lollard reference to the spiritual Church:

> And all þoo þat worsshipen not here fadir or hire moodir, or þat helpen hem or counforten hem not in body and in soule in here neede at here power, or þei þat worsshipen not here gostly moodir holy chirche as þe au ten to doo, þei breken þe feerth comaundement.[34]

Much of the discussion of the Decalogue, though, can be said to have a wholly personal resonance. Unlike much of Lollard discourse, his treatise is not at all concerned with the transgressions of the institution, and instead it reflects

30 Hudson, *Premature Reformation*, p. 4.   31 Clanvowe, *The Two Ways*, ll. 625–7.   32 Hudson, *Premature Reformation*, p. 167.   33 Clanvowe, *The Two Ways*, ll. 645–50.   34 Ibid., ll. 657–63.

solely on how the individual may engineer his or her own salvation. At the same time, however, Clanvowe manages to include himself in a group of the persecuted, whom he says are being charged for their adherence to traditional spiritual virtues and scriptural belief.

Perhaps more tellingly, however, the personal and individual salvation set forth by Clanvowe is expressed in an essentializing manner. Essentializing rhetoric is

> the mode of discourse by which the Lollards distinguish themselves from their opponents by referring to themselves using wholly positive tags, and applying their pejorative antonyms to their opponents. The Lollards therefore refer to themselves as the children of God, and their opponents as children of the fiend; they claim to be true men of religion while their opponents are false.[35]

If we are to understand the narrow way to heaven as signifying personal salvation attained by living according to the Decalogue and repenting when one strays – namely the way of evangelical Lollardy – then the broad way to hell could be interpreted as the way of the institutional Church. This broad path, according to Clanvowe, is taken by many, whereas the narrow way to heaven is found by few. Furthermore, Clanvowe asserts that the broad way is the way on which we are already travelling, and that we can only leave it by grace. Of course, this kind of excursus is perfectly well aligned with the orthodox penitential schemes: the broad way could be interpreted as the way of the flesh, and the narrow the way of the spirit, but there is one other detail of the text that suggests the narrow way to be the way of the Lollards and the broad way to be that of the orthodox Church.

There is nothing explicitly heterodox about the use of essentializing rhetoric; what is subversive about it, though, is that contextually it is often used by the Lollards to condemn the earthly Church. Clanvowe makes extensive use of essentializing rhetoric in his treatise. In fact, thematically the entire text is one elaborate essentialization. The treatise opens with a call for the examination of the two ways: the way to eternal life, and the way to damnation. It clearly calls the reader to an alternative mode of living, and while it seems that the focus is a moral one, Clanvowe explicitly identifies it with accusations of Lollardy. Again:

> swich folke þat wolden fayne lyuen meekelich in þis world and been out offe swich forseid riot, noise and stryf, and lyuen symplely, and vsen to eten and drynken in mesure, and to clooþen hem meekely, and suffren paciently wroonges þat ooþere folke doon and seyn to hem, and hoolden

35 McCormack, p. 18 n.16, citing Hudson, 'A Lollard Sect Vocabulary?' in *So Many People, Longages and Tonges: Philological Essays in Scots and Medieval English Presented to Angus McIntosh* (Edinburgh, 1981), pp 15–30.

hem apayed with lytel good of þis world, and desiren noo greet naame
of þis world, ne no pris ther of, swiche folk þe world scoorneth and
hooldeþ hem lolleris and loselis, foolis and schameful wrecches. But,
sikerly, God holdeth hem moost wise and most worsshipful, and he wole
worsshipen hem in heuene for evere, whan þat þoo þat þe worlds wors-
shipeþ shuln bee shaamed and pyned for euere in helle, but ef þat þai
amenden hem heere eer þanne þei passen out of this world. And, þer-
fore, taake we sauour in þoo þinges þat been so goode and so worsshipful abouen and recche we neuer þou þe world scoorne vs or hoolde
vs wrcecches, ffor þe world scoorned Crist and heeld hym a fool.[36]

It is clear from this passage that the way that leads to the bliss of heaven is
the way of the Lollards. Those who face similar accusations to this are those
that take the narrow way, those true in belief.

Clanvowe has therefore made a very daring distinction between the Lollard
way (which, he asserts, leads to eternal life), and the other way, which implicitly leads to hell. He guards himself, though, by problematizing his applica-
tion of the term 'lolleris', which reads as though it were intended in its older
sense of 'idlers'. Nonetheless, he maintains the essentializing distinctions
throughout his treatise, differentiating repeatedly between the broad way leading to death and the narrow way leading to life; between the way of the pain
of hell and the way of the bliss of heaven; and between the ways of God and
the ways of the fiend.

Other elements of essentializing rhetoric recur, and occasionally antonyms
are implied rather than stated. Clanvowe refers to 'trewe byleeue', that helps
a man withstand the false teaching of the fiend.[37] He refers to the 'trewe con-
seil of the gospel',[38] perhaps in opposition to the false counsel of worldly institutions, and identifies true judgement and right rule in opposition to their
absent antonyms of disapprobation.[39] Thus, while Clanvowe does not explicitly condemn the Church, he does indicate that the Lollard way is the true
way of faith, and that any other approach to salvation is essentially flawed.

Rather than specifically expounding any Lollard doctrine, then, Clanvowe
merely argues for the way of Lollardy over the way of the orthodox Church.
His treatise is fundamentally about the salvation of the individual, and, he
asserts, the individual may choose one of the two ways. If he decides to travel
by the narrow path, then he may be slandered as a fool and a Lollard, but if
he chooses the broad path (which he appears to define as anything other than
the Lollard route), he will be led to the pains of hell. This text is clearly not
designed to fulfil the purpose of the dissemination of Lollard tenets. It reads
more like a justification for holding to the Lollard way. It does not provide
the reader with significant insight into the tenets of Lollardy to which

36 Clanvowe, *The Two Ways*, ll. 503–22.   37 Ibid., ll. 278–9.   38 Ibid., l. 345.   39 Cf. l. 501.

Clanvowe subscribed, but we can judge from the doctrinal temperance of the text that Clanvowe's position was moderate.

The reader in search of insight into whether the Lollard Knights held to the doctrine of real presence will be disappointed. Clanvowe's text refuses to give this away. Rather, it serves as an apologia for holding to the Lollard way – the new way of faith – and it promises that this way leads to salvation. Lollardy was in no way homogeneous as a movement, and this text provides no form of insight into the form or level to which Clanvowe and his fellows subscribed. It is clear, however, that Clanvowe considered himself to be a member of a fellowship of like-minded individuals, and that he was convinced that they had found the path to heaven. Aston and Richmond suggest that 'Lollardy survived primarily because gentry patronage of its exponents persisted', and when we read Clanvowe's treatise, we can be assured of the commitment with which some members of the knightly class stood behind those who responsible for disseminating its doctrine.

Shakespeare, Thomas More and the
Princes in the Tower

EILÉAN NÍ CHUILLEANÁIN

This essay starts from the depiction of the two murdered princes in the Tower of London in Shakespeare's *Richard III*, and goes back to Shakespeare's source in Thomas More's *History of Richard III*, from which the playwright copied the arguments about the taking of the younger of them out of sanctuary. The intention is to explore the ways in which More is complicating a tradition of immunity attached to consecrated places and persons, how this is changed in Shakespeare's dramatic presentation, and how on closer examination important elements of Shakespeare's treatment are foreshadowed in More's juxtaposition of two versions of immunity: the claim of sanctuaries and the claim of childhood.

The entry into the Westminster sanctuary of Edward IV's widow and children, including her younger son, was a political move, which More represents as such. In his account, the tactic is countered, on the surface, by specious political arguments, by implied criticism of inflated religious claims by church establishments, and by an evidently rational suggestion that sanctuary is a social problem. There is also the unspoken threat of brute force that threatens its inmates. Concerns about the wisdom of privileging sanctuaries, in a context remote from the fraught confrontations of the *History*, also surface in More's *Utopia*, where a wise and disinterested churchman, Cardinal Morton, suggests their limitation. They were in fact largely abolished in 1540. A contemporary scandal, the death of a London merchant, Richard Hunne, in the Bishop of London's prison, the recourse to the sanctuary of Good Easter, in Essex, by his suspected murderers, and their escape from legal punishment due to their clerical status, sharpens More's irony, in both texts, in relation to the phenomenon of sanctuary and its use and abuse. A classical historical text, nowadays known as Tacitus' *Annales* I–VI, newly discovered and published at the moment of the writing of *Utopia*, provides another view of sanctuary and the sacred, which was also a potent influence on More's text.

The image associated with the children's murder in Shakespeare's *Richard III* is a memorable one. The murder is not shown in the play, and the wretched details of the children's smothering with bedclothes, their final struggles, their naked bodies inspected by their uncle's agent, and the indecision as to where they should be buried, which appear in the version of More's *History* printed in his 1557 *English Works*, are passed over. Instead, there is a pathetic description of their appearance just before the event, which perhaps

reflects the discourse of martyrdom and innocence behind More's final comment, 'they gave up to God their innocent souls into the joys of heaven, leaving to the tormentors their bodies dead in the bed'.[1] In its soft-coloured
voyeurism the scene of the sleeping children suffuses the words of the villainous James Tyrrell with feeling:

> Dighton and Forrest, whom I did suborn
> To do this ruthless piece of butchery,
> Although they were flesh'd villains, bloody dogs,
> Melting with tenderness and kind compassion
> Wept like two children in their deaths' sad stories.
> 'Lo, thus,' quoth Dighton, 'lay those tender babes.'
> 'Thus, thus,' quoth Forrest, 'girdling one another
> Within their innocent alabaster arms:
> Their lips were four red roses on a stalk,
> Which in their summer beauty kiss'd each other.
> A book of prayers on their pillow lay;
> Which once,' quoth Forrest, 'almost changed my mind;
> But O! the devil' – there the villain stopp'd
> Whilst Dighton thus told on: 'We smothered
> The most replenished sweet work of nature,
> That from the prime creation e'er she framed.'   [IV, iii][2]

The fact that it is the organizer of the murder, Tyrrell, who speaks here in
soliloquy, connects him other villainous gazers: with Macbeth, with Tarquin
in *The Rape of Lucrece,* and even with Iachimo in *Cymbeline.* The description
is doubly distanced since Tyrrell is relating the words of his hitmen, including their allusion to the sacred, in the prayer-book on the boys' pillow, which
almost but not quite deflects the assassins. The innocence of the victim is a
spectacle, invoking religious reverence though mediated by a villain.

   If we consider the story of Edward IV's sons as found in Shakespeare's
most important source, More's *History of Richard III,* we find that the claim
of childhood to protection in virtue of its innocence is juxtaposed with other
claims to immunity which were the subject of contemporary public debate,
but had largely faded from public consciousness by Shakespeare's day: the
ecclesiastical immunities of sanctuary and benefit of clergy. Shakespeare follows More, who manoeuvres the reader into seeing the children as possessing
a sacredness independent of any particular religious trappings. However we
shall find that there is hovering in the background another, pre-Christian reli-

1 Thomas More, *History of Richard III and Selections from the English and Latin Poems* (here-
with *History*), ed. R.S. Sylvester (New Haven, 1976), p. 88.   2 William Shakespeare, *The
Histories,* ed. Peter Alexander (London, 1956). All quotations from this edition.

gious sanction which also failed to protect an innocent child. More shocks the reader into a realization of the special claims of childhood as more pressing than the legalities invoked by various actors in his narrative.

The *History* is an apparently unfinished work, of which the various versions in English and Latin end at about the moment of Richard III's seizing of the throne, rather than narrating the history of his reign.[3] It appears to have been begun after (I shall suggest fairly soon after) 1514; some versions contain additions which may have been made as much as ten or fifteen years later.[4] What may well be the earliest English text does not contain the murders of Edward IV's children; neither does the Latin. The victims of Richard's earlier tyrannies, after he has been declared Protector on his brother's death, are politically active figures like Hastings, Dorset and Rivers; the fall of Hastings especially is narrated with tragic energy. However the reader is aware from the beginning of the impending major atrocity, and much of the *History's* impact comes from the attempts to stave it off; the historical irony which flashes through the work, illuminating the mismatch between intention and result, between professed and real motives, is given its lurid gleam by the crime against innocence.

The argument about innocence is foregrounded in a paradoxical form in relation to sanctuary. The attempt to persuade Queen Elizabeth to yield her son out of Westminster takes place in the context of a political reality: the crime of murder will be of use to Richard only if he can eliminate both boys, since if the younger survives he will succeed his brother as heir to their father's crown. The discussion of sanctuary by the Protector's Council (in an episode which has been found to loom disproportionately large in the *History*) includes positions skewed by sectional interest, but also apparently reeking of superstition and taking the reader away from the immediate crisis to contemplate the interlinking between superstitious credulity and human folly and crime.

Repeatedly in this work, superstitious beliefs are countered by reasonable and enlightened arguments, mockery or simple scepticism. The reader may nod approvingly, as when Lord Hastings gives a lecture on the silliness of taking omens seriously, when warned by Lord Stanley about a dream he's had, of

---

3 See notes to pp 83 and 84 of Sylvester's 1976 edition. One version in English ends with the cynical comments of the Londoners on Richard's manoeuvres to gain the throne; the Latin concludes with his coronation 'with the same provision that was appointed for the coronation of his nephew', p. 84. The 1557 printing contains the murders, and ends with an incomplete conversation between the duke of Buckingham and his prisoner Bishop (later Cardinal) Morton, tending to persuade Buckingham to side against Richard (pp 94–6).   4 See *The Yale Edition of The Complete Works of St Thomas More* (hereafter *Complete Works*), vol. II, *The History of King Richard III* , ed. R.S. Sylvester (New Haven, 1963), pp lxiii–v; Alison Hanham, *Richard III and his Early Historians, 1483–1535* (Oxford, 1975) argues for a later date for the work's commencement. As will be clear, I find her position unconvincing, especially in view of the parallels between this work and *Utopia*.

them both being attacked by a boar (the boar being Richard's crest). Hastings
sensibly ignores Stanley's dream; whereupon, on the following day, Richard has
him summarily beheaded. When Richard accuses Hastings of treason he displays his own arm as evidence that it has been withered by witchcraft, although
'no man was there present but well knew that his arm was ever such since his
birth'. Earlier, in the narrative of Edward IV's marriage to the widowed
Elizabeth Grey, his mother, the duchess of York, attempts to argue that a king
because of 'the sacred majesty of a prince, that ought as nigh to approach priest-
hood in cleanness as he doth in dignity' should only marry a virgin, but the
suggestion is mockingly dismissed by her son; earlier still the *History* repeats
the ominous portent of Richard's birth feet foremost and 'not untoothed' with
a sceptical comment.[5] More has at the point of writing this work already earned
a reputation for his Lucianic wit and his impatience with superstition.[6] In the
History, portents decorate the narrative, as flourishes appropriate to Humanist
historical writing, while being simultaneously exposed to learned mockery.

But the debate preceding the unwilling yielding of the child Duke of York
out of the sanctuary is full of a direr irony. All the sensible arguments are on
the side of those who propose to violate the sanctuary; the reader is invited
to share their impatience with the invocation of legends and relics. The problem is their motivation, which is to circumvent the Queen's plan to protect
both children by retaining custody of the younger. More's account of the case
for and against overruling her is ample and oratorical, by contrast with the
briefer treatment in Shakespeare's play, which elides the contrast between
pious role-play and hard power politics. Yet the fact that Shakespeare does
not jettison the argument about sanctuary entirely (he might have substituted
an emotional scene of the mother's parting from her son, since this was also
available to him in More) suggests that as an asylum for the innocent (an earlier moment in *Richard III* has shown the Queen resolving to take refuge
there) he wants to keep the idea of sanctuary in his audience's mind.

In the Shakespeare version we do not enter Westminster Abbey but we
follow the earlier stages of the debate. We are given a précis of the arguments
for and against respecting the sanctuary. The cardinal of York rather per-
functorily declares for its inviolability; he will try to persuade the Queen to
part with her young son:

> but if she be obdurate
> To mild entreaties, God in heaven forbid
> We should infringe the holy privilege
> Of blessed sanctuary! not for all this land
> Would I be guilty of so deep a sin.

---

5 *History,* pp 50, 48, 63, 8.   6 See, for example, R. Pace, *De Fructu qui ex Doctrina Percipitur,*
ed. Frank Manley and Richard S. Sylvester (New York, 1967), pp 104–8.

Buckingham, Richard's accomplice, makes a tortuous case that the Prince
cannot claim sanctuary precisely because he is *not* an adult criminal:

> You are too senseless-obstinate, my lord,
> Too ceremonious and traditional
> Weigh it but with the grossness of this age,
> You break not sanctuary in seizing him.
> The benefit thereof is always granted
> To those whose dealings have deserved the place,
> And those who have the wit to claim the place:
> This prince hath neither claim'd it nor deserved it;
> And therefore, in mine opinion, cannot have it:
> Then, taking him from thence that is not there,
> You break no privilege nor charter there.
> Oft have I heard of sanctuary men;
> But sanctuary children ne'er till now.

The Cardinal caves in immediately:

> My lord, you shall o'er-rule my mind for once.
> Come on, Lord Hastings, will you go with me?   [III, i]

He and Hastings go off, there is a dialogue with the young king to show his
maturity and regal quality, and then York is produced, playful and disre-
spectful, a perfect part for a child actor.

More's version of the episode is much more gloomy, but the argument
made by Buckingham is the same: sanctuary is for adult criminals, those
'whose dealings have deserved the place' and who 'have the wit' to claim it
(in Shakespeare's words), not (in More's) for a child 'whose innocence to all
the world his tender youth proveth', and who is a 'babe ... [without] discre-
tion to require it'.[7] Enlightened arguments against sanctuaries are put into the
mouths of Richard and Buckingham, who declare themselves shocked at the
shelter they give to criminals and social misfits 'as though God and Saint
Peter were the patrons of ungracious living ... unthrifts riot and run in debt
upon the boldness of these places', wives run away from their husbands, and
thieves come out of sanctuaries to rob. The archbishop of York makes an
impassioned defence of the tradition, producing an argument that appeals (in
a detail which Shakespeare jettisoned) to a miracle story:

> [The] holy ground was more than five hundred year ago by Saint
> Peter, his own person in spirit, accompanied with great multitude of

angels, by night so specially hallowed and dedicate to God (for the proof whereof they have yet in the abbey Saint Peter's cope to show) that from that time hitherward was there never so undevout a king that durst that sacred place violate, or so holy a bishop that durst it presume to consecrate.[8]

Buckingham's clinching argument against the privilege makes the point that Shakespeare borrowed, 'And verily I have often heard of sanctuary men. But I never heard erst of sanctuary children.'[9] The Archbishop agrees to try persuading Queen Elizabeth to part with her child, and More's account of the second stage of the debate is set in the sanctuary itself, where the mother's fears are far from being assuaged by the prelate's apparently sincere assurances that her child will be safe; but she shrewdly and sadly concludes that she cannot keep him and resigns herself to his departure. Here the arguments are sharply put; in her words, 'man's law serveth the guardian to keep the infant. The law of nature wills the mother keep her child. God's law privilegeth the sanctuary, and the sanctuary my son.'[10] But neither the queen nor the archbishop mentions the physical fact: the sanctuary is watched and guarded by Richard's troops, and she cannot resist force if force is used.[11] While the politicians she has to deal with speak of 'womanish fear' and 'womanish frowardness', More repeatedly calls Elizabeth 'wise', and shows her to have a more accurate sense of her own and her enemy's powers and of his intentions than any of the other players.[12] But her despairing decision to trust to the influence of the Cardinal and the lords to protect her child does not save him.

From the images of women and children in the *History* I will presently turn to the contemporary experience of those adult males who benefited from sanctuary, to suggest that the association between sanctuary and the privileges of the clergy which appears in the particular series of events I will be adducing is reflected both in the *History* and in *Utopia*. Part of my argument is based on the connection between these texts, and on a belief that they are close in date, that the *History* with its often satiric strategies was written when More had recently published or was about to publish *Utopia*, with its marked indebtedness to the Greek satirist Lucian. He had brought out his own version of some dialogues of Lucian in 1506 and was in 1518 to issue his *Epigrams*, several translated from the same writer. More's contemporary admirers identify him with the Lucianic mode of mockery, and Lucian's influence on *Utopia* is notorious.[13]

Numerous parallels exist between the *History* and *Utopia*; most often remarked upon are the appearance in both of Cardinal Morton, More's child-

8 *History*, p. 28.   9 *History*, p. 33.   10 *History*, p. 39.   11 *History*, pp 23, 34.   12 *History*, pp 29, 49, 62.   13 See Pace, quoted n. 6 above; also E. Ní Chuilleanáin, 'Motives of translation: More, Erasmus and Lucian', *Hermathena*, 183 (2007), 49–62.

hood patron, and the theme of tyranny. I will discuss these below, as well as the appearance in both works of the suggestion that sanctuary needs to be reformed. Both compare politics to drama, and a similar comment on kingship appears in both (and in the 1518 *Epigrams*); Edward IV answers his mother's plea that he should marry a foreign princess because of 'great possibility of increase of his possessions' by observing that 'we have already title by that means, to so much as sufficeth to get and keep well in one mans days', while Raphael Hythlodaye in *Utopia* imagines himself telling the king of France that 'the single kingdom of France by itself was almost too large to be governed well by a single man'.[14]

Part II of *Utopia*, written in 1515, is described as originating in conversations with learned acquaintances in Antwerp, in a lull in the negotiations during More and Tunstall's historical embassy to Flanders. The pleasure of enlightened dialogue is highlighted in Part I by the contrasting accounts of political corruption and prejudice in Europe and England. In this fiction as in the correspondence of the humanists, we are presented with the kind of world in which the manuscript of the *History* might have circulated, alongside new books and editions. 1515 is the year of the first publication, under the direction of Pope Leo X, of Philippus Beroaldus' edition of Books I–VI of Tacitus' *Annales* (then labelled as Books I–V), with Books XI–XVI, which were already known, in the edition of Franciscus Puteolanus.[15]

We know that More knew the *Annales* (he quotes Tacitus in a letter of 1515 to Martin Dorp); Daniel McKinney's edition of the Latin *Historia Ricardi Tertii* has identified many parallels which are suggestive, in particular the characterization of Richard in terms reminiscent of the portrait of the Emperor Tiberius' minister Sejanus, in Book II of the *Annales*. R.S. Sylvester pointed out that Book III contains a reference to the abuse of sanctuary. *Annales* 3. 60–2 describes how numerous Greek cities cited 'ancient superstitions' in support of their sanctuaries which sheltered slaves, debtors and those accused of serious crime.[16] Renaissance readers and editors of Tacitus and Suetonius noted their accounts of Tiberius' reform of sanctuaries. Giovanni Battista Egnazio picks it out in the list of contents to his 1516 edition of Suetonius' *Lives of the Twelve Caesars* while the elder Beroaldus in his notes on Suetonius had written a disquisition on the origin of sanctuaries, and noted like Buckingham that they offered 'receptacula flagitiosorum & inuitamenta maleficiorum.'[17]

---

14 Thomas More, *Utopia*, ed. E. Surtz (New Haven, 1964), pp 42, 49; *History*, pp 83, 65; cf *Epigrammata* (1518), p. 263.   15 *P. Cornelii Taciti libri quinque noviter inventi atque cum reliquis eius operibus editi* (Rome, 1515).   16 *Complete Works*, vol. 2 (*History of Richard III*), lxxxvii–xc. Sylvester refers to *Annales* 3.36, which in fact speaks of guilty Romans and slaves clasping the emperor's image to escape punishment.   17 Tacitus, *Annales*, p. 45; C. *Suetonij Tranquilli XII Caesares. Index rerum memorabilium per singulos Tranquilli Caesares ab Ioanne Baptista Egnatio Veneto compositus* (Venice, 1516); *Commentationes conditae a Philippo Beroaldo in Suetonium*

A more dreadful reminiscence is reported by Nicholas Harpsfield, in his account of More's refusal to attend the coronation of Anne Boleyn. More quoted (inaccurately) one of Tacitus' most shocking stories (*Annales*, V.9; Suetonius refers to something similar), the rape of the young daughter of Sejanus, who was killed with all her family after her father's fall. It was ordered that the little girl should be raped because there was no precedent for the execution of a virgin – the fact that she had committed no crime being less relevant than her intact status.[18] Richard Marius takes this as an example of More's equation of virginity with purity, Geoffrey Elton finds More's use of the story 'harsh and crude'.[19] I want to consider More's deliberate deployment of the taboos surrounding innocence and guilt in his own society, and in antiquity, and the shadow of this event among the narrative strategies which build the reader's apprehension, in the *History of Richard III*, of an impending unthinkable inhumanity. Alongside contemporary interest in the historical role of sanctuary and superstition, the rape in Tacitus presented More with ideas about a culture's designation of what is 'unheard-of' or 'crime' in the view of the ancient historians. Suetonius, who was known since the Middle Ages, had told of girls raped before execution as among Tiberius' cruelties; he had not however individualized the victims.[20] It is Tacitus who specifies that there were two children, identifies their fate as connected the fall of Sejanus, and distinguishes between an older one, a boy who knew what was happening, and the girl who thought she was going to be punished for a childish fault. More's princes are not given any memorable lines, but the elder registers protests at what is happening while the younger is passive, both like Sejanus' children inextricably linked to an implacable fate.[21] And a Tacitean sense of the irony of history, the 'mockery of human plans in every transaction' [*Annales*, III, 18] pervades the *History of Richard III*.[22]

The theme of tyranny which is prominent in the 1518 *Epigrams* (and which surfaced too in his 1506 Lucian translations) is so evident in Tacitus that it seems superfluous to name it – it appears in every account of a modern dictator.[23] Like the emperor Tiberius however, Richard III was a tyrant in a

Tranquillum (Bologna, 1506), p. 130.   18 N. Harpsfield, *The Life and Death of Sr Thomas Moore, Knight: Sometymes Lord High Chancellor of England*, ed. E.V. Hitchcock (Oxford, 1932), pp 148–9; *Annales* fol. 63v, 'Tradunt temporis eius auctores, quia triumuirali supplicio inauditum habebetur: a carnefice laqueus iuxta compressam: exin oblisis faucibus, id ætatis corpora in Gemonias abiecta.'   19 R. Marius, *Thomas More* (New York, 1985), p. 439; G. Elton 'Thomas More, Councillor' in R.S. Sylvester (ed.), *St. Thomas More, Action and Contemplation* (New Haven, 1972), pp 87–122, at p. 114.   20 Tacitus says 'quia triumuirali supplicio adfici virginem inauditum habebetur', fol. 63v; Suetonius 'quia more tradito nefas esset uirgines strangulari', fol. 79v.   21 *History*, pp 20, 87, 88.   22 *Annales* fol. 37v, 'Mihi quanto plura recentium, seu veterum reuoluo, tanto magis ludibria rerum mortalium cunctis in negociis obseruantur.'   23 See for example, http://kotare.typepad.com/thestrategist/tacitus/, which associates Tacitus' emperors with Hitler and Mugabe. Accessed 7 October 2008.

traditional society, with rituals, traditions, and assemblies and occasions for rhetorical self-justification. Tacitus' Tiberius 'allowed the senate the appearance of its old power', encouraging it to adjudicate on the petitions in favour of the Greek temple sanctuaries.[24] Similarly Richard is shown by More engaging in serious debate with the members of his Council on the appropriateness of sanctuaries in Christian churches.

The irony here is not simple. Reservations about the church's claim for the inviolability of sanctuaries might be expected from More as a lawyer. The privilege of sanctuary had been upheld by the church throughout the Middle Ages (Durandus, the thirteenth-century authority on liturgy, says that a church carries with it the privilege of protecting those guilty of blood crimes who have recourse to it against the state and other enemies, and refers back to Joab in the Old Testament who 'took hold of the horn of the altar');[25] but while secular rulers took account of the privilege, there was a tendency to limit it to certain churches. Under Edward II, in a statute of 1316 (some elements of which go back to 1280), the rules under which criminals were allowed to take sanctuary were codified; offenders who abjured the realm [promising on oath to leave the kingdom] and, fleeing to a church for refuge, claimed privilege of sanctuary, were to be allowed to have the necessaries of life and were to be at liberty to go out of the church to relieve nature. Violation of the right of sanctuary carried automatic excommunication.[26] The system appears to have persisted into the early modern period; the late sixteenth-century account of the Rites of Durham specifies that the whole of Durham Cathedral was a sanctuary until the Reformation, with three hundred sanctuary men in residence at the end of the fifteenth century.[27]

There was however a debate, in the decade in which More (in my view) wrote both the *History of Richard III* and *Utopia*, on the subject of sanctuary, and the related one of clerical immunity from prosecution in secular courts. John Guy quotes a pronouncement by Henry VIII of about 1519, which sounds as if he'd been reading More's *History*, when he invokes the founders:

> I do not suppose that St. Edward, King Edgar, and the other kings and holy fathers who made the sanctuary ever intended the sanctuary to

24 *Annales*, p. 45, 'vim principatus sibi firmans imaginem antiquitatis Senatui præbebat.' **25** G. Duranti, *Rationale Divinorum Officiorum*, ed. A. Davril O.S.B. & T.M. Thibodeau (Turnhout, 1995), vol. I [Corpus Christianorum, Continuatio Mediaevalis CXL], I.i, 49, pp 27–8, 'ecclesia consecrata reos sanguinis ad se confugientes … defendit ne vitam perdant aut membra. Unde legitur quod Ioab in tabernaculum fugit et cornu altaris apprehendit.' **26** See J. H. Denton, 'The Making of the "Articuli Cleri" of 1316', *English Historical Review*, 101:400 (1986), 564–95, at 580–1. **27** See *Rites of Durham*, Surtees Society, 1903, pp 35, 42–3; also 'Westminster Abbey: The Sanctuary and Almonry', *Old and New London: Volume 3* (1878), pp 483–91. Online source: http://www.british-history.ac.uk/report.asp?compid=45169. Accessed 17 September 2006.

serve for voluntary murder and larceny done outside the sanctuary in hope of returning, and such like, and I believe the sanctuary was not so used in the beginning. And so I will have that reformed which is encroached by abuse, and have the matter reduced to the true intent of the making thereof in the beginning.[28]

What may also have made sanctuary (the question of clerical immunity from prosecution was already, as we shall see, a live issue) especially controversial in the middle of the decade is the history of the Londoner Richard Hunne and the actions of those believed to be responsible for his death. This case involved both sanctuary and clerical crime; More discusses the first in the *History* and the second in *Utopia*.

In the background to the Hunne case is the attempt by the Tudor government to check some of the privileges of the minor clergy. In 1512 Parliament had passed an act making clerks in orders, of lower status than subdeacons, liable to prosecution in the ordinary courts for most crimes of murder. After a heated dispute between Convocation, the assembly of the clergy, and Parliament, after the abbot of Winchcombe had declared in 1515 that the act of 1512 was 'clean contrary to the law of God', and the Pope had denounced it (while urging bishops to be careful whom they admitted to minor orders), the act was not renewed. But King and Parliament had declared, and never went back on, their view that the common law should extend to the clerical criminal who was not an in 'major orders', thus not a participant in the sacred ceremonies of the Mass.

On the day, 5 December 1514, when the dead body of Hunne, a merchant tailor and suspected heretic, was found in the bishop of London's prison, or certainly before the end of that month, the jailer and summoner, Charles Joseph, fled into sanctuary at Good Easter in Essex.[29] He reappeared some

28 John Guy, 'Thomas Cromwell and the Intellectual Origins of the English Revolution', quoting J.H. Baker (ed.), *The Reports of Sir John Spelman*, Selden Society, 2 vols (London, 1977–8), vol. II, Introduction, pp 342–3. 'Matters had come to a head in the wake of a local feud in 1516 when John Pauncefote, a Gloucester justice, was shot and mutilated on his way to the sessions at Cirencester. The murderers and their supporters caused a public outcry by taking sanctuary.' Online source: http://www.tudors.org/undergraduate/65-thomas-cromwell-and-the-intellectual-origins-of-the-henrician-revolution.html. Accessed 7 October 2008.   29 See John Foxe, 'A full declaration and history of the whole discourse and lamentable handling of Richard Hun, within lollardes tower in London' in John Foxe, *Ecclesiasticall History contaynyng the Actes and Monuments of thynges passed in euery Kynges tyme in this Realme* (London 1570), pp 930–6. Online source: http://www.hrionline.ac.uk/johnfoxe/index.html. Accessed 7 October 2008. 'The deposition of Richarde Horsnaile bailife of the sanctuary toune called Goddesture in Essex', p. 395, 'The said Richard saieth, the Friday before Christmas day last past that one Charles Ioseph, somner to my Lord of London, became a sanctuary man, and the aforesaide Frydaye, he regestred his name, the sayde Charles saiying it was for the sauegarde of his body, for there be certaine men in London so extreme aginste him for the death of Richard Hun, that he dare not

time later and confessed to murdering Hunne, in the company of the Bishop's chancellor, Dr Horsey, a clerk in holy orders, and another man named John Spalding, the bell-ringer of the cathedral. Richard Marius suggests that, as well as Dr Horsey, Joseph and Spalding may have been in minor orders.[30] Marius, like other modern scholars, agrees with the verdict of the inquest held on 6 December, which concluded that Hunne was murdered. The church's case, upheld by More fifteen years later in his *Dialogue Concerning Heresies*, was that he committed suicide. In any case, Joseph was either a murderer or a malicious perjurer. But the ecclesiastical powers moved at once to protect him, and to prevent men like him and especially Dr Horsey from being exposed to a trial at common law. Horsey was ultimately punished with a heavy fine and a remote parish.[31]

In the aftermath of Hunne's death practical negotiation took place. Henry VIII gave way to clerical pressure (the bishop of London's petition to Wolsey, claiming extreme prejudice against the clergy, 'assured am I if my Chaunceller be tried by any twelue men in London, they be so maliciously set, *In fauorem heretice prauitatis,* that they will cast and condemne any clerke, though he were as innocent as Abell')[32] by pardoning Horsey, but insisted that Hunne's goods, which would have been forfeit if he had been found to have killed himself, should be restored to his daughter and son-in-law. The royal order for restitution is made according to Foxe in response to pressure from Parliament; it emphasizes the supremacy of the laws of England: 'hetherto ye haue made no recompence, accordyng to our lawes, as myght stand with equitie, Iustice, right, and good conscience, and for this cause due satisfaction ought to be made by our lawes'.[33] We seem, reading the documents quoted by John Foxe, to be close to the views of the major players, people with whom More was familiar, about the rights and wrongs of what had happened. Negotiation and compromise should not obscure the fact that a case for the need to continue the clerical privilege was vigorously put, and that on the other side an appeal was made to 'equity justice, right and good conscience' which must prevail.

Richard Hunne was called a heretic after he refused to pay a small offering that the church demanded at the funeral of his infant son. Though More in his later account was to assert that the charge was justified, since Hunne did frequent heretical groups, it is important to read the *History of Richard III* and *Utopia* in the light of the issues that seemed pressing at the time they were written, including those raised by the Hunne case, rather than in those

abyde in London: Howbeit the said Charles saieth, he knowledgeth him selfe giltles of Huns death, for he deliuered the keyes to the Chaunceler by Huns life, also the sayde Bailife saieth, that Charles paide the deutie of the saide regestring, both to hym and Syr Iohn Studely Vicar.' **30** Marius, *Thomas More*, p. 145. **31** J.D.M. Derrett, 'The Affair of Richard Hunne and Friar Standish', appendix to More, *Complete Works* ix, *The Apology*, ed. J.B. Trapp (New Haven, 1979), pp 215–46, at 236. **32** Foxe, *Ecclesiasticall History*, p. 935. **33** Foxe, *Ecclesiasticall History*, p. 936.

of the early English Reformation, and to ask whether the religious economy
described in *Utopia* is not organized to make just such unedifying and
unsavoury events as those which led to Hunne's death impossible. The
marked absence in either *The History of Richard III* or *Utopia* of any endorsement of the systems of sanctuary and clerical immunity as they were practised
in England, a practice questioned in the decade 1510–20 by both king and
parliament, shows More in the pre-Reformation period sharing the scepticism
of contemporary politicians about their value, but like King Henry focusing
on the contrast between the original or ideal purpose of a privilege and its
abuse, rather than calling for radical abolition.

The Utopian state does not penalize the members of minority religious
groups. The country has no physically holy places that get in the way of a
rational policy on crime, the clergy are rewarded with honour and with immunity from prosecution (More comments, in case the reader had missed the difference between them and the rabble of clerical hangers-on in contemporary
London, that 'It is easier for them to observe this custom because their priests
are very few and very carefully chosen'), but like other Utopians have no use
for money; they have no ecclesiastical prisons and no disreputable minor func-
tionaries like Spalding and Joseph. Holiness inheres in people and their
actions, not in places. Something like the privilege of sanctuary attaches to
the Utopian priests, but it neither belongs to a place nor extends to criminals;
it is enemies in battle, foreigners, who are saved. In war the priests 'restrain
the fury of their own men against the routed enemy. Merely to see and to
appeal to them suffices to save one's life; to touch their flowing garments pro-
tects one's remaining goods from every harm arising from war.'[34] The
Utopians' conduct of their international affairs is explicitly contrasted with
the European, in terms which draw attention to the recent examples of per-
fidy at the highest level of the church in the behaviour of the recently dead
Pope Julius II. The Utopians never enter into treaties because they find kings
in their hemisphere are inclined to go back on their word:

> In Europe, however, and especially in those parts where the faith and
> religion of Christ prevails, the majesty of treaties is everywhere holy
> and inviolable, partly through the justice and goodness of kings, partly
> through the reverence and fear of the Sovereign Pontiffs. Just as the
> latter themselves undertake nothing which they do not most conscien-
> tiously perform, so they command all other rulers to abide by their
> promises.[35]

In Book I of *Utopia*, written after Book II with its detailed description of
the ideal state, there is a direct reference to sanctuary. More's fictional nar-

34 More, *Utopia*, p. 141 and note.   35 *Utopia*, p. 116.

rator Raphael describes a meeting with Cardinal Morton, encountered in the *History* as a prisoner of Richard's, later Chancellor in the reign of Henry VII, in whose household More lived as a child.[36] The Cardinal is praised for his wisdom and humanity, and one of the subjects discussed elsewhere in Book I, the effectiveness of the humanist-philosopher as adviser to rulers, is illustrated; when Raphael argues against capital punishment for theft, he is shouted down by his fellow-guests at the great man's table, until it appears that the Cardinal agrees with him, that the imaginary 'Polylerites' system of penal servitude might well work in England instead of wholesale hanging, 'after limitation of the privileges of sanctuary'. The company at dinner changes its mind immediately.[37]

More's subject in Book I of *Utopia* is practical politics. If the talk at the cardinal's table is less philosophical, and the speakers less disinterested, than in the dialogue of humanists in Peter Gilles' garden which provides the framing narrative for the description of the ideal state, it offers an example of how a new idea might be conveyed into a national discourse of crime and punishment. It rebuts Raphael's own position, that power is invariably deaf to philosophy, which he goes on to illustrate with a parody description of the king of France's counsellors vying with each other to think up crooked ways of grabbing territory in Italy.[38] The cardinal's openness to unfamiliar ideas suggests that the political realm may not everywhere be as hopeless a field for the wise man as Raphael had suggested, and his proviso about sanctuary may thus be seen to be a sensible modification in the context of reform, and in tune with the thinking of More, the legal establishment, and the king whose service More was about to enter. Morton's cautious dialogue with his powerful custodian Buckingham, at the end of the 1557 text of the *History*, remotely foreshadows the beginning of a new era of wise counsel.

To return, then, to the sanctuary scenes in the *History of Richard III*. Here, the strong pathos of the parting of the mother and child, the threatening catastrophe, certainly do not amount to an argument for continuing the tradition of sanctuary. When Queen Elizabeth is actually moving into Westminster, and More exerts himself to imagine the moment in its real confusion, as a large train of people moves house and the nominal mistress sits uselessly on the margins, we are far from a numinous or sacred space: 'much heaviness, rumble, haste and business, carriage and conveyance of her stuff into sanctuary ... the queen herself sat alone alowe on the rushes, all desolate and dismayed.'[39] The fact, as More knows and as contemporaries recognized, is that sanctuary was far from impermeable, and sacred and secular spaces, clerical and lay interests constantly jostled and overlapped, in the late medieval world.

But while the case for sanctuary is shown to be a poor one, the literary strategies of the *History* construct a different version of immunity. In part this

36 *Utopia*, p. 19.   37 *Utopia*, pp 39, 34–5.   38 *Utopia*, pp 40–2.   39 *History*, p. 22.

is done by the way in which both the mother and children are patronized and silenced. Her 'maternal fear' is dismissed as 'womanish' instability and her eloquent arguments are followed by her silent decision to risk her son since she cannot defend him. As she hands him over she weeps; the child 'weeping as fast', just as earlier his elder brother 'wept' when his servants were sent away and others put in their places[40] – though Prince Edward is given a few mature lines of speech, his weeping suggests he is still really a child. Some of the words used about the children belie their actual ages, of ten and thirteen, which More gives accurately (they are in fact too old to be *doli incapax* by the usage of their time); he allows Buckingham to call York 'yonder babe' and speaks of the murder as 'the dolorous end of these babes'.[41] Attention and narrative suspense are focused on the younger of the two, and since they cannot be political agents, the image of very early childhood is inaccurately projected.

More's reference in later life, at a time when the lessons of Roman history must have seemed especially apposite, to the account in Tacitus of the killing of Sejanus' children, suggests that his humanist culture made available an image of doomed innocence in the princes, which is not dissociated from religious systems of immunity but which by juxtaposing pre-Christan with Christian systems invites the reader to consider the reasons for their validity. More's presentation of the arguments about the manipulation of sanctuary and his Tacitean references create the context in which childhood innocence can be seen as an absolute, independent of context. If the readers of *Utopia* were expected to recognize references to contemporary politics as well as classical precedents in dialogue and fantasy, the smaller group for whom More wrote, and rewrote in a second language, and added to, the manuscript *History*, should have been equally aware of the density of his allusions.

The treatment of sanctuary and clerical immunity has shown places and persons acquiring immunity by consecration, which happens at a determined time and place. This enables a negotiation with the profane world whereby certain adult persons enter the sacred world permanently or temporarily. The system is shown to serve the interests of a cadre in society, the clergy, in a context of explicit contemporary relevance which has little claim to promote justice. Even the fates of the two murderers illustrate this; one 'yet walketh on alive' at the time of writing; the other 'rotted away piecemeal' ... in sanctuary, at St. Martin-le-grand.[42]

The position of children is different from that of those who claim such immunities. Their innocence is non-negotiable, as infants, powerless, almost speechless, they are outside time, as Shakespeare put it, the 'sweet work of nature,' framed in 'the prime creation'. It is this that makes them sacred. The

---

40 *History*, pp 42, 20.   41 *History*, pp 32, 85.   42 *History*, p. 89. Cf. More, 'A Mery Jest', *History of Richard III and Selections from the English and Latin Poems*, p. 104, where a spend-thrift gets into debt and takes refuge in 'saynt Katheryne' to avoid arrest.

fading relevance of the issue of sanctuary means that by Shakespeare's time it is the pathos of the princes as victims that is foregrounded; the image of the two unconscious, sleeping children in the Tower amounts to a statement that it is childhood itself, not any particular place or relationship, that possesses the radiant innocence which strikes, though it fails to melt, the murderers' hearts. However, the fact that the sanctuary argument survives in Shakespeare has a double effect. It provides the story of the princes with a narrative tension, while the audience watches the grown men debate the fate of the children; and it gives the princes a residual aura of the ecclesiastical sacred, which utterly fails to protect them from the malice of their uncle.

The 'English Brut Tradition' in an Irish and Welsh Context

JOHN J. THOMPSON

In this essay I want to consider a series of issues related to the reception among seventeenth-century readers of the fifteenth-century Latin and English material celebrating English history, now found in Dublin, Trinity College Library MS 505.[1] The manuscript is composite and brings together a carefully conflated version of the ME Prose *Brut*, in its second part (B), that is now prefaced (in part A) by a series of illustrated Latin genealogical diagrams, many with accompanying annotation derived from Galfridian sources. John Scattergood has already acquainted us with this key codicological feature of the manuscript as part of his discussion of the function of its illustrations.[2] Alongside the genealogical and historical material preserved in part A, he sees the fascinatingly varied townscapes included in the decorative roundels accompanying the text as facilitative 'eyes of memory' for fifteenth-century and later scholarly readers. As such, both his account of the diagrams and illustrations in MS 505, and my own attempt to build upon it here, are characteristic of a much larger set of critical preoccupations – especially within contemporary English studies – that have profoundly shaped the scholarly methodologies of nearly all of the contributors to this volume who claim an interest in late medieval reading habits and the archaeology of the medieval book. John's published work on manuscript studies has been seminal in this regard, particularly in terms of his steady and reliable focus on combining historical and textual detail to inform his and our views of the Middle Ages. Indeed, it is worth remembering that the possibility of writing about the later reception of ME literary texts, as well as – or even, as here, in preference to – the circumstances of their production and earliest dissemination, reflects a research agenda that would hardly have been deemed relevant or possible fifty years ago.[3] Understanding the literary-historical impli-

Earlier versions of this essay were given at Trinity College Dublin (June 2009) and Queen's University Belfast (October 2009). I take sole responsibility for the views expressed here but I am very grateful to colleagues for their lively discussion and occasional disagreement on these occasions and also to the editors of the current volume for their much-appreciated patience and assistance.
1 See the manuscript description in M.L. Colker, *Trinity College Library Dublin: Descriptive Catalogue of the Medieval and Renaissance Latin Manuscripts* 2 vols (Aldershot, 1991), 2, pp 935–38. For the textual affiliations of MS 505's *Brut* copy, see Lister M. Matheson, *The Prose Brut: the Development of a ME Chronicle* (Tempe, AZ, 1998), pp 285–7. 2 '"The Eyes of Memory": the Function of the Illustrations in Dublin, Trinity College Library MS 505', in John Scattergood, *Manuscripts and Ghosts: Essays on the Transmission of Medieval and Early Renaissance Literature* (Dublin, 2006), pp 228–51. 3 For the rapid development of book history in medieval

cations of manuscript study through the afterlives of medieval texts and manuscripts is now an even more pressing concern that will continue to reshape fundamentally our understanding of the place and importance of English medieval manuscript study and the 'History of the (pre-modern) Book'.

In his most recent writings, Scattergood has described the role and relevance of the manuscript scholar more imaginatively, in markedly less institutionally-bound terms, and with broader brush strokes than I have deployed in the previous paragraph. In the introduction to his volume of selected essays entitled *Manuscripts and ghosts*, for example, he argues that the letters on the page of the manuscript book articulate 'the words of those who are absent, and can by extension cause the presence of the speakers to be imagined'.[4] There is no mention here of the quasi-scientific disciplines of dialectology and palaeography, the exponents of which have played important and pioneering roles in the invention of codicology, itself an unquestionably more subjective quasi-discipline than those from which it is ultimately derived.[5] Instead, these words in generous praise of the scholarly imagination describe the task of picking up a medieval manuscript with the intention of reading it (here using the idea of reading in both its literal and figurative senses) as a task that might be faced by any modern reader. The task is described in terms that will certainly seem familiar to readers of poetry or the novel, as well as to those more wedded to examining theories of consumption in material culture than to the prolonged and often painful study of palaeography and diplomatic.[6] But just as there are different ways to read novels and poetry, so too there are numerous possibilities to 'coax into presence' the voices of the past by careful examination of the written word in manuscript form. That there are different justifications and reasons for so doing is a factor that must also be borne in mind. Much will depend on the modern scholarly interests and training a reader brings to the task of reading a medieval book. Also it would seem that some medieval books are always going to be more amenable than others to the modern scholarly desire 'to interrogate the writing of the past so that it will speak and inform the present'.[7] So it is with an understanding of these challenging issues in mind that I begin this essay by admitting to having uncovered a series of unresolved issues related to the later ownership and reception history I have here imagined for MS 505. All the same, it seems fair to add that the voices of the past I am attempting to 'coax into presence' in this essay have not been heard before by modern scholars of

studies and its implications for a larger historically-inflected English literary history than is yet currently available, see Ralph Hanna's polemical and seminal comments in 'Analytical Survey 4, Middle English Manuscripts and the Study of Literature', *New Medieval Literatures* 4 (2001), 243–64; also 'Middle English Books and Middle English Literary History', *Modern Philology* 101 (2004), 157–78.   4 Scattergood, *Manuscripts*, Preface, p. 18.   5 See Hanna, 'Analytical Survey' for bibliographical details.   6 For the latter, see the recent stimulating comments on the practice and study of western palaeography in Malcolm B. Parkes, *Their Hands Before Our Eyes, a Closer Look at Scribes* (Aldershot, 2008).   7 Scattergood, *Manuscripts*, Preface, p. 18.

the medieval period. I think that this is simply because they have left such few traces in the relevant documentary record. And notwithstanding many years of scholarly progress in these matters, the fact remains that we have not always trained ourselves to look closely enough at the likely impact on post-medieval readers of the potent interpenetration of past and present, myth and history, signalled by the later histories of medieval texts on the British history now extant in old books such as MS 505.[8]

Much regarding the earliest provenance of MS 505 remains uncertain. It was originally produced in two parts, with both parts brought together early for a single decorative campaign where townscape illustrations were added in pen and ink outline drawings, usually also painted with coloured washes, now found in both the genealogical diagrams in A and as a full-page frontispiece on p. 86 for the ME prose *Brut* in B. That single decorative campaign probably took place not long after the Latin genealogical sequence in A was compiled and there are some signs in both A and B that it may even have been suspended, and then abandoned as unfinished 'work in progress', in the newly-composite manuscript. It may be relevant in this context that the English regnal genealogies in A continue as far as the progeny of Edward IV, with his son Thomas referred to as earl of Huntingdon, a designation suggesting that this material was probably completed between the years 1471 and 1475 when Thomas held that title. At this point some other lists were then added, giving details of biblical and ancient rulers from Adam, emperors and popes, and archbishops of Canterbury, beginning with Augustine and ending with a partially erased entry for Thomas Bourgchier (who was archbishop from 1454 to 1486). The ME prose *Brut* that follows in B represents a relatively *de luxe* version of the much-copied ME prose item. It begins with the heading 'How thys lond was first callyd Albyon and of whom hyt had that name he schal here as folowythe aftyrward', preceded by the frontispiece within which three roundels convey information about 'Anglia', such as its geographical dimensions and the number of its shires and bishoprics.[9] And this *Brut* version ends with a description of the murder of James I of Scotland in 1437, an event in the relatively recent past that was probably still within living memory at the time when the MS 505 copy was made.

That the compiler of the MS 505 version had already attempted to give as full an account as possible of English regnal history is also hinted at because

8 For one such attempt to do so at Queen's Belfast, through a publicly-funded collaborative research project intended to support early career scholars, see Stephen P. Kelly and Jason O'Rourke, 'Culturally Mapping the Middle English Prose *Brut*: a report from the "Imagining History" Project', *Journal of the Early Book Society* 6 (2003), 41–60; also http://www.qub.ac.uk/imagining-history, accessed 9 April 2010.   9 This detail endorses Scattergood's view (*pace* Colker, *Trinity College* 2, pp 937–98) that the full-page illustration on p. 86 in MS 505 depicts the artist's representation of 'England' rather than providing a composite image of 'London' (Scattergood, *Manuscripts*, p. 246).

this copy is a careful conflation of two distinctive textual traditions, the first a so-called 'Peculiar version' exemplar of the prose *Brut* that is followed closely as far as the reign of Henry III; the MS 505 copy is then supplemented by a 'Common Version' source that offered a more expansive account of events in the later reigns of English kings, from Henry III to Richard II.[10] In most important respects, therefore, the prose *Brut* material in B might be said to follow a broadly similar trajectory through Galfridian and English history as the Latin genealogical sequence that precedes it in A. If the two parts were originally produced as entirely separate commissions, a general similarity of historical theme and 'shape' may even offer the most obvious rationale for originally bringing them both together to form the present composite manuscript. Despite the obvious attention to detail that went into the design and copying of the texts and illustration of the material in MS 505, I can see little or nothing to suggest the identity of an original commissioner or owner for either part of the manuscript.

On the other hand, there are still good indications of sixteenth- and seventeenth-century interest in the book. The Welsh associations of MS 505 are perhaps the most immediately striking signs of this later readerly interest. These are suggested by a series of astrological symbols on p. 1, accompanied by a scrap of Welsh verse on the zodiac that is ascribed and dated 'per me Llewys Dwnn 1593'.[11] Dwnn (also known as Lewys ap Rhys ab Owain) was a prolific Welsh-language poet, genealogist, and self-styled deputy herald of Wales, who was associated with some of the most influential landed families in the principality.[12] It was through such contacts that in February 1585 he secured a patent issued by the English-speaking Clarenceux and Norroy kings-at-arms then in post, affording him suitable recognition for his scholarly efforts.[13] Among other details, this lengthy and verbose English-language document grants:

> that he in respecte of his former trayveyles thouroughowte the most part of the said Countrey for the atteyninge unto the knowledge of the lynes pedegrees and descentes of the chiefest families and kinredes within that principalitie (the bookes and gatherings wherof we have

10 Terminology for classification based on Matheson, *The Prose Brut*, esp. pp 49–56, 98, 278, 285–87. 11 Described, transcribed and translated by Colker, *Trinity College* 2, p. 938. 12 Michael Siddons, 'Dwnn, Lewys (b.c.1545, d. in or after 1616)', *Oxford Dictionary of National Biography* (Oxford, 2004) [http://www.oxforddnb.com/view/article/8340, accessed 9 April 2010]. I am very grateful to my colleague at Queen's University Belfast, Dr Rhian Andrews, for assistance with the peculiarly anglicized form of Welsh that Dwnn deploys for his pedigrees. 13 These were, respectively, Robert Cook (Clarenceux; d. 1593) and William Flower (Norroy; d. 1588); for background details and the text of the patent, see *Heraldic Visitations of Wales and Part of the Marches ... by Lewys Dwnn*, ed. S.R. Meyrick, 2 vols (1846) 1, pp xxii–xxv, esp. xxiii–xxiv.

seene) may the rather vpon their comendac'on and his paynfull dilig[ence] heretofore vsed together in regard of his skill in the Welshe or Brittishe tongue be by vs encouraged and allowed to contynew and goe forward in makinge his collections thoroughowt the said principalitie ... and by these p[ate]ntes do allowe him the said Lewis ap Rhis to record, register, and make entrances of all the discentes, marriages, funeralles and obits of the knightes, esquires, and gentlemen inhabitinge within the said principalitie or the Dominions and Lordships marchers therof: omittinge all highe lynes dedvced from farre aboue all memorie, which for great part ar found to be coniecturall, vnlesse evidences, histories or matter of good credict be showed for approbac'on therof.

Notwithstanding this final injunction to avoid fanciful speculation, Dwnn was obviously as fascinated as earlier generations of Anglophone and Latin readers by the mythic British origins of the Tudor royal line. In the prefatory comments attached to his 1586 collection of family pedigrees for Camarthan, Pembroke and Cardigan, he even offers some account, in Welsh, of the human and magical qualities that marked out for greatness the twenty-four knights in Arthur's court.[14] And, in the *Llyfr Achau*, another set of manuscript pedigrees with which he is associated (not in Dwnn's hand but copied, in part, we are informed, from the pedigrees in one of his stray manuscript collections), we find details of the heraldic devices associated with the Nine Worthies, Brutus, Lear and Cymbeline, among others, here given in support of an English royal pedigree extending from the remotest imagined reaches of the British past.[15] Yet it is also clear that Dwnn was a serious scholar who attempted to clarify the inherited status and titles of leading Welsh families, many of whom based their exaggerated claims for descent from princely blood on nothing more convincing than local traditions and consensus, or, sometimes, careless or optimistic reading of the available sources. Dwnn apparently took very seriously his quasi-antiquarian scholarly role and the responsibilities outlined in his patent during his visitations to these families. He was often careful too to ensure that the heads of the households he visited signed the family pedigrees he had prepared for them as a mark of verification and approval.[16] Similarly to many of the genealogically-inclined local scholars who went before or came after him, he obviously had a high regard for such

14 *Heraldic Visitations*, vol. 2, p. 10.   **15** *Heraldic Visitations*, vol. 2, pp 8ff.   **16** Presumably this custom offered itself as an alternative to the professional habit of requiring the person registering a pedigree to sign the submitted document to make it official, a heraldic practice apparently initiated by Robert Cook, the Clarenceux king of arms who was one of the signatories on Dwnn's patent; see J.F.R. Day, 'Cooke, Robert (d.1593)', *Oxford Dictionary of National Biography* (Oxford, 2004, online edn, January 2008) [http://www.oxforddnb.com/view/article/6148, accessed 9 April 2010]. An unnumbered plate in *Heraldic Visitations* 2, following p. 334 offers facsimile versions of some of the autograph signatures accompanying Dwnn's work.

archive work on British antiquities and regarded it as an important and sci-entific contribution. Alongside the Arthurian references in the 1586 collection, for example, he usefully lists the names of the previous generations of Welsh poets, musicians, scholars and genealogists who had gone before him, 'ar rain a sgrivenysant am holl Ynys Prydain yn fangol, ag I mae llyfrau yw gweled etto gidai dysgiblon hwynt' ('and those wrote minutely of the whole Isle of Britain, as their books yet to be seen in the possession of their disciples tes-tify').[17] He then formally records another important debt: 'henwau y Pendevigion y kefais I ganthynt weled hen Regords a llyfrau y tai o grefydd, a barasai yr abadiaid ar prioriaid I kynnyll ai sgrifenu' ('names of the aristoc-racy, by whom I was permitted to see old records, and books from religious houses, that had been written and their materials collected by Abbots and Priors'). This list of the heads of notable families in Glamorgan and South Wales, who not only rescued old books after the dissolution of the monaster-ies but also offered their hospitality to him, is then followed by some more general comment on the difficulties he occasionally faced in other households where he was only granted limited opportunity to complete research on the family holdings and experienced little or no hospitality in return for his efforts. As if to underline the point, Dwnn's account of the churlish gentry behaviour he sometimes experienced on his journey through south Wales is then artfully followed by his reference to far off days and the superlative qualities of the knights then happily resident in Arthur's court.

I have discussed elsewhere how our work on the 'Imagining History' proj-ect in Belfast has demonstrated that there was considerable Welsh and met-ropolitan genealogical interest shown in the Tudor period in the versions of the British history preserved by manuscripts of the ME prose *Brut*.[18] Of par-ticular interest in this respect is the *Brut* text now extant in Aberystwyth, National Library of Wales, MS 21608, which can be linked in the fifteenth century to the Ruthyn area of Denbighshire but eventually also seems to have attracted metropolitan attention. That was largely perhaps due to the appar-ently much-publicized secretarial work among Welsh archives undertaken by the genealogical commissioners set up by Henry VII.[19] Now the evidence of similar such genealogical interests at the level of a range of different Welsh

---

17 *Heraldic Visitations*, vol. 2, pp 7–8 for the Welsh text and translation. Dwnn shows by this that he was acquainted with the works of an earlier generation of bards such as Gutuyn Owain, Ieuan Brechfa and Howel Swrdwal, and that, in turn, he was trained by an older generation of teachers, 'o brydyddion perffaith awduredig graddol oll' ('perfect poets, duly authorized, and all graduated'), that included Howel ap Sir Mathew, William Llyn and Owain Gwynedd.   18 'The Middle English Prose *Brut* and the Possibilities of Cultural Mapping', in Margaret Connolly and Linne R. Mooney (ed.), *Design and Distribution of Late Medieval Manuscripts in England* (Woodbridge, Suffolk, 2008), pp 245–260.   19 Kelly and O'Rourke, 'Culturally Mapping', pp 41–60; see also William Marx (ed.), *An English Chronicle, 1377–1461: A New Edition* (Woodbridge, Suffolk, 2003), pp xv–xxii; Matheson, *The Prose Brut*, pp 290–3.

aristocratic and gentry households (as evidenced by Dwnn's scholarly career
and the reports of it in his later Welsh-language writings) can offer useful sup-
porting evidence for this continuing early modern fascination with medieval
texts in 'the Brut tradition'. Not only does this type of evidence assist us in
understanding the likely nature of Dwnn's interests, as a Welsh-language poet,
in the illustrated genealogical diagrams and composite Latin/English version
of the British history now preserved in MS 505, but it also offers some clue
as to how he may have come across the manuscript in the first place. This
was likely to have been on one of his many different scholarly visits to Welsh
households in search of 'books from religious houses, that had been written
and their materials collected by Abbots and Priors'. It seems almost inevitable
that MS 505 started life over a century before Dwnn had commenced his visitations as one of these very books.

Dwnn's verse on the zodiac in MS 505 is signed by him and dated 1593,
but he regularly seems to have added his autograph and snippets of verse in
other manuscripts, perhaps merely as confirmation that the manuscript details
had been authenticated by him rather than, necessarily, as an ownership mark.[20]
By 1593, both the Clarenceux and Norroy kings-at-arms who had originally
authorized his role as Welsh deputy herald were dead and no attempt was
made to renew Dwnn's patent by their successors. Nevertheless, his scholarly
work on the muniments of leading families in south-west Wales continued
apace until 1613, some three years before his death. Moreover, it is clear from
the signatures attached to Dwnn's pedigrees that the heads of the households
he visited generally approved of and supported his scholarly endeavours,
although, strictly speaking, his pedigrees and the other genealogical information he painstakingly compiled during his lifetime was amateur work that had
no formal status with the heralds belonging to the College of Arms after 1592.
Dwnn's manuscript pedigrees instead seem to have remained available for sympathetic perusal and copying by other leading genealogical scholars and enthu-
siasts in Wales. Such men were enthusiastic amateur genealogists but they were
sometimes also members of the local gentry families whose lively interests in
the remaining evidence confirming their origins and pedigree scholars working with Dwnn's training and dedication had once so well served.[21]

The later history of MS 505 remains unclear for the period immediately
following Dwnn's interest in the manuscript until it arrived in Trinity College
Library in 1741 as part of bishop John Stearne's bequest (where it was
number 32 in the folio series of Madden/Stearne manuscripts).[22] The

20 See also n. 16 above.   21 For the range of surviving manuscripts containing his work, see
the bibliographical details in the *DNB* entry for Dwnn (n. 12 above).   22 Colker, *Trinity College*
2, p. 938; William O'Sullivan, 'John Madden's Manuscripts' in Vincent Kinane and Anne Walsh
(eds), *Essays on the History of Trinity College Library Dublin* (Dublin, 2000), pp 104–15; see also
John Bergin, 'Stearne (Sterne), John (1660–1745)', *Dictionary of Irish Biography*, ed. James
Mcguire and James Quinn (Cambridge, 2009) [http://dib.cambridge.org.ezproxy.qub.ac.uk/

Madden/Stearne manuscripts are so called because they include a library of items of mainly Irish genealogical, monastic and historical interest that reflect the antiquarian collecting zeal of John Madden, Trinity graduate, one-time president of the College of Physicians (an organization founded by Stearne's father), and member of the Dublin Philosophical Society. Following Madden's death in 1703, Stearne had purchased this collection from Madden's widow, augmented it with further library items, and updated Madden's earlier cata-logue, before presenting it to Trinity College. In addition to MS 505, the Stearne bequest included a number of other medieval manuscripts with sim-ilarly obscure or partially incomplete sixteenth-century provenance histories (the volumes that are now Dublin, Trinity College Library MSS 178, 314, 427, 657, 667 and 689), as well as books, or parts of books – now MSS 584, 593, 845/3 – that can with certainty be shown to have once belonged to the impressive collection assembled by James Ussher, archbishop of Armagh.[23]

The bulk of Ussher's library came to Trinity College in 1661, five years after Ussher's death and following a complex series of events both during and after Ussher's lifetime that had led to a number of different kinds of early losses to the collection.[24] Some of these losses are more susceptible than others to innocent explanation and can be attributed to such details as Ussher's habits of scholarly book lending and gift giving, for example, rather than to the vicis-situdes his books have also undeniably endured due to wanton destruction, theft and vandalism. Indeed, the presence in the Stearne bequest of items for-merly in Ussher's collection may well reflect at some level the ties that bind in the Ussher/Stearne/Madden family network: Stearne's grandmother was Archbishop Ussher's niece, and, in June 1642, during a troubled and danger-ous time in Ireland, it was Ussher who, through a personal recommendation to the master of Sidney College Cambridge, assisted Stearne's father to remove himself from Dublin at short notice without taking his Trinity degree.[25] Stearne senior matriculated at Cambridge the month after Ussher intervened, graduating BA in 1642 and MA in 1646, before finally abandon-ing Cambridge for Oxford in the face of the perceived and continuing threat to the university from Parliamentary forces. This was shortly after the time when the archbishop had similarly left Ireland with part of his extensive book collection in tow, severely inconvenienced in his own scholarly work because of the effects of the onset of civil war in both Ireland and England.

viewReadPage.do? articleId=a828, accessed 12 April 2010]. **23** Alan Ford, 'Ussher, James (1581–1656)', *Oxford Dictionary of National Biography* (Oxford, 2004, online ed, October, 2009) [http://www.oxforddnb.com/view/article/28034, accessed 10 April 2010]; John McCafferty, 'Ussher, James (1581–1656)', *Dictionary of Irish Biography* [http://dib.cambridge.org.ezproxy. qub.ac.uk/viewReadPage.do? articleId=a8774, accessed 12 April 2010]. **24** T.C. Barnard, 'The Purchase of Archbishop Ussher's Library in 1657', *Long Room* 4 (1971), 9–14; William O'Sullivan, 'Introduction', in Colker, *Trinity College* 1, pp 21–45. **25** John Bergin, 'Stearne (Sterne), John (1624–69)', *Dictionary of Irish Biography* [http://dib.cambridge.org.ezproxy.qub.

There remains the question, then, of how MS 505 might have found its way into Irish hands during these troubled times. One possibility, I think, lies in Archbishop Ussher's travels in south Wales following his decision to leave Oxford, where he had been with the king since Charles I had left London and Parliament had voted to abolish episcopy. During this period Ussher had continued to preach on the topic to congregations largely sympathetic to the royalist cause and to conduct research on the origins of the episcopate in the early church. This seems to have been part of his vain attempt to find a middle way that might yet lead the opposing parties out of the rapidly-developing religio-political impasse.[26] By February 1645 Ussher had left Oxford and travelled to Cardiff, where he was the guest of his royalist son-in-law, Sir Timothy Tyrell. He stayed there until July of that year. When the city fell to the Parliamentarians he hurriedly left and took up an invitation to continue his research in the library of the Stradling family at St Donat's Castle in Glamorganshire.[27] Although he probably had little choice in the matter, the invitation from the recently widowed wife of Sir Edward Stradling (d. 1644) enabled Ussher to extend his enforced Welsh sojourn in a pre-eminent aristocratic household that, not unnaturally, held royalist sympathies and still kept a decent library. On the journey to St Donat's, however, Ussher and his party fell foul of thieves who attacked the company and stole a number of his possessions, including many of his books and manuscripts, most of which were subsequently recovered after a local appeal for their safe return. Ussher's biographer notes that 'in the [St Donat's] library he made many choice collections of the British or Welsh Antiquities' and for much of this time Ussher must surely have had his pick of such volumes to aid his recuperation from serious illness, assist him in his studies, and simply pass the time.[28] By the end of that year – truly Ussher's *annus horribilis* – parliament had ordered his arrest, together with Bishops John Bramhall of Derry and Roger Mainwaring of St David's, on charges of attempting to draw the inhabitants of Glamorganshire

ac.uk/viewReadPage.do? articleId=a8286, accessed 12 April 2010].   26 For Ussher's spirited defence of episcopacy in these years see Alan Ford, *James Ussher, Theology, History and Politics in Early-Modern Ireland and England* (Oxford, 2007), esp. pp 223–56.   27 He was invited to St Donat's by Mary, daughter of Sir Thomas Mansell of Margam and the recently-widowed wife of Sir Edward Stradling, speculator and royalist army officer, for whom see Lloyd Bowen, 'Stradling, Sir Edward, second baronet (bap. 1600, d. 1644)', *Oxford Dictionary of National Biography*, online edn [http://www.oxforddnb.com/view/article/26625, accessed 14 April 2010].   28 *The Life of the Most Reverend Father in God, James Ussher ... with a Collection of Three Hundred Letters*, ed. R. Parr (1686), p. 60. The St Donat's library had long been treated as a lending library for Stradling family acquaintances and visiting antiquaries with interests in chronicles, genealogies, monastic records, antiquities, heraldry and literature; see G.C.G. Thomas, 'The Stradling Library at St Donat's, Glamorgan', *National Library of Wales Journal* 24 (1985–86), 402–19 (Ussher's scholarly reading of the Stradling copy of Trevisa's translation of Higden's *Polychronicon* is described, p. 405); R.A. Griffiths, 'The rise of the Stradlings of St Donat's ', *Morgannwg* 7 (1963), 15–47.

away from their obedience to Parliament.[29] Although he was never arrested and charged with the offence, Ussher spent his remaining time in Wales as, technically, both an outlaw at large and also a scholarly house guest and book borrower at St Donat's.

Sixty years previously, the hospitality of an earlier generation of Stradling family members had similarly caught Llewys Dwnn's imagination when the wandering Welsh scholar reported that he had found at St Donat's a hospitable and supportive environment in which to consult family records and old books from ancient religious houses. As such, the name of Sir Edward Stradling (d. 1609) heads Dwnn's 1586 honour roll that records by name the aristocratic hosts for his Glamorgan visitations.[30] It takes little further imagination to conjecture that it was probably in the Stradling library collection at St Donat's, but under very different personal circumstances, that both Llewys Dwnn and Sir James Ussher caught their first glimpses of the composite and nicely illustrated medieval volume on the British history that we now know as MS 505.

One further major episode in the seventeenth-century history of MS 505 requires some attention since it undeniably links the attractive townscape images in the manuscript to the history of the town of Belfast.[31] Such links to the latter are certainly implied by the sequence of records relating to members of the Chichester family that has been reasonably carefully added to MS 505 by a single anonymous later seventeenth-century hand. The list occupies p. 2 of the manuscript, which had been originally left blank, but the page is now filled by a record, firstly, of the marriage of Edward, Lord Viscount Chichester, to Anne, daughter and sole heir of John Coperstone of Eggsford, esq. in 1605 (3 James 1). There then follows five birth records: for Arthur Chichester, the aforementioned Edward's son and heir, who is now viscount and earl of Donegall, born 1606 (4 James 1); Elizabeth Chichester, married to Sir William Wrey, born 1607 (5 James 1); Mary Chichester, married to Thomas Wise, esq., born 1608 (6 James 1); John Chichester, esq., born 1609 (7 James 1), and Edward Chichester, born 1611 (9 James 1).

---

29 William M. Abbott, 'James Ussher and the "Ussherian" Episcopacy, 1640–1656: the Primate and His Reduction Manuscript', *Albion* 22 (1990), 237–59 (pp 254–5). 30 R.A. Griffiths, 'Stradling, Sir Edward (c.1529–1609)', *Oxford Dictionary of National Biography* (Oxford, 2004, online ed, January 2008) [http://www.oxforddnb.com/view/article/26624, accessed 14 April 2010]. See also Welsh text and translation in *Heraldic Visitations* 2, pp 7–8. Also named in Dwnn's Glamorgan list is Sir Edward Mawnsel (doubtless an ancestor of Mary, widow of Sir Edward Stradling who played host to Ussher during his 1645–46 visit to St Donat's), together with Sir William Havard of Cardiff and Sir John Gams; also Rhys ap Meurig of Cottrel, Ieuan ap Siankin of the Gladlys, and Anthony Powell of Tir yr Iarll, all classified as gents. 31 I am here building on the brief comments in Thompson, 'Middle English Prose *Brut*', pp 257–58. The standard history is J. Bardon, *A History of Ulster* (Belfast, 1992), where members of the Chichester family are referred to passim.

The Chichester family were originally from Devon and the birth records in MS 505 identify, preserve, and perhaps even celebrate, the West Country associations of some family members to a larger narrative of Ulster Plantation possession and ownership. Edward, Lord Viscount Chichester (d. 1648), was the brother of Arthur (first Baron Chichester, lord deputy of Ireland from 1605 to 1616, and scourge of the Irish rebels in Ulster).[32] Edward married Anne Coplestone, the daughter of John Coplestone of Eggesford, Chulmleigh, Devon, and was the father of Arthur Chichester, first earl of Donegall, also Elizabeth, Mary, John and Edward, all mentioned in the family record in the note. His eldest son, Arthur, was dead by 1675, after which the reference to his current status as earl and now viscount would not have made much sense. The earldom of Donegall was granted to Arthur by Charles I in March 1647.[33] And a *terminus ante quem* of 1648 can be established for the note in MS 505 by the fact that Arthur officially assumed the title of viscount on his father's death in 1648, when he became the second Viscount Chichester of Carrickfergus and third Baron Chichester of Belfast.

Mary, Edward's sister, returned to her family roots when she married Sir Thomas Wise of Mount Wise, Plymouth, High Sheriff for Devon, while Elizabeth, Edward's eldest sister, became the wife of Sir William Wrey. Wrey was originally from Trebitch in Cornwall but became MP for Belfast in 1639.[34] He worked closely with Henry Le Squire (d.1643), probably originally from St David's in Exeter, but now a wealthy, energetic and prominent new Belfast resident and loyal Chichester supporter. Coincidentally, his will (proved 1643) provides us with another fascinating glimpse of just how generous Le Squire was to the Chichester family members named in the birth record in MS 505. The relevant sections of it read as follows:

> ... Item. I bequeath to my most honored Lord and master, Edward Lord Viscount Chichester, and to my most honored Lady Mary Chichester, to either of them, a piece of plate of the value of £10; to Mr John Chichester and Mr Edward Chichester a piece of plate of £5 a peece, to be raised out of my goods or any other plate remaining in Isle of Man.

32 John Mccavitt, 'Chichester, Arthur, Baron Chichester (1563–1625)', *Oxford Dictionary of National Biography* [http://www.oxforddnb.com/view/article/5274, accessed 9 April 2010]; Raymond Gillespie, 'Chichester, Arthur (1563–1625)', *Dictionary of Irish Biography*, ed. James Mcguire and James Quinn (Cambridge, 2009) [http://dib.cambridge.org.ezproxy.qub.ac.uk/viewReadPage.do? articleId=a1642, accessed 12 April 2010]. 33 J.M. Rigg, 'Chichester, Arthur, first Earl of Donegal (1606–1675)', rev. R.M. Armstrong, *Oxford Dictionary of National Biography* (Oxford, 2004, online edn, January 2008) [http://www.oxforddnb.com/view/article/5275, accessed 9 April 2010]. 34 George Benn, *A History of the Town of Belfast from the Earliest Times to the Close of the Eighteenth Century*, 2 vols (London and Belfast, 1877, repr. Belfast, 2008), 1, pp 94–5, 238.

Item. I give to Mrs Mary Chichester my amatist ring, and to Mrs
Elizabeth Chichester my silver *aqua vite* cupp, and to her daughter Mrs
Mary a ring of the value of 20*s*.

Item. I give to the Corporation of Belfast the Remainder due upon
an account of my disbursements for their Maces, Seale, and Coat of
Armes, and will that the Mace I have bee delivered to the Sufferane
for the Towne's Use …

Le Squire's extraordinary generosity to the corporation of Belfast is also quite
understandable since he had prospered in this brave new urban environment.
As one of Belfast's most prominent citizens he had been elected town sover-
eign in 1635, 1636, and again in 1639; Le Squire also served as agent and
seneschal to Edward, first Viscount Chichester, and was the lawyer responsible for securing the disputed Ulster titles and estates of the Chichester family
during the unsettled period leading up to and following the 1641 rebellion.[35]
In short, Le Squire's whole career in Belfast displays his loyalty and service
to the corporation of Belfast and to the Chichester family members who were
steadily securing the Belfast garrison as their power base through the growth
and development of their new plantation town.

One would obviously like to make some closer connection than has yet
proved possible between this record of Chichester family power and influence
based largely on the new garrison town emerging on the shores of the Lagan
and the mid-seventeenth-century whereabouts of MS 505 before it had
become part of the Madden/Stearne bequest to the library at Trinity College.
Given the likelihood that Ussher may have consulted MS 505 in Wales and
borrowed it from the Stradling library at St Donat's shortly before the
Chichester family birth records had been inserted in the volume, his subsequent ownership of the book seems a strong possibility.[36] Likewise, one can
speculate that among the extensive network of scholarly associates and family
members who had access to Ussher's books both during and after his lifetime,
there was surely someone who would have appreciated making a link between
the Chichester family members recorded in the note on p. 2 of MS 505 and
the series of medieval English townscapes imaginatively included in the decorative roundels in part A of the book. These acted as the facilitative 'eyes of
memory' for later scholarly readers aware of the genealogical significances of
remote British history, and may just possibly have held some iconic signifi-

35 Ibid., vol. 1, pp 193, 201–2, 231–33, 238–40, 242. The extracts from Le Squire's will can be
found on p. 239 and the details of the mace he donated to the town corporation are given on
pp 231–2. For his prominent place in the list of burgesses who served as sovereigns see 'The
Names of the Sovereigns and Burgesses of Belfast since the Year 1612', *The Belfast Monthly
Magazine* 4:20 (1810), 176–80.   36 For one of Ussher's notebooks that stayed in Wales, see
William O'Sullivan, 'Two Clogher Constitutions', *Clogher Record* 15 (1996), 145–55.

cance for seventeenth-century readers, permitting them to reflect on the continuing impact of English urban settlement on their present lives.[37] The cultural mapping processes that have allowed me to reach this climactic point in
this discussion will certainly also allow me to characterize MS 505, for perhaps the first time, as a medieval book that enjoyed a fairly perilous journey
from its original point of origin to its current location in Trinity College
Library. If its twenty-first-century readers can accept some of the imaginative
possibilities discussed in this essay, then a truly extraordinary Irish dimension
can now be added to the evidence of English and Welsh interest in the multi-
layered Latin and vernacular confection of religious, classical, medieval British
and English history that MS 505 uniquely represents.

37 In this sense, both John Madden and John Stearne junior – seventeenth-century scholars,
book collectors, book borrowers, and book cataloguers, and sometime Ulster residents with access
to books in Ussher's collection – would seem the most obvious but not the only possible persons who might have shared this inclination.

Wordsworth and Chaucer's *Manciple's Tale*

KAREN HODDER

It might seem strange to be offering a tribute to a distinguished scholar of the Middle Ages on the subject of Wordsworth. However, it is well-known that John Scattergood's reading, interests and expertise are phenomenally wide, as are his sympathies; and he encouraged my growing enthusiasm for nineteenth-century medievalism before it became the current rather fashionable field of research. Other reasons why this choice of subject might prove an apt one will emerge in the course of the following essay, including that commitment to the politics of art which have informed so much of what both the Romantic poet, Wordsworth, and the modern critic, Scattergood, have written.

Unusually for the period in which he was born, Wordsworth survived with all his wits about him until he was eighty years old, and outlived the majority of his family, friends and contemporary writers. Inevitably, over his long adult life, his political opinions changed considerably, moving, as often happens, from left to right. The radical thinker who could calmly contemplate the execution of the French monarch in the cause of a greater social good became the energetic campaigner for the election to parliament of Lord Lowther's Tory sons and a close friend of the Tory art-patron Sir George Beaumont. Given the existence of *The Prelude*, Wordsworth's great autobiographical account of 'the growth of a poet's mind', as it is subtitled, there is less excuse for attaching him exclusively to one of those symbolic categories of age so popular in the Middle Ages than almost any other figure in the history of English poetry. In the mass of critical writing devoted to the analysis of that 'growth' Wordsworth scholars, who have naturally been more concerned with the contemporary context, have so far given scant attention to a significant aspect of Wordsworth's poetic development, namely his respect for Chaucer and lifelong, if intermittent, involvement with one whom he described in 1810 as the 'Morning Star' of English literature.[1]

A brief foray into Wordsworth's correspondence and critical utterances soon justifies any generalization about his admiration for the medieval poet, and many references to his affinity with Chaucer can be traced via Caroline Spurgeon's *Five Hundred Years of Chaucer Criticism and Allusion, 1357–1900*.[2]

---

1 *The Friend*, 20, (4 January 1810), 305, cited in W.J.B. Owen and J. Worthington Smyser (eds), *The Prose Works of William Wordsworth* (Oxford, 1974), 3 vols, II, p. 12. 2 Caroline F.E. Spurgeon, *Five Hundred Years of Chaucer Criticism and Allusion, 1357–1900*, 3 vols (New York, 1960). Spurgeon makes it clear that, apart from Byron, Wordsworth's distinguished literary peers, including Coleridge, shared his enthusiasm for Chaucer. Spurgeon, I, p. lxiii. Only a few of

Chaucer's name is frequently linked by Wordsworth with those of Shakespeare and Milton and invariably in laudatory terms: for instance 'My love and reverence for Chaucer are unbounded' he exclaims in a typical letter written to Henry Crabb Robinson in 1840.[3]

Nor was Wordsworth's interest in medieval writers limited to Chaucer: a number of medieval texts, including ballads, romances and political poetry, feature in his library and were therefore probably read by him during the period at the beginning of the Nineteenth Century when he was also studying Chaucer. His copy of *Percy's Reliques* was acquired in Hamburg while he was not at all well off and was therefore presumably of some personal significance.[4]

The basis of Wordsworth's admiration for Chaucer will be touched on later, but suffice it to say here that such praise was not just a matter of ritual genuflection before an ancient shrine, nor was appreciation always expressed in solemn language:

> Beside the pleasant mills of Trompington
> I laughed with Chaucer; in the hawthorn shade
> Heard him, while birds were warbling, tell his tales
> Of amorous passion ...   *The Prelude*, 1805, Book III, 276–9.[5]

In this way Wordsworth describes with hindsight how he enjoyed reading Chaucer's *Reeve's Tale* during his undergraduate years at Cambridge between 1787 and 1791. Duncan Wu has demonstrated that the poet may, indeed, have had the opportunity to peruse Chaucer's works before 1787 in the 'black letter' edition of 1561 (usually known as 'Stowe's edition'), in Hawkshead School library.[6] Wu remarks that he sees 'no serious reason to doubt [Wordsworth's] claim' that he also read Chaucer at Cambridge, though it is improbable that the circumstances were exactly as Wordsworth recollects them in *The Prelude*.[7] However, although it is unlikely that Wordsworth's acquaintance with Chaucer was very profound at this point, it is nevertheless striking that he chose to link the medieval poet's name with the narrative of his own poetic development.

Most significantly of all, though, Wordsworth's response to reading Chaucer's poetry can be examined via that group of translations which he made and revised over a period of nearly forty years. They were:

them, however, expressed that enthusiasm as actively as Wordsworth.   3 Ernest de Selincourt (ed.), *The Letters of William and Dorothy Wordsworth: The Later Years 1821–1853* (Oxford, 1978), 4 vols, revised and ed. Alan G. Hill, VII, Part 4, p. 11.   4 Chesney L. Shaver and Alice C. Shaver, *Wordsworth's Library, A Catalogue* (New York, 1979), pp 113, 149, 198, 285.   5 Jonathan Wordsworth, M. H. Abrams and Stephen Gill (eds), *The Prelude, 1799, 1805, 1830* (London, 1979), p. 104.   6 Duncan Wu, *Wordsworth's Reading, 1770–1803* (Cambridge, 1993), pp 27–8. 7 See Stephen Gill, *William Wordsworth, A Life* (Oxford, 1990), p. 7.

The Prioress's Tale
Dove Cottage MS13; DC MS35; marginalia, Folger Library edition of Anderson, Coffman A56.
Published 1820,1827,1832, 1836, 1845, 1850.
The Manciple's Prologue and *Tale*
DC MS13; DC MS 36; DC MS 89
Not published during Wordsworth's lifetime.
The Cuckoo and the Nightingale
DC MS13
Published 1841,1842,1845,1846,1850
Troilus and Cressida (*Troilus and Criseyde*), extract, Book V, 519–686.
DC MS 24
Published 1841, 1845, 1846, 1850.

Apart from this evidence of Wordsworth's serious interest in Chaucer, we know from various sources, and notably from the journals of Dorothy Wordsworth, that family readings of Chaucer's and other medieval poetry took place, and that none of them was apparently daunted by the original language. For example, on 26 December 1801, the day after Dorothy's birthday, there was a reading of *The Miller's Tale*.[8] *The Knight's Tale* was another favourite, of which no manuscript translation by Wordsworth survives.[9] Entries in Dorothy Wordsworth's Grasmere Journal during December 1801 and February and April 1802 suggest a period of intense and steady work by Wordsworth on these translations, often taken up at night after a day's walking or visiting, which would have necessitated the use (and expense) of artificial light.[10] Although William habitually composed and revised his poems during his walks, the Chaucer translations would, of necessity, be made indoors: quite apart from avoiding the winter cold, a translator usually needs to have his base text near at hand.[11]

Study of Wordsworth's work on Chaucer has been immeasurably facilitated by the publication of Bruce Graver's scholarly edition for Cornell University Press of all the poet's surviving translations of Chaucer and Virgil.[12] Graver's edition includes reading texts, transcriptions, textual variants and facsimiles of manuscripts. For the first time, Chaucer's originals can be compared with a definitive collection of Wordsworth material that offers more than the piece-

8 Pamela Woof (ed.), *The Grasmere and Alfoxden Journals* (Oxford, 2002), p. 53.   9 Ibid., p. 137.   10 For a succinct summary of the attention given to the Chaucer-related activity see Bruce Graver (ed.), *Translations of Chaucer and Virgil by William Wordsworth* (Ithaca, 1998), pp 11–12.   11 The one used by Wordsworth was rather large and heavy, namely the first volume of Robert Anderson's *A Complete Edition of the Poets of Great Britain*, 13 vols (London, 1793). Two copies of this work associated with Wordsworth survive: see Wu, *Wordsworth's Reading*, p. 4.   12 Bruce Graver (ed.), *Translations of Chaucer and Virgil by William Wordsworth* (Ithaca, 1998).

meal insights into the nineteenth-century poet's treatment of his predecessor's work, which were all that was possible before the Cornell edition.

A glance at some of the MSS, particularly those of *The Prioress's* and *Manciple's Tales*, shows how difficult Graver's own task must have been, especially when it is considered that the editor had then to compare these, the majority of which are fragmentary and in a variety of hands, with other copies, printed and reprinted versions and marginal annotations in editions of Chaucer used by Wordsworth and in Wordsworth's own copies of his poems.

Wordsworth was an inveterate reviser of everything he composed, transcribed or had copied by others, greatly complicating an editor's task. The 'reading texts' of Wordsworth's translations provided by Graver are based on 'the first form of the poem published under Wordsworth's supervision or ... the earliest finished version of the poem' and it is those texts which are quoted below.[13]

Before proceeding any further I should perhaps comment, both on my own use of the term 'translation' for Wordsworth's versions of Chaucer's poetry and, briefly, on some general issues connected with the kind of exercise they represent.

The relatively recent growth of what might be called 'translation studies' has established translation as a capacious term, applicable to everything from metaphrase to imitation.[14] 'Translating', is, in fact, the term which Dorothy Wordsworth used when describing her brother's work on Chaucer;[15] though, later on, he and other contemporaries tended to use the term 'modernization'.[16]

The genre of translation, which Reuben Brower has described as 'the unacknowledged half-sister of "true" literature',[17] has continued to attract serious scholarly and creative attention until the present day; as well it might, when the teaching of linguistically 'difficult' texts, including those in Latin and Greek, Old and Middle English, and even the works of Shakespeare, is under siege in our secondary and tertiary educational institutions. Although it seems to be taken for granted that new generations are quite capable of absorbing idioms from the demotic of a diverse contemporary linguistic culture, there is an assumption that Chaucer is 'too difficult': that because he sometimes uses unfamiliar words, or familiar words in a different sense from us, his original poetry will be incomprehensible or, at best, misleading to a modern lay reader.[18]

---

13 Ibid., p. xxv.   14 Reuben A. Brower (ed.), *On Translation* (Cambridge, MA, 1959), p. 5.   15 Woof, *Grasmere and Alfoxden Journals*, p. 45.   16 As in the anthology by various hands, R.H. Horne (ed.), *The Poems of Geoffrey Chaucer Moderniz'd* (London, 1841), of which more below, p. 150.   17 Brower, *On Translation*, p. 4.   18 Peter Ackroyd uses arguments like these in the 'Note on the Text' of his own recent lively prose rendering of *The Canterbury Tales*; and he omits Chaucer's 'Tale of Melibee' and 'Parson's Tale' 'in the belief they will not be missed'. Such a decision seems incompatible with his wish 'to intimate or express the true nature of the original.' *The Canterbury Tales by Geoffrey Chaucer* (London, 2009), pp xix–xxii.

There are, of course, also differing views about the value of the exercise of translation. Brower claimed that:

> A translation which was made by a master and which was markedly successful in its time, offers an excellent subject for seeing how a writer responds to alien literary traditions and how he domesticates them by adjudicating between the claims of past and present.[19]

This might seem to apply appropriately to Wordsworth's work on Chaucer. 'Domesticate', however, is a troubling word, implying as it does something tamer, something nearer to home – the very opposite of that positive experience of the 'alien' which is often the *raison d'être* of literary experience.

More recently, those who have examined translations of Chaucer's works in particular have focused more attention on the potential *audience* for such translations. It is suggested that that is more probably being targeted under the influence of the sort of educational pressures just referred to, than out of the 'love and reverence' alluded to by Wordsworth.[20] Steve Ellis, who is concerned with twentieth-century modernizers and translators seeking a wider, and usually younger readership for Chaucer, concludes gloomily that translating his works merely 'provides a substitute for Chaucer rather than a bridge to him.' In that critic's opinion few translators have any claim to being considered a 'master', let alone a master poet.[21]

In the space available here it is not possible to invite the reader to judge the quality of Wordsworth's translations at length. Instead of detailed textual analysis, therefore, this essay offers a kind of literary history of those translations, together with some comment on what, in my opinion, they meant to Wordsworth. This second point is, of course, the more significant.

In homage to our dedicatee, John Scattergood, I shall pay closest attention to *The Cuckoo and the Nightingale* and *The Manciple's Tale*. He edited the first of these poems for his Master's degree, when he successfully attributed it to Sir John Clanvowe and re-titled it *The Boke of Cupid*;[22] but in Wordsworth's time the author of the poem was, of course, still thought to be Chaucer. *The Manciple's Tale* is the text which I shall be connecting with a story about the growth of Wordsworth's 'responsibilities'.

---

19 Brower, *On Translation*, p. 5. **20** Steve Ellis, *Chaucer at Large: The Poet in the Modern Imagination* (Minneapolis, 2000). He considers that translators should be honest about their intended audience: 'you cannot at the same time write for those unable to read Chaucer's original text while claiming to find fresh generations of readers for it' (p. 99). Cf. Ackroyd's view that 'translation can be a form of liberation, releasing an older work into the contemporary world and thereby infusing it with new life' (Ackroyd, *The Canterbury Tales*, p. xix). **21** Ellis, *Chaucer at Large*, pp 98–120. Ellis is least enthusiastic about prose translations of Chaucer (p. 103). **22** V.J. Scattergood (ed.), *The Works of Sir John Clanvowe* (Cambridge, 1965).

In 1974 John Scattergood published a fine article about Chaucer's Maniple and his tale which, like many of his essays on Chaucer and other medieval and renaissance texts, led to a re-evaluation of that poem and has affected its interpretation ever since.[23] The Manciple's is also a tale with which Scattergood's name is associated via his edition and notes on this text for the Riverside edition of Chaucer.[24]

Beginning with a brief prefatory context for Wordsworth's translations: Wordsworth belongs to a long tradition of attempting to render Chaucer more accessible via translation and modernization, a tradition of which he himself was quite aware. Betsy Bowden's collection of eighteenth-century modernizations of *The Canterbury Tales,* for example, makes it possible to compare Wordsworth's with those of many of his lesser-known predecessors, including Andrew Jackson and William Lipscomb (who both attempted *The Manciple's Tale*).[25] The latter also tackled Wordsworth's best-known Chaucerian subject, *The Prioress's Prologue* and *Tale.*

Wordsworth's correspondence shows that he was extremely conscious of the precedent set by Dryden, and that he felt he was aiming at something different. For example, in a letter to Henry Crabb Robinson dated 23 January 1840, written when revising his Chaucer translations, Wordsworth summed up his attitude to those of Dryden: 'Dryden and Pope have treated these originals admirably and in a manner of their own, which, though good in itself is not Chaucers' (sic).[26] This is, in fact, one of the politest of Wordsworth's numerous allusions to Dryden's translations, a poet of whom in general he disapproves.[27]

Three of the most important aspects of Dryden's attitude toward the medieval poet were his acceptance of Chaucer's status as English poetry's Homer or Virgil; his belief that Chaucer's language had become inaccessible to the majority of readers, and his notorious judgment that Chaucer was 'a rough diamond' in need of polishing, a poet overtaken by the progressive sophistication of the English language. If Wordsworth fervently accepted the first of these premises, he certainly disagreed with the others, and he and Coleridge evidently concurred, given the observation offered in the Preface to *Lyrical Ballads* (1800) that Chaucer spoke a language 'universally intelligible'[28]

23 V.J. Scattergood, 'The Manciple's Manner of Speaking', *Essays in Criticism,* 24:2 (1974), 124–46.   **24** *The Riverside Chaucer,* gen. ed. Larry D. Benson (Boston, 1987), pp 952–4.   **25** Betsy Bowden (ed.), *Eighteenth Century Modernizations from 'The Canterbury Tales'* (Rochester, NY, 1991), pp 156–8, 196–8, 241–4.   **26** Edith J. Morley (ed.), *The Correspondence of Henry Crabb Robinson with the Wordsworth Circle* (Oxford, 1927), 2 vols, I, p. 397.   **27** See, for example, Wordsworth's letter to Sir Walter Scott of 7 November 1805. Ernest de Selincourt (ed.), *The Letters of William and Dorothy Wordsworth,* I, revised Chester L. Shaver (Oxford, 1967), p. 611; and to the same recipient, 18 January 1808: 'Chaucer I think he has entirely spoiled, even wantonly deviating from his great original, and always for the worse.' *Letters,* ed. de Selincourt, II, Part 1, revised Mary Moorman (Oxford, 1969), p. 191.   **28** W.J.B. Owen and J. Worthington

which seems to have been based on a new optimism about the prospect of being comprehended if one were to preserve words such as 'eke', 'lemman' or 'ywis', as Wordsworth does in his early translations of Chaucer, but does not use elsewhere in his poetry.

Wordsworth's resistance to the theory of Chaucer's unintelligibility may have been influenced by the recognition that advances had been made by eighteenth-century philological and editorial scholars. Urry's edition of 1721 and Tyrwhitt's, published 1775–8, were both equipped with glossaries; and Spurgeon credits Tyrwhitt, in particular, with helping to disperse much of the ignorance about Chaucer's versification.[29] Middle English grammar, too, had begun to be analyzed and better understood. By 1820 Wordsworth may also have become aware that a revaluation of Chaucer's poetry was taking place in London literary circles and that Leigh Hunt's views about the manner in which it should be modernized largely coincided with his own.[30]

Graver points out that Wordsworth's policy of translating is:

> radically different from his predecessors: rather than letting Chaucer speak contemporary English [he] constructs a self-consciously archaic poetic idiom, one that never lets his readers forget that they are reading a medieval poem. He is experimenting with modern English, bending it out of its natural shape, to preserve as fully as possible the genuine language of Chaucer.[31]

This might seem paradoxical, yet it is entirely understandable if one sees Wordsworth as being engaged with Chaucer in order to enrich his own poetic idiom as well as interpreting Chaucer's.

In his article on *The Manciple's Prologue* and *Tale* John Scattergood opened our eyes to their political potential and, even more strikingly, to the verbal subtlety of Chaucer's writing, claiming that 'Chaucer is particularly interested in the Manciple because the Manciple's ways of using words bears some relation to the strategies he himself uses as a poet'.[32] Similarly, for Wordsworth and Coleridge, Chaucer was perceived as exemplifying certain practices, and these they were ideologically committed to adopting in their own poetry, as stated in the 1800 Preface to *Lyrical Ballads*, published just before Wordsworth began making his translations. There Chaucer was specifically invoked in support of the declared aim 'to imitate and, as far as is possible, to adopt the very language of men'; and that famous note qualified a passage in which Chaucer's style, by implication, was associated with other merits such as 'simple and unelaborated expressions' and 'a language arising out of

Smyser (eds), *The Prose Works of William Wordsworth* (Oxford, 1974), 3 vols, I, p. 130. **29** Spurgeon, *Five Hundred Years of Chaucer Criticism*, I, pp liv–v. **30** Graver, *Translations of Chaucer*, p. 17. **31** Ibid., p. 11. **32** Scattergood, 'The Manciple's Manner of Speaking', 143.

repeated experience and regular feelings'; and was contrasted with that of
poets who 'separate themselves from the sympathies of men, and indulge in
arbitrary and capricious habits of expression'.[33]

The motives behind Wordsworth's selection of particular Chaucer poems
for translation remain a matter for speculation. However, as well as repre-
senting a variety of subject-matter, genre and tone which shows Wordsworth
exploring Chaucer's full verbal range, they also suggest that Wordsworth was
interested in metrical experimentation. For example, he renders this original
stanza from Chaucer's *Troilus*:

> O sterre, of which I lost have al the light,
> With herte soor wel ought I to biwaille
> That evere derk in torment, nyght by nyght,
> Toward my deth with wynd in steere I saille,
> For which the tenthe nyght, if that I faille
> The gydyng of thi bemes bright an houre,
> My ship and me Caribdis wol devoure.
>
> Chaucer *Troilus and Criseyde*, Book V, (638–44)[34]

as

> O Star, of which I lost have all the light,
> With a sore heart well ought I to bewail,
> That ever dark in torment, night by night,
> Toward my death with wind I steer and sail;
> For which upon the tenth night if thou fail
> With thy bright beams to guide me but one hour,
> My ship and me Charybdis will devour.
>
> Wordsworth *Troilus and Cressida*, (120–6)[35]

Here we see Wordsworth characteristically attempting to preserve Chaucer's
original verse-form and word order as well as much of his vocabulary. What
is more, the verse form is one of Chaucer's most complex: *Troilus*, *The
Prioress's Tale* and *The Cuckoo and the Nightingale* are all composed in rime
royal. This is a very unusual metre in English poetry, especially in post-Tudor
periods; and it is not commonly used by Wordsworth. However, in 1801, the
year in which he first experimented with translating Chaucer, Wordsworth
published *Resolution and Independence* (also known as *The Leech Gatherer*) in
which he, too, uses rime royal. Anthony Conran has attributed this usage to
an 'unusual interest in stanza forms' and detects the influence of *The Cuckoo*

---

33 Owen and Smyser (eds), *The Prose Works of William Wordsworth* I, p. 130.   34 *The Riverside Chaucer*, pp 568–9.   35 Graver, *Translations of Chaucer*, p. 59.

and the Nightingale on other aspects of Wordsworth's poem, arguing that the 'medieval influence' of Wordsworth's courtly Chaucerian translation extends to 'the dialectical approach to the construction of *Resolution and Independence*'.[36]

Wordsworth used a base version of *The Cuckoo and the Nightingale* which included the *Envoy to Alisoun,* only later identified by Chaucer's editors as a separate poem, although it looks as though Wordsworth was alert enough to recognize the error, since one manuscript of his translation has 'Finis' at the end of Clanvowe's poem.[37]

As well as the assistance which his attention to Chaucer gave to the 'growth of a poet's mind', I would argue that Wordsworth had a considerable emotional investment in Chaucer's poetry. His attachment to it would have been encouraged by those of his many friends and acquaintances who were also enthusiastic about aspects of medievalism: Coleridge, Southey, Keats, Leigh Hunt, Sir Walter Scott, Sir George Beaumont, Henry Reed, Benjamin Haydon – to name only a few.

Of the two copies of Anderson's edition of Chaucer which we know Wordsworth used, one, belonging to Coleridge and annotated by both of them, would have been available to Wordsworth from 1797 when he moved to Alfoxden.[38] The other, inscribed in his own hand 'William Wordsworth from his dear brother John' reflects the literary tastes which William shared with his favourite brother, a sea-captain, who read the medieval poet's works on many of his voyages before 1805 when, to the intense grief of the Wordsworth family, he was drowned; its poignant existence is suggestive of the special place Chaucer seems to have had in the brothers' hearts, as well as that which John Wordsworth had in William's.[39]

My conclusion concerns the more cheerful story of Wordsworth's relationship with *The Manciple's Tale*. He began translating this in 1801 and probably finished and revised it in 1840.[40] It was the only one of his Chaucer pieces not published in his lifetime, and there were particular reasons for this.

---

36 Anthony E.M. Conran, 'The Dialectic of Experience: a Study of Wordsworth's *Resolution and* Independence', *PMLA* 75 (1960), 66–74 (68). Conran's case would appear to be strengthened by the fact that Elizabeth Barrett seems to have derived a model of Chaucer translation practice from Wordsworth, like him exploring the unusual verse forms used by the early poet in order to ally herself to the famous English classical tradition represented by Chaucer; and adopting a similar style of paraphrase to Wordworth's. See Karen Hodder, 'Elizabeth Barrett and the Middle Ages' Woeful Queens', in Leslie J. Workman and Kathleen Verduin (eds), *Medievalism in England II*, Studies in Medievalism 7 (Cambridge, 1995), pp 105–30.   37 Wordsworth did not work directly from medieval manuscripts, of course, and his base text, Anderson's edition, is at fault here. However, by lucky chance, variant readings of *The Cuckoo and the Nightingale* came his way and he was able to improve later reprintings of his translation with their aid. See Graver, *Translations of Chaucer*, pp 23–5.   38 Wu, *Wordsworth's Reading*, p. 4.   39 Ibid.   40 Graver, *Translations of* Chaucer, pp 13–14.

In 1839 Wordsworth was approached by an oleaginous admirer called Thomas Powell and asked to contribute to a collection of Chaucerian translations aimed at a popular market. This was eventually published in 1841 under the title *The Poems of Geoffrey Chaucer Moderniz'd*. I have published an account of this production elsewhere so will simply summarize a few points here.[41]

Chaucer Moderniz'd is not without interest for a twenty-first century reader, not least because Wordsworth, Leigh Hunt and Elizabeth Barrett were among the contributors, and Wordsworth approved of its general aims. Unfortunately, however, it appeared at the moment when the fashion for 'modernising' Chaucer was about to yield place to good, scholarly editions of his original texts, accompanied by explanatory notes and essays (although Wordsworth himself would die nearly fifty years before the publication of Skeat's edition). And *Chaucer Moderniz'd* was almost bound to fail from a number of causes.

Thomas Powell seems to have been trying to inveigle Wordsworth into 'fronting' this enterprise via its editorship, or at least by inducing him to make a major contribution to it, and was obliged to apologise for overreaching himself in this respect.[42] But it was too late in the day for Wordsworth to want to be involved in a major project and eventually the collection was edited by R. H. Horne, 'a gentleman unknown to me', Wordsworth said.[43] However, Wordsworth promised to send Powell all his previous Chaucer translations apart from his *Prioress's Tale* which had already been published in all collected editions of his poems.[44] The translation of the previously unpublished *Manciple's Tale*, however, was to prove a problem.

Chaucer's tale describes how Phoebus' tame, white, speaking crow witnesses its master's wife's adultery and reports this in the most tactless and indelicate terms, provoking Phoebus to slay his wife in a rage, only immediately to regret his action bitterly and banish the crow with curses, which is why all crows henceforth have been black. A Chaucerian tale of sex and violence, no less – and about to be offered to a popular Victorian audience, of all people.[45] The issues raised by sex, in particular, gave all those contributors

41 Karen Hodder, '"Dispersing the Atmosphere of Antiquity and Attempting the Impossible": R.H. Horne's *Geoffrey Chaucer Moderniz'd*', *Book Collector* 51:2 (2002), 222–39.   42 Graver, *Translations of Chaucer*, pp 19–22.   43 Letter to Henry Reed, 13 January 1841: Leslie Nathan Broughton (ed.), *Wordsworth and Reed, The Poet's Correspondence with his American Editor, 1836–1850* (New York, 1933), p. 43. Horne was not unknown to the contemporary poetry-reading public, however: see Ann Blainey, *The Farthing Poet* (London, 1968).   44 This suggests that Wordsworth himself considered the poem had merit, despite its adverse early critical reception. 45 It seems likely, from the cheap and compact format of *Chaucer Moderniz'd* that it was hoped it might be adopted by the popular lending libraries such as Mudie's (founded in 1840). Powell, in his correspondence with Wordsworth, refers to aiming at a 'family Chaucer.' Unpublished letter of 23 October 1840, at Dove Cottage Library, Grasmere, quoted with the kind permis-

who had chosen to translate some of Chaucer's fabliaux quite a headache, and necessitated some special pleading from Horne in his Preface in order to include them.[46] The consequence for *Chaucer Moderniz'd* was bowdlerization.

Wordsworth's tussles with the translation of some lines in *The Manciple's Tale* show in the textual variants written in his own hand and those of several amanuenses.[47] Most problematic of all were the instances of indecency in Chaucer's fabliau, especially lines 238–9[48] and line 256.[49] The second of these examples involves the climactic revelation by the tale-telling crow in Chaucer's poem: 'For on thy bed thy wife I saw him swyve', when the bird uses the most unequivocally obscene word in Chaucer's vocabulary.[50] Wordsworth substitutes 'For on thy bed I saw him with thy wife'; or 'The guilt I witnessed saw him with thy wife' before finally settling for 'Saw him in guilty converse with thy wife'.[51] This modernization does considerably weaken the force of the original via its changed word order, but the actual vocabulary is not, perhaps, as innocent it might appear to us. Leigh Hunt, who simply cut this line when he took over the translation of the tale for *Chaucer Moderniz'd*, had used the phrase 'improper conversation' as a substitute for 'fornication' in *The Friar's Tale*, one of his other translations. Both that phrase and Wordsworth's 'guilty converse' would, I think, have infallibly suggested to a contemporary audience that formula of nineteenth-century divorce courts: 'criminal conversation' or 'crim.con.' – the lawyers' technical synonym for adulterous intercourse.[52]

The efforts of Wordsworth's wife, Mary, allied with his friends Isabella Fenwick and Edward Quillinan, were responsible for preventing the publication of Wordsworth's translation of *The Manciple's Tale* in Powell and Horne's volume. However, although it was a useful pretext for them to hang their objections on the question of the propriety of the text, and despite its being one which Wordsworth was prepared to accept, considerations of decency were not the only motive. Justifiable reservations about the intentions of the gentlemen editors were probably a greater factor.[53]

sion of the Trustees of the Library. **46** Horne (ed.), *Chaucer Moderniz'd*, pp xv–vi. **47** Graver, *Translations of Chaucer*, pp 81–103. **48** *The Riverside Chaucer*, p. 285; Graver, *Translations of Chaucer*, p. 65, ll. 134–5. **49** *The Riverside Chaucer*, p. 285; Graver, *Translations of Chaucer*, p. 66, l. 52; Wordsworth also worried about Chaucer's ll. 204–5 (Graver, *Translations of Chaucer*, p. 64, ll. 100–01) on account of the word 'lemman' ('lover') which, while it has connotations of adultery and lust, is not actually coarse per se. See *The Riverside Chaucer*, p. 954, note 204–6. **50** Hans Kurath, Sherman M. Kuhn and Robert E. Lewis (eds), *Middle English Dictionary* A–T (Michigan, 1952–2001), s.v. 'swyve'. **51** Graver, *Translations of Chaucer*, p. 66, l. 52. This line was a perennial problem: the bookseller Jackson, publishing in 1750, offers a modernization which succeeds in being far more obscene than Chaucer's original. In 1795 Lipscomb, the clerical tutor/chaplain to the Duke of Cleveland opted for decent curtailment of the crow's bird's-eye view. Bowden, *Eighteenth-Century Modernizations*, p. 157. **52** See Roderick Phillips, *Untying the Knot: A Short History of Divorce* (Cambridge, 1991), pp 64–5. **53** Graver, *Translations of Chaucer*, p. 25.

Powell's involvement, especially, rang alarm bells: he was a mediocre poet and lionizer who grossly flattered Wordsworth, gave celebrity parties – with embezzled money, it was later discovered – and had *bought* his own translations. Soon after this Chaucerian venture, his financial misdemeanours were discovered and he only escaped prison by feigning insanity and decamping to New York.[54]

As correspondence between Mary Wordsworth, Isabella Fenwick and Edward Quillinan shows, and that between Powell and Wordsworth also demonstrates, Powell was rightly suspected by Wordsworth's family of duplicitously trying to exploit his insinuating connection with the more famous man, soon to be appointed poet laureate. Wordsworth's family was obviously concerned lest he should act in a way which would be detrimental to his own reputation while enriching, literally and figuratively, a man of whom they disapproved. The family debate is of some interest: in a letter of March 1840 to his daughter Dora (Quillinan's wife) Wordsworth says:

> Tell Mr Quillinan, I think he has taken rather a narrow view of the spirit of the Manciple's Tale, especially as it concerns its morality. The formal prosing at the end and the selfishness that pervades it flows from the genius of Chaucer, mainly, as a characteristic of the narrator whom he describes in the Prologue as eminent for shrewdness and clever worldly prudence. The main lesson and the most important one, is inculcated as a poet ought chiefly to inculcate his lessons not formally, but by implication.[55]

Similarly, in a conversation with his friend Barron Field about this matter, Wordsworth is reported to have 'referred to the part the Crow plays in the Manciple's Tale, and praised the father-poet's dramatic skill and courage'.[56]

These comments constitute acute criticism on Wordsworth's part of Chaucer's ironic technique: he seems to have recognized that the medieval poet adopted a variety of narrative 'voices' within a single poem, and thus anticipated modern critical writing on Chaucer's use of personae. After the suppression of his translation of *The Manciple's Tale* Wordsworth continued to believe in its merits and wrote to Powell that respect for his friends' views, rather than his own judgment, was responsible for withholding it.[57] Wordsworth, like John Scattergood, was responsive to 'the Manciple's manner of speaking' and the survival of his translation of the tale furnishes an appropriate link between the Romantic poet and the modern Chaucer scholar.

54 Blainey, *Farthing* Poet, p. 114.   55 Hill, *Letters: Later Years*, VII, Part 4, p. 129.   56 Unpublished *Memoir*, cited in Bruce E. Graver, 'New Voice on Blake', *Blake: An Illustrated Quarterly* 24:3 (1990/1), 93.   57 Hill, *Letters: Later Years, VII*, Part 4, p. 71.

Index